KANT AND THE SCANDAL OF PHILOSOPHY

The Kantian Critique of Cartesian Scepticism

Kant considered it scandalous that philosophy had been unable to find a rational proof of the existence of the external world. Arguably, the scandal continues today, because scepticism remains a widely debated and extremely divisive issue among contemporary thinkers. Although scholars have devoted considerable attention to Kant's arguments against Cartesian scepticism, the literature still presents gaps and inaccuracies that obscure a full understanding of this issue and its significance for contemporary philosophy. In *Kant and the Scandal of Philosophy*, Luigi Caranti corrects this omission, providing a thorough historical analysis of Kant's anti-sceptical arguments from the pre-critical period up to the 'Reflexionen zum Idealismus' (1788–93).

Caranti demonstrates how reconstructing Kant's critique of scepticism is crucial for understanding the origin of his philosophy and for avoiding serious mistakes that continue to serve as obstacles to the proper understanding of the *Critique of Pure Reason*. In particular, Caranti shows how the sceptical challenge leads Kant to the critical stage of his thought. Moreover, this study responds to recent criticism of transcendental idealism, showing how it can serve as the main premise of a powerful anti-sceptical argument whose main structure is suggested by Kant in the 1781 Fourth Paralogism. Erudite and engaging, *Kant and the Scandal of Philosophy* fills an important void in the literature and breathes new life into this field of inquiry.

(Toronto Studies in Philosophy)

LUIGI CARANTI is a Marie Curie Fellow at Philipps-Universität and a research associate at Libera Università Internazionale degli Studi Sociali Guido Carli.

LUIGI CARANTI

Kant and the Scandal of Philosophy

The Kantian Critique of Cartesian Scepticism

UNIVERSITY OF TORONTO PRESS
Toronto Buffalo London

© University of Toronto Press 2007
Toronto Buffalo London
utorontopress.com

Reprinted in paperback 2019

ISBN 978-0-8020-9132-1 (cloth)   ISBN 978-1-4875-2551-4 (paper)

Toronto Studies in Philosophy
Editors: Donald Ainslie and Amy Mullin

Library and Archives Canada Cataloguing in Publication

Title: Kant and the scandal of philosophy : the Kantian critique of Cartesian scepticism / Luigi Caranti.

Names: Caranti, Luigi, author.

Series: Toronto studies in philosophy.

Description: Series statement: Toronto studies in philosophy | Paperback reprint. Originally published in hardcover in 2007. | Includes bibliographical references and index.

Identifiers: Canadiana 20190216638 | ISBN 9781487525514 (softcover)

Subjects: LCSH: Kant, Immanuel, 1724–1804. | LCSH: Kant, Immanuel, 1724–1804. Kritik der reinen Vernunft. | LCSH: Idealism, German. | LCSH: Skepticism.

Classification: LCC B2799.I42 C37 2019 | DDC 193–dc23

University of Toronto Press acknowledges the financial assistance to its publishing program of the Canada Council for the Arts and the Ontario Arts Council, an agency of the Government of Ontario.

Contents

Introduction 3

1 The Problem of Idealism in the Precritical Period 10

2 The Nature of Transcendental Idealism and Its Foundations 36

3 The Antisceptical Argument of the Fourth Paralogism 80

4 The Problem of Idealism between 1781 and 1787 114

5 The Refutation of Idealism 126

6 The Refutation of Idealism in the Reflexionen 152

Conclusion 173

Notes 177
Bibliography 207
Index 215

KANT AND THE SCANDAL OF PHILOSOPHY:
THE KANTIAN CRITIQUE OF CARTESIAN SCEPTICISM

Introduction

How to respond satisfactorily to Cartesian scepticism has been one of the central problems of philosophy since the first appearance of the *Meditations*. It is little exaggeration to say that all of the important philosophers since Descartes have found it necessary to deal with the sort of radical scepticism he drew to the attention of the erudite world with his hypothesis of the Evil Genius. The search for a 'solution' to Descartes's problem has resulted in a number of 'refutations of scepticism' that are as ingenious as they have turned out to be vulnerable to the replies of sceptics. Recent accounts, such as Hilary Putnam's[1] and Barry Stroud's,[2] bear witness both to the ongoing efforts to silence what Kant called the 'scandal of philosophy' – that is, the inability to prove beyond doubt the existence of the external world – and to the awareness that perhaps we must learn to live with this embarrassing theoretical result.

In this continuing debate, weighty epistemological issues have entered to the scene, well beyond the specific question of whether it is possible to prove the existence of the external world, and the sceptical problem has shown itself to be a vitally important approach to testing the validity of general philosophical assumptions. Indeed, many contemporary philosophical perspectives have betrayed their weaknesses precisely in their efforts to refute Cartesian scepticism. Thus, the constant re-emergence of scepticism from the rubble created by those who thought they had toppled it forever provides an opportunity for us to examine anew the epistemological options that contemporary philosophy offers us.

I contend that our inability to silence scepticism once and for all suggests an extremely important lesson for contemporary philosophy, a lesson this book tries to spell out. To begin with, this inability flows from a failure to embrace the essence of Kant's philosophical legacy – that is, transcendental idealism. In fact, as I will show, this philosophical perspective, heir to the 'Copernican revolution,' is truly (as Kant himself puts it) 'the only refuge' against the threat of skepticism. Moreover, and even more importantly, precisely because it plays such an indispensable role in meeting the challenges of skepticism, we should approach transcendental idealism as a serious option for contemporary epistemology, however strongly it has been dismissed on recent years.

As a necessary framework for this project, I will historically reconstruct and critically evaluate Kant's arguments against Cartesian skepticism from the precritical period up to the 'Reflexionen zum Idealismus' (1788–93). Despite the attention that Kant's interpreters have always devoted to these arguments, and the merits of recent studies, gaps and inaccuracies continue to obscure a proper understanding of the subject, as well as its vast significance for Kant's entire philosophy and its relevance to contemporary thought.

The main defect of past treatments has been that no one has offered a systematic account of Kant's precritical arguments against skepticism.[3] Yet such an account is crucial if we are to avoid those serious mistakes which even today prevent us from understanding properly the *Critique of Pure Reason*. The problem of skepticism is not an isolated one with little or no bearing on the basic tenets of Kant's mature philosophy. Quite the contrary – there is abundant evidence that after Kant introduced the phenomena/noumena distinction in his 1770 *Dissertation*, the challenge put to him by skepticism was what drove him to reshape the foundations of his thought.

In a nutshell, this is how it happened. In 1770, Kant had failed to refute skepticism by identifying phenomena with mental entities, and by affirming things in themselves as the mind-independent objects that caused them (the strategy of the *Dissertation*); realizing this, he was forced to modify radically his notion of phenomena in such a way as to make a new antiskeptical argument possible. This new notion was precisely the idea that the immediate objects of our external experience (outer phenomena or appearances) are not mental entities, but rather genuine, mind-independent objects. This idea, which he introduced over the course of the silent decade, constituted his first step towards the antiskeptical argument of the First Edition of the *Critique of Pure Reason*, the Fourth Paralogism. At the same time, it was nothing less than the basis on which Kant's entire critical philosophy would come to rest.

If we bear in mind this evolution of the notion of phenomena throughout the silent decade, we can avoid common and still widespread misunderstandings of the *Critique*. First and foremost, the attribution to Kant of some versions of phenomenalism conflicts with the direction of this evolution. This invites us to consider the *Critique* – even in its First Edition – as the culmination of an antiphenomenalistic progress, rather than as the manifestation of Kant's commitment to this doctrine. Moreover, many troublesome parts of the *Critique* – parts that are usually taken as clear evidence of Kant's commitment to phenomenalism (especially the Fourth Paralogism) – appear in a completely different light when we view them against the background of this evolution. Far from being a deeply flawed effort to refute Cartesian scepticism by affirming some version of Berkeley's *esse est percipi*,[4] the Fourth Paralogism is in fact an expression of the empirical form of realism that characterizes the final stage of Kant's development.

Once we have abandoned the phenomenalistic reading, we can begin to see that the Fourth Paralogism contains material for a powerful refutation of scepticism. To be sure, we must construct this argument out of the material that Kant offers but does not articulate thoroughly. In fact, the Fourth Paralogism provides an antisceptical strategy that is clearly unsatisfactory. It does, however, offer the thesis of the immediacy of outer perception and the crucial intuition that the Evil Genius hypothesis amounts precisely to an illegitimate inquiry into the nature of the thing in itself. I will try to show that these two theses in combination bring us to a compelling refutation of scepticism.

By arguing in favour of this conclusion, I am placing myself in direct contradiction with almost all of Kant's interpreters. Previous analysts of this subject can be divided into two main groups: those who consider his efforts to refute scepticism ultimately unsatisfactory[5]; and those who are convinced that Kant succeeded in refuting scepticism only with the Second Edition argument, the Refutation of Idealism.[6] The Fourth Paralogism – the argument Kant presented in 1781 – is generally dismissed because of its supposed commitment to phenomenalism, which would obviously undermine its antisceptical aims. In contrast to both groups, I contend that Kant does in fact have a powerful argument against scepticism, but that it is not to be found in the Refutation of Idealism, nor in its refinements in the 'Reflexionen.' Rather, we can perceive it in a line of thought contained in the Fourth Paralogism. I thus claim that the Second Edition argument, notwithstanding its intuitive appeal, ultimately fails and indeed can be salvaged only if we borrow antisceptical resources from the Fourth Paralogism.

The problem with any interpretation that favours the argument of the Fourth Paralogism over the 1787 Refutation of Idealism is that the latter may be construed as independent of transcendental idealism,[7] whereas the former undoubtedly rests on its truth. Both the idea of the immediacy of outer perception and the possibility of dismissing the 'big hallucination' hypothesis in the way suggested presuppose the truth of transcendental idealism. Given the general dissatisfaction with this theory – which is uttered not only by philosophers who work outside a Kantian framework, but also by many Kant specialists – it is important to shake the confidence with which that condemnation is uttered. This requires both an analysis of the nature of transcendental idealism and an evaluation of Kant's own arguments for it. I intend to offer readers a rather detailed treatment of the first issue, but I will be obliged to limit greatly my discussion of the second. The reason for this is quite simple: the proof of the non-phenomenalist nature of Kant's idealism can be handled within a reasonable space, as a mere *step* in a larger project; however, an adequate analysis of transcendental idealism's foundations – that is, of the direct argument in the Aesthetic and the indirect argument in the Dialectic – would transform this study into something completely different from what I intend. At the same time, however, I cannot dispense completely with a defence of transcendental idealism, given how central it is to the logical structure of my argument against scepticism. Thus I am obliged to propose a compromise: I will limit my discussion to the direct argument of the Aesthetic, and defer to others the task of defending the indirect argument of the Dialectic.[8] This choice is necessary not just because of space considerations; also, the thesis of the immediacy of outer perception, which plays such a crucial role in Kant's argument against scepticism in the Fourth Paralogism, can be fully grasped only through the apriority and the intuition arguments of the Metaphysical Exposition.

The reader will not find an exhaustive defence of transcendental idealism in this book, but *can* expect a thorough analysis of the significance of Kant's famous remark that transcendental idealism is 'the only refuge' against Cartesian scepticism. I intend to show that the failure of all past efforts to refute scepticism (including Putnam's allegedly Kantian argument against the 'Brains in the Vat' hypothesis) is not surprising, given their often unconscious embrace of a transcendentally realist tenet regarding the mind–world relation. This will support the intuition – central to this book's program – that the problem of scepticism suggests a new, 'indirect' argument in favour of transcendental idealism. Until philosophy takes this stance seriously, it will always struggle to address the 'scandal' (Kant's own famous term) of being unable to refute rationally the Evil Genius hypothesis.

This book has six chapters. In the first, I reconstruct Kant's precritical arguments against scepticism. Kant's strategy from 1755 to 1781 undergoes profound changes that give the impression of sheer inconsistency. If these changes are seen in the general context of the development of Kant's philosophy, however, they appear as natural consequences of the different philosophical positions that Kant embraced over time. The first task of this chapter thus will be to show how these antisceptical arguments reflect the broader context of Kant's overall intellectual development. In addition, I will show how, after 1770, the sceptical challenge did much to lead Kant to two crucial achievements: (a) his mature interpretation of the transcendental distinction between appearances and things in themselves as a distinction between two perspectives on the same set of objects, as opposed to a distinction between two sets of objects; and (b) his abandonment of any commitment to phenomenalism.

In the chapter 2, I build on this result and show that the idealism that Kant argues for in the First Edition of the *Critique* has nothing to do with phenomenalism. I will contrast the formal nature of Kant's idealism with the material nature of Descartes's and Berkeley's idealisms, along the lines suggested by Kant himself in his reply to the famous Garve–Feder review. In the second part of the same chapter I address the foundational arguments of the Aesthetic and try to defend Kant's foundations from contemporary critics. This chapter as a whole is meant to show that transcendental idealism is a compelling philosophical option that can serve as a premise for an equally compelling antisceptical argument.

In chapter 3 I offer just this argument. One important question I will have to answer concerns Kant's reasons for placing the refutation of scepticism in the Paralogisms in general and in the Fourth Paralogism in particular. I will argue that this placement is extremely significant, because it suggests a connection between scepticism and transcendental illusion. Since Kant does not explain this connection, I will try to spell it out by suggesting that the mistake connected to transcendental illusion – the conflation of a subjective condition of thought with an objective feature of the world – is the basis of Descartes's cherished thesis of the superiority of inner experience over outer experience. After this, I focus on the thesis of the immediacy of outer perception, which is

Kant's approach to discrediting Descartes's superiority thesis as well as a necessary albeit insufficient ingredient of Kant's overall refutation. In order to show the originality of Kant's position, I compare it with Reid's affirmation of the same thesis. Finally, I complete the antisceptical argument and rebut what I see as a crucial but also last-resort counter-objection available to the sceptic. The chapter ends with a comparison of Kant's and Putnam's antisceptical arguments.

In chapter 4, I analyse the development of Kant's antisceptical strategy from 1781 to 1787, paying particular attention to the arguments in the *Prolegomena* and in the Metaphysics Mrongovius, a series of lectures Kant gave during these years. The chapter also contains a suggestion as to the alleged reasons why Kant replaced the Fourth Paralogism with the Refutation of Idealism in the Second Edition of the *Critique*. Obviously, an analysis of this point is crucial to my interpretation, which, you will recall, turns on the idea that the Fourth Paralogism is a far superior argument to the Refutation. I therefore owe readers and explanation why Kant replaced a good argument with a bad one.

Chapter 5 analyses the 1787 Refutation of Idealism. In the first two parts, I analyse this proof by focusing on its placement in the general context of the Second Edition and in the specific context of the Postulates of Empirical Thought. I then assess the soundness of the Refutation. After an overview of the proof, I analyse its most important (and controversial) points, such as the kind of self-knowledge that Kant assumes, whether he is entitled to attribute it to Descartes, the nature of 'the permanent' (*das Beharrliche*) that is supposed to determine the temporal structure of one's inner experience, and the reason why the permanent cannot be an inner object. My conclusion from this analysis will be that even if we remove pseudo-difficulties that could undermine the success of the Refutation, the proof is still vulnerable to a crucial sceptical reply that Kant foresees and attempts unsuccessfully to silence. The chapter ends with an attempt to 'salvage' the Refutation by applying the antisceptical resources of the Fourth Paralogism.

In the sixth and final chapter I will focus on Kant's late arguments against idealism in the 'Reflexionen zum Idealismus' (1788–93). I attempt to answer two main questions: Why did Kant return to the problem of idealism if this was supposed to have been solved by the 1787 Refutation of Idealism? And do the arguments in these Reflexionen actually improve on Kant's strategy? Regarding the first question, I will argue that Kant returns to the problem of idealism mainly because he lacks confidence that he has truly silenced the sceptics through his 1787 argument. Regarding the second question, after identifying ten different arguments and grouping them into three main antisceptical lines of thought, I will conclude that these late refinements of Kant's strategy fail to significantly improve Kant's critique. At times, they even seem to push the antisceptical strategy back to a precritical, dogmatic stage. This ultimately negative assessment of the 'Reflexionen zum Idealismus' clashes with the interpretation suggested by Paul Guyer, who finds in them not only Kant's sole successful refutation of the sceptic, but also the central premise of Kant's entire epistemology. The chapter ends with my reply to Guyer.

Few would doubt today that the problem of scepticism is one of the unavoidable and recurrent questions that philosophy is called to address. And ever fewer would deny that this problem was central to Kant. If the arguments of this book are sound, the efforts my readers will have to make to go through abstract reasoning, long hermeneutical analyses, and at times tiresome historical reconstructions will be repaid by a fresh way to look at the problem. This new perspective will confirm – of this at least I am sure – the crucial importance of the sceptical problem for contemporary philosophy and, I hope, the urgency of finding a solution. In offering my own solution to Kant scholars, I expect fierce resistance for at least two reasons: because of my unconventional preference for the first-edition argument of the Fourth Paralogism, which scandalously even becomes the clearest expression of Kant's mature position, and (much more seriously) because of my unabashed dismissal of any conflation between Kant's transcendental idealism and his phenomenalism, even in the 1781 edition of the First Critique. Outside the relatively restricted circle of Kant specialists, I expect even stronger resistance due to my attempt to rehabilitate the formal kind of idealism that Kant presented as an attitude of philosophical modesty, as epistemology's contribution to the decentralization of human beings that Copernicus had started. Today, for quite mysterious reasons, this position appears more scandalous, less 'acceptable' than controversial forms of idealism such as the one presented by John McDowell. The almost universal resistance that I foresee is frightening but at the same time reassuring, in that it gives me hope that I have reached some original results. Whether originality is here married with correctness I leave it to my readers to decide.

1 The Problem of Idealism in the Precritical Period

At first glance, Kant's precritical confrontation with the problem of idealism seems to be characterized by sheer inconsistency. Moments of confidence as to the possibility of countering the sceptical doubt are followed by moments of despair, and vice versa. Kant's antisceptical arguments are first proposed, then withdrawn, then restored, and again abandoned. When we approach these profound changes in the context of the development of Kant's philosophy, however, they become less mysterious. Rather, they appear as natural consequences of the different philosophical positions that Kant embraces over time. Thus the primary task of this chapter is to show how the various arguments that Kant devotes to the problem of idealism fit with the broader context of his overall intellectual development. Once this general context is provided, Kant's precritical positions no longer appear as a puzzling succession of conflicting arguments, but rather, hopefully, as an intelligible and coherent albeit non-linear development.[1]

Yet this is not the only challenge that Kant's precritical treatment of idealism poses for us. The problem of idealism is not simply a specific problem with little or no bearing on the development of the central tenets of Kant's mature philosophy. Quite the contrary, especially after Kant introduces the distinction between sensibility and understanding in the 1770 *Dissertation*, the sceptical challenge constitutes the main force that leads him to reshape the foundations of his philosophy – that is, to provide a new and truly critical interpretation of the appearances/things in themselves distinction. In particular, realizing that he had failed to refute scepticism by identifying appearances with mental entities and by affirming things in themselves as the mind-independent objects that 'underlie them,' Kant was forced to arrive at a new sense of that distinction which would make possible a fresh antisceptical argument. This new sense was, quite simply, the idea that the immediate objects of our experience – that is, appearances – are not mental entities, but rather genuine, mind-independent objects and that, correlatively, things in themselves are just those objects considered in abstraction from the sensible forms of our cognition. This new sense amounted to the first step in the antisceptical argument that Kant would present in the Fourth Paralogism. At the same time, it constituted nothing less than the foundation of Kant's critical philosophy. Indeed, as we shall see when we examine the Fourth Paralogism, this new interpretation of the appearances/things in themselves distinction is identical with the notion of empirical realism, which, in turn, is nothing but transcendental idealism. On our reading, then, the precritical confrontation plays the crucial role of dictating the reinterpretation of the phenomena–noumena distinction – a distinction that Kant had already introduced (but, as we shall see, misinterpreted) in his 1770 *Dissertation*.

There are six main passages from the precritical period in which Kant discusses the problem of idealism. They are contained in the following texts: *Nova Dilucidatio* (1755), Metaphysics Herder (1762–4), *Dreams of a Spirit-Seer* (1766), *Dissertation* (1770), letter to Herz (1772), and Metaphysics L_1 (mid-1770s). The subsections of this chapter discuss each of these texts.

The Causal Argument of the *Nova Dilucidatio* (1755)

As its title suggests, the *Principiorum primorum cognitionis metaphysicae nova dilucidatio* is devoted to a discussion of the most fundamental metaphysical principles. In the Leibnizian framework in which Kant works, these are the principles of contradiction and sufficient reason (Kant wanted to rename the latter 'the principle of determinant reason'). Having defended the latter principle from the usual charge that it would make human freedom and accountability impossible, Kant spells out two new metaphysical principles that supposedly flow from it. One of these is the 'principle of succession': 'No change can occur to substances, unless they are in connection with others: it is precisely this reciprocal dependence that determines a reciprocal change in their state.'[2] The proof of this principle is a reductio ad absurdum. It turns on the idea that, given the internal determinations of a substance and their 'reasons' (R) – here understood in the sense of causes that produce such determinations – if we abstract from all external influence, we are forced to postulate the presence in the substance of other reasons, opposed to (R), to explain the occurrence of a change in the internal state of the substance. In other words, we are forced to postulate the coexistence in the substance of reasons (R) and of reasons (-R), which is absurd. Indeed, the presence of (-R) would counterbalance (R), thus making impossible for the substance to be in the original state. It follows that inner changes in a substance must arise from the external influence of another substance.

Given this, Kant believes that 'for the first time' the existence of external things is proven with a degree of certainty that escaped other 'more healthy' philosophies that attempted the same proof. As he puts it:

> I discover that for the first time the real existence of bodies, which a philosophy a little more healthy [sanior] did not manage to defend against the idealists if not *via* probability, follows from our principles in the most transparent way. The mind, namely, is subject through means of internal sense to internal changes; since these changes cannot ... arise from its own nature considered in isolation and apart from connection with other things, those other things must be present outside the mind, and the mind must be connected with them in a mutual relation.[3]

In other words, internal changes in the mind cannot arise unless some external object causes them. This line of thought – which I hereafter call the 'causal argument' – seems to run through the whole precritical period up to the *Dissertation* and is clearly abandoned only in the first edition of the *Critique* with the familiar consideration that any inference from the effect to the cause is invalid.[4] However, we should resist the impression that the young Kant is relying on an inference from effect to cause without any awareness of the risks involved in this procedure.[5] As our brief discussion of the proof of the principle of succession has indicated, Kant has ruled out the possibility of a self-produced change of the inner states of a substance (in this case of the mind) by arguing that this would presuppose the coexistence of two contradictory reasons in the substance itself. Quite independently of the cogency of this proof, this shows that Kant was well aware of the need to rule out the possibility of self-produced inner changes (as with hallucinations).

What, then, is the flaw in the argument of the *Nova Dilucidatio*? And why did Kant, as we shall see, abandon that argument? It is not difficult to see that Kant's proof of the principle of succession, on which everything turns, is contradicted by experience. It is a simple empirical fact that we are capable of self-determination of our mind. When we imagine something, we do not take the change in the state of our mind to be produced by an external cause. Trying to be faithful to Kant's setting, we could say that our mind is able to introduce in itself new 'reasons' that were not present at a preceding stage, in such a way as to produce a change in its states. There is no need to assume that those 'reasons' were pre-existing in such a way as to conflict with those responsible for the present state of the mind. The whole point of imagining is precisely to introduce spontaneously these 'reasons/causes' independently of external influence. Put briefly, Kant's proof requires us to deny the entire faculty of imagination as we know it.

Let us now consider how the causal argument fits with the context of Kant's philosophy in the 1750s and how that philosophy underwent a profound change in the early 1760s. In doing so, we shall see how Kant came to realize the weakness of his causal argument and consequently chose to abandon it. To begin with, let us recall that in 1755 Kant is still operating within the framework of Leibnizian–Wolffian rationalism. At the same time, however, he is trying to adjust some if its main tenets. For example, the very idea that changes in the inner states of a substance must arise from an external cause constitutes a substantial departure from the Leibnizian school to which, by and large, Kant belongs. Indeed, famously, according to Leibniz monads do not interact with one another. Not surprisingly, Kant contends that his principle of succession, by establishing a real influence among substances, removes the need for Leibniz's pre-established harmony. A mutual physical influence among substances is also one of the central tenets of the *Monadologia Physica* (the title is telling), which appears just one year after the *Nova Dilucidatio*. Thus this refutation of idealism has the interesting characteristic of containing in a nutshell the central tenets of Kant's overall philosophy of these years. On the one hand, the very problem of the refutation is expressed in terms of a relation between two substances/monads – something that clearly echoes the Leibnizian framework within which Kant's operating; on the other hand, it also rests on the idea of a physical influence among monads, which constitutes the main thrust of Kant's critique of that philosophical framework.

Furthermore, note that the idea of proving the existence of a cause starting with the effect this alleged cause produces seems to be a common strategy for the young Kant. A similar logical path is discernible in

Universal Natural History and Theory of Heavens, also published in 1755. In this work Kant reiterates Leibniz's thesis that the universality and inviolability of the rules of nature is the best proof of the existence of God. Not miracles, then, but the strict mechanical laws of nature constitute sufficient evidence for the existence of a wise Creator.[6] From the natural order and its fixed rules (the effect), we infer the existence of God (as the cause of such an order); in the same way, from the inner changes of our mind, we infer the existence of the (external) causes of such changes. In both cases, the inference is from the effect to the cause; and in both cases we have the same attempt to rule out the possibility that other causes are producing the effect from which the inference started. We have already seen how this works in the causal argument against idealism. In the present proof, it is implicitly but clearly assumed that *only* God can be responsible for the lawfulness of nature. Only His infinite wisdom is a cause adequate to such an effect.

A last but crucial point needs to be made before we can place the 1755 refutation of idealism in the context of the general development of Kant's thought. This proof can be taken as the result of the general style of thinking that Kant adopts in these years. As Cassirer has pointed out, Kant never stands closer than in the 1750s to the ruling eighteenth-century intellectual model, according to which philosophy is a way to solve problems by appealing to enlightened common sense.[7] A clarification and a refinement of concepts present in any mind is the key to solving old and heavily discussed philosophical problems. Kant's present style is very different from the analytical rigour that he will adopt after 1763 and that – with the sole exception of *Dreams of a Spirit-Seer* – he will never abandon. This style is often responsible for arguments that can hardly be accepted with the same confidence with which Kant presents them. Sometimes we even have examples of reasoning that amount to a *petitio principii*, such as the central thesis of the 1759 *Versuch einiger Betrachtungen über den Optimismus*. Here the Leibnizian position that we live in the best of all possible worlds is defended on the grounds that the opposite view amounts to the assertion that 'the Supreme Wisdom has preferred the worst to the best' – something that is against the 'principles of sound understanding.'[8]

Towards the Abandonment of the Causal Argument

It is precisely by changing his style of thinking and becoming suspicious of the possibility of solving old metaphysical problems by using refined common sense that Kant will abandon the causal argument against idealism. Let us recall that in the early 1760s Kant was forced to think about the problem of the metaphysical method by the question posed by the Academy of Berlin on the amenability of the metaphysical sciences to the same degree of clarity as the mathematical sciences. Crucial for the period we are discussing is the fact that Kant came to realize that metaphysics – including the kind of metaphysics he had been doing – was not on firm foundations. No progress in this discipline could be made without a profound change in its method. The main thrust of the methodological reform that Kant proposed to the philosophical world through the prize essay was that metaphysics needs to be extremely cautious in its inferences. One must not start from definitions, says Kant, as is traditionally done, and then infer conclusions that are plausible only for the features that were arbitrarily introduced in the definitions. We must, rather, insert in a concept the features that *experience* has taught us belong to that concept (for example, we must insert solubility in aqua regia into the concept of gold because we have experienced that gold has this property). In this way, there is hope that metaphysics can reach a degree of certainty comparable to that of the mathematical sciences.[9]

This idea of avoiding unwarranted inferences that hold only because we have arbitrarily inserted into the concept certain features is the key to understanding the flaw in the *Nova Dilucidatio* argument. This is precisely the mistake that the 1755 causal argument can be charged with. Kant's reasons for ruling out causes of our inner determinations other than external ones (such as the imagination) were based on an a priori definition of the mind. Kant had arbitrarily stipulated that a mind cannot produce out of itself a 'reason' (not R) that, at the moment of its coming to be, would remove the pre-existing reason (R). His (by the new standards) dogmatic method had led him to overlook or deny a very simple empirical fact: that the mind sometimes *does* produce its internal changes, as happens in familiar cases of imagining (or hallucinating). It follows that Kant in 1755 was guilty of the very methodological mistake that he would stigmatize in his 1764 prize essay. He started with an a priori definition of the substance 'mind,' without considering the features that experience teaches us about it, such as the capacity for self-affection; thus he was led to wrong inferences, which would have been avoided had he consulted experience from the very beginning.

While Kant's specific criticism of the metaphysical method centred on the need to avoid a priori definitions, his general criticism targeted the groundless confidence that metaphysics can solve old and perennial problems. If we keep in mind the confidence of the 1755 argument, also this criticism can also be seen as an a posteriori self-criticism. A passage in *Der einzige mögliche Beweisgrund zu einer Demonstration des Daseins Gottes* (1763) sounds much like an autobiographical note: 'There is a time, in which in a science such as metaphysics one has confidence to explain and prove everything; there is another time in which one embarks in such enterprises only with fear and diffidence.'[10] By considering this radical rethinking of the explanatory power of metaphysics, one can understand Kant's abandonment of the 1755 argument and make sense of the profound change in his attitude towards scepticism in the Metaphysics Herder (early 1760s).

The Metaphysics Herder (1762–4): The Impossibility of Refuting Idealism 'Logically'

In the section of the Metaphysics Herder devoted to cosmology and, within this, in the subsection on the parts of the universe, Kant inserts the following crucial passage. Given its importance, let me quote it in full:

> An egoist thinks that I, who am thinking here, am the only simple being, without connection <*nexu*> with others. [An] idealist, that there is merely a spiritual world. Origin of *idealism*, the truth that the body without thoughts constitutes no world. So Bishop Berkeley, in the treatise *On the Use of Tarwater for Our Body*, doubted whether there are any bodies at all. He alleges that all bodies are mere appearances of bodies in our soul. And that with much plausibility.
> 1. for all sensation of bodies outside us is merely *in* us, e.g., beauty, ugliness, merely in our sensation, therefore the various judgments [on] color, not in the body, but rather merely in the refractions of the light rays, as the prism teaches. – It is foolish to recommend to him the proof of a beating, because he would also hold it to be lively appearances in him. The proof from experiences is ineffective, because he also holds them merely to be lively representations.
> 2. As in a dream, since one imagines things which nevertheless are not, far more lively than [when one is] awake: since an affection concerning absurdities is greater. And were dreams actually in mutual agreement, who would not hold them for occurring things? But could God not have

arranged it so that our life is in mutual dream, and that our death would be only an awakening? In Locke's day an honest, learned man who had never lied passed himself off with all certainty as Socrates, who can refute this? – The weapons of truth, wisdom, goodness of God, are too dull against idealism, and even serve it. For would it not be a shorter way of wisdom, all the same, to effect by representations than by bodies?

Thus *logically* he cannot be refuted, but rather by the assent of other human beings and one's own conviction.'[11]

It is well known that Kant modelled his lectures on Baumgarten's *Metaphysica* (1739). Sometimes Kant simply repeats a definition that Baumgarten gives in his work. It follows that we must be very careful to avoid attributing to Kant opinions that he might simply repeat from Baumgarten without embracing them. If we compare the part in the *Metaphysica* corresponding to the passage that interests us, however, we find that Kant takes from Baumgarten only the definition of 'egoista.'[12] But the rest is Kant's addition. We never find in the *Metaphysica* an appreciation of Berkeley. Also, in another passage Kant seems to be granting to idealism a theoretical strength that is not acknowledged by Baumgarten. Having repeated Baumgarten's definitions of 'mundus egoisticus' and 'mundus idealisticus,' Kant notes that the imperfection (by which Kant means lack of reality) of the idealistic world is difficult to prove. Indeed, we would have to prove that our world, composed of spirits *and* bodies, is more perfect than the idealistic world because 'spirits without bodies could not have the same series of thoughts.' Far from believing that this proof is possible, however, Kant thinks that a world in which our thoughts are obtained without the contributions of bodies would be better because 'the same ends are obtained by a shorter way.' This is another appreciation of the idealist position that Kant adds. Therefore, one can hardly doubt that the concessions he grants to idealism in the text reflect his considered judgment.

Having ascertained that much, we can begin to analyse the passage. The first thing to notice is the confession of impotence in giving a *logical* antisceptical proof. Such a confession may sound surprising if one considers that it comes from the same thinker who was convinced in 1755 that he had found a 'most transparent' way to ground the existence of the external world. But if one bears in mind the profound transformations that Kant's thought had undergone, one will not be surprised that Kant was no longer satisfied with his earlier argument. The idea that the 'proof of the beating' is impotent against idealism, and the reference to the dream argument, are obvious objections to the 1755 causal argument from the new methodological standpoint. If we start with simple data of experience, we soon realize that self-produced modifications of the mind are natural phenomena. In turn, we realize that the sceptical doubt will not be countered by any argument that starts with a representation in us (such as the vivid pain arising from a beating) and then points to the apparent cause of it. As the dream argument shows, we would have the same 'lively appearances' also in cases in which our world is nothing but 'dreams ... in mutual agreement.'

As we have already pointed out, Kant did not merely ignore such objections in 1755. Consider that the principle of succession is supposed to rule out the possibility of self-produced alterations in a substance. But the proof of the principle of succession, it will be recalled, was a clear example of, by later standards, 'bad' metaphysics. Indeed, it owed its entire plausibility to an a priori definition of the mind turning on the idea that two contradictory 'reasons' cannot coexist in it. We have seen that the need to avoid a priori definitions was the essence of the reforms to the philosophical method that Kant proposed in his prize essay. Thus the passage we are considering here is the natural result of these reforms.

We have other confirmations that Kant's position on idealism fits with the broader context of his philosophy. To begin with, the early 1760s were characterized by Kant's abandonment of the causal-teleological proof of the existence of God. Indeed, the *pars destruens* of the 1763 *Beweisgrund* strongly suggests that despite its intuitive appeal and its utility for the common understanding, any proof that starts with the beauty and order of nature and that climbs to God as the only possible creator cannot reach the desired conclusion. That is, one cannot infer from the harmony and beauty of nature to the existence of God. This is because – as Kant had already shown in the *Universal Natural History and Theory of Himmels* – such features could be the mechanical effects of the inherent laws of matter.[13] When one focuses on the presumed effects of divine wisdom, one remains open to the objection that a cause other than the divine could produce such effects. Kant's rejection of the physico-teleological proof tells us that in the early 1760s, he became well aware of the risks inherent in any argument that moves from the effect to its alleged cause.

To be sure, Kant insists in the *Beweisgrund* that we *can* infer the existence of a wise creator (although not that of God) from the order of nature.[14] But the central idea of this work is that God's existence is a precondition of all possibility, not that God is the only cause that could produce the order of nature. It follows that Kant's proof does not at all rest on an inference from effect to cause. In general, he is now much more cautious in his inferences. His new methodology demands extreme caution. His abandonment of the causal argument against idealism and of the teleological argument for God's existence must be viewed as the outcome of a new stage in his philosophical development – a stage characterized, as Cassirer has aptly put it, by 'a higher stage of reflection and critical self-awareness.'[15]

As we have already seen, Kant in his 1764 prize essay recommended to philosophers a sort of empirical method: never infer from pre-given definitions, but only from features of an object ascertained through experience.[16] We must heed this empirical orientation of Kant's methodology if we are to make sense of one last crucial aspect of the passage from Metaphysics Herder. Kant does not say that since idealism cannot be refuted *logically*, it cannot be refuted at all. Quite the contrary – he suggests, albeit very briefly, that there are alternative ways to refute it: 'the assent of other human beings and one's own conviction.' This formula is rather vague, but Kant seems to have in mind something like the immediate, unproblematic conviction about the existence of objects around us. And the phrase 'the assent of other human beings' seems to suggest that our conviction can be strengthened by the general agreement among human beings that there are material objects independent of us. Thus Kant appears to be relying on the immediate evidence of the senses not triggered by philosophical sophistry. In this way, he is applying his methodological orientation towards empiricism to the problem of idealism. That problem's solution involves relying on convictions produced by the senses, even if we are aware that such convictions cannot be logically grounded. Kant seems to think that if we cannot refute idealism *logically*, we can still refute it *empirically*.

Unfortunately, Kant's present position is highly paradoxical, as is easy to see. Because it is based ultimately on sense data, his 'proof' is exposed to the traditional difficulties faced by any empiricist attempt to ground realism. One could say that the entire development of classical empiricism, from Locke's realism to Hume's scepticism, is summed up in the passage we are discussing. Modern empiricism began with efforts to consider 'ideas' or mental representations as the immediate objects of our knowledge. Early in its development, with Locke, it confidently took sense data as a certain proof of the existence of external objects that corresponded to them. Locke took for granted that external objects exist so that they can 'convey into the mind several perceptions of things, according to those various ways wherein those objects do affect them.'[17] In his view, external objects, along with the internal operations of our minds, were what 'supplies our understandings with all the *materials* of thinking.'[18] But in its ultimate stage, with Hume, classical empiricism arrived at scepticism precisely *because* of its focus on subjective sense data or 'ideas.' How could we go beyond these 'ideas' in our mind? In the *Treatise*, Hume pointed out that 'properly speaking, 'tis not our body we perceive, when we regard our limbs and members, but certain impressions, which enter by the senses.'[19] It follows that the senses 'give us no notion of continu'd existence, because they cannot operate beyond the extent, in which they really operate.'[20] The senses do nothing to inform us about the existence of independent objects. Locke's idea that there is an independent source for the materials that occupy our mind amounted to a trespass beyond the sphere of impressions.

Analogously, Kant's proof suggests that we rely on our empirically grounded conviction (and the convictions of others) – this, even though he has just cautioned us that no empirical evidence can be used against Berkeley's argument. Kant was perhaps still too enthusiastic about his new empirical method to fully understand its limits. This enthusiasm, however, was to vanish soon. Kant's growing awareness that it would be a paradox to refute idealism 'empirically' left him with a single option: to dismiss the entire problem, to stop treating it seriously and start ridiculing those whose speculations led them to doubt (or even worse, deny) the existence of external objects. This is indeed what Kant does against the 'idealist' Swedenborg.

Dreams of a Spirit-Seer (1766): Idealism Is as Ridiculous as Swedenborg's Visions

In 1766, Kant quarrelled with a very peculiar 'idealist,' the 'visionary' Swedenborg. Certainly, *Dreams of a Spirit-Seer* is more concerned with removing spiritual substances from the sensible world – the spirits that Swedenborg claimed to see – than with grounding the existence of material substances. Indeed, this polemical essay does not explicitly discuss idealism. Kant criticizes Swedenborg because, given his explanation of how one can form visions of spirits, the consequence is that 'he denies to this world its independent subsistence, and therefore held it to be only a systematic appearance, arising from the constitution of the spirit world' – something that makes him an 'idealist.'[21] Yet Kant does not mount a *modus tollens* – that is, he does not demonstrate the existence of bodily beings in order to prove that Swedenborg's account is false. Rather, he simply assumes their existence. It is precisely this lack of argumentation that highlights Kant's attitude towards idealism at this stage. *Dreams of a Spirit-Seer* constitutes the culmination of the new orientation in Kant's thought that took root in the early 1760s. By 1766, Kant has completely reconstructed his views about the possibility and even the goal of metaphysics. This science must be the science of the 'limits of reason,' as Kant would later famously declare. Kant now leaves no important issues to metaphysics. Philosophy can be a critical discipline, but not a doctrine. All of the long-asked questions that Kant had thought metaphysics could answer, even if that science were to be reconstituted according to his suggestions in the Prize Essay, now seem of a piece with Swedenborg's visions. Accordingly, we must address them with the same ironical tone with which Kant treated Swedenborg.

In this context, it should come as no surprise that we find in Kant no actual argument against idealism, but only a lampooning of Swedenborg for reducing material things to epiphenomena. Indeed, for Swedenborg material things are merely the gross perceptions of those who lack his higher faculty for seeing the real constituents of the world – that is, spirits.[22] As we have noted, Kant seems to see no point in providing reasons to reject the idealism to which Swedenborg is committed. Instead, he is content to highlight the embarrassing consequences of Swedenborg's ideas. In 1766, consistently with his disillusionment with all traditional metaphysical questions, Kant approached the sceptical challenge simply by relying on the immediate commonsensical reaction to it: the idea of doubting or denying the existence of the external world need not be taken seriously. After all, there is no doubt that reason can conceive of the most bizarre philosophical fantasies. Only ordinary experience can narrow what is conceivable down to what is real. Reason can conceive the most abstruse relations between cause and effect. Experience is the only criterion we have for rejecting them. Interestingly, Kant points out that if we do not appeal to experience, the claim that my will causes the moon's orbit to stop is no less *intelligible* than the claim that my will causes the motion of my arm. Only experience tells me that the former is a fantasy.[23] Similarly, the claim that some sort of Evil Genius causes my representations is not less intelligible than the claim that external objects are the usual causes of our representations. Again, the only difference is that experience informs me that the latter kind of causal relation is the only one that takes place.[24]

Echoing the position of the Metaphysics Herder, Kant seems to be relying on our immediate 'conviction' to silence the sceptics and thus ridicule Swedenborg. But note well that here, Kant is taking this approach to the extreme. Whereas the Metaphysics Herder at least took the sceptical challenge seriously, now the entire problem of idealism is no longer considered worthy of serious reflection. Again, Kant simply views it as an embarrassing consequence whose absurdity is self-evident: idealism is as absurd as Swedenborg's visions, and both must be ridiculed rather than seriously criticized.

This dismissive attitude towards idealism was perhaps forced on Kant by his commitment to a broadly construed empiricistic framework. His insistence in 1764–6 on the importance of grounding philosophy on empirical data committed him to the usual aporiae of all empiricistic philosophy: if our knowledge is reduced to sense data and to inferences from them, then the problem of how to move beyond these subjective sense data will always arise. In the Metaphysics Herder, Kant thought he had solved this problem by inferring to 'the assent of other human beings and one's own conviction.' But as we have seen, an inner contradiction threatened that solution. The orientation of Kant's thought now led him to the only option left: since neither a 'logical' nor, strictly speaking, an 'empirical' solution to the problem is possible, the best attitude is simply to dismiss it.[25]

That this is Kant's strategy is also confirmed by his remarks in the third chapter of *Dreams*. Having attempted in the first chapter a serious metaphysical refutation of Swedenborg, Kant now sympathizes with those readers who prefer his scientific argument to the metaphysical one because the latter is guilty of the same abstraction against which it was directed: 'For it creates at once grave suspicion for one to attempt seriously to expound the fancies of a visionary, and the kind of philosophy which is found in such bad company is open to question.'[26]

This is precisely the attitude that we wanted to point out. It is impossible to refute logically metaphysical fantasies such as spirit-seeing or idealism; furthermore, it is a sign of intellectual decadence even to take them seriously. Spirit-seeing or idealism, we might conclude, are such hyperbolic and implausible possibilities that, although they can be consistently held, they are not worthy of our attention. The price for meeting the challenges posed by them is to sink into equally abstract and confused speculations. Never was Kant's attitude closer to Hume's disappointment with philosophical reflection. At the end of the first book of his *Treatise*, Hume noted the risks inherent in grounding scepticism

Idealism in the Precritical Period   23

on rational arguments similar to those he had put forward, and thus made the furthering of his philosophical enterprise conditional on a radical change in his philosophical method: abstract reasoning must be abandoned altogether, *even if it aims at establishing the position one wants to defend*.[27] Here, Kant is recommending a similar stance towards highly abstract philosophy: do not try to solve its vain problems with its own methodology, because this will inevitably lead you to the same impasse you wanted to avoid. In addition, since you would be using the same intellectual tools, you would look no different from the champions of metaphysical sophistry you wanted to ridicule.

Ironically, the more we emphasize Kant's dismissive attitude towards metaphysics and its various problems (including idealism), the harder it becomes for us to explain why only a few years later, in the 1770 *Dissertation*, he returned in grand style to metaphysics – in particular, to a metaphysical argument against idealism. To this historical mystery we must now turn.

The *Dissertation* (1770): A Restoration of the Causal Argument?

The *Dissertation* has always constituted one of the most serious challenges for any interpretation of Kant's precritical thought. The problem lies in the fact that having instructed metaphysicians to abandon all hope of attaining knowledge of the supersensible world, to direct their efforts at determining the limits of human reason, and to confine philosophical research to the realm of experience, Kant now claims that knowledge of the intelligible world is possible, that metaphysics is about determining the first principles of this world, and that the primary concern should be to remove empirical concepts from our descriptions of the intelligible world. Interpreters have ingeniously attempted to show that what seems to be an insoluble and unexplainable reversal of philosophical commitment is actually part of a continuous development and that, on closer examination, there is no real shift between *Dreams* and the *Dissertation*.[28] Regardless of how well these efforts have succeeded, we face a similar challenge with regard to the development of Kant's treatment of the problem of idealism. We have already seen that from the time of the Metaphysics Herder, Kant seemed to have abandoned all hope of refuting scepticism in the way he did in the *Nova Dilucidatio*. We have seen that after 1762, Kant is well aware that it is impossible to refute scepticism by pointing to the cause of our impressions. No matter how lively these impressions are, and no matter how puzzling our mind alterations are (if we do not assume that some external object determines them), the dream argument tells us clearly that we could have fleeting impressions in our mind in complete absence of external factors. In 1770, however, Kant presents an argument that seems to entirely ignore such awareness: 'Now although phenomena are properly species of things and are not ideas, nor do they express the internal and absolute quality of objects, none the less cognition of them is most veridical. For first of all, in as much as they are sensual concepts or apprehensions, they are witnesses, as being things caused, to the presence of an object, and this is opposed to idealism.' (Ak. 2: 397).

Let us suspend our discussion on whether this is a mere repetition of the argument in the *Nova Dilucidatio*, mysteriously advanced after the remarks of the Metaphysics Herder. We need first to understand what Kant is saying in this passage, which is much less clear than it seems at first glance. In particular, we need to understand precisely what 'bears witness' to the presence of an object, what this object is, and what kind of relation occurs between the two. On these questions, interpreters are not unanimous. Some think that Kant here is taking phenomena to be genuine, mind-independent objects. Others reject this reading as committing Kant to a patent nonsense.[29] It is crucial for us to choose between these two alternatives, because the interpretation of Kant's treatment of idealism in the *Dissertation* largely depends on how we read this passage. Moreover, once we are clear about what Kant is saying, we will be able to determine whether he is mysteriously repeating the argument of the *Nova Dilucidatio*.

Guyer champions the non-phenomenalistic reading. He thinks that Kant is saying here that the ideality of space and time does not entail that the things in space and time are dependent on the subject – that is, that they are mental entities.[30] Thus he seems to take phenomena in this passage to be 'objects of experience' – that is, genuine objects existing outside the mind. To be sure, I shall show that 'phenomena' or 'appearances' must be so understood in the first *Critique* (incidentally, something that Guyer denies[31]). It is highly doubtful, however, that Kant in this passage is already taking phenomena in this sense. Actually, on Guyer's reading the passage becomes meaningless. As Hoyos Jaramillo has rightly pointed out, it hardly makes sense to say that idealism is refuted because a phenomenon, understood as a genuine mind-independent object, bears witness to the presence or existence of another object. On such a reading, the latter object would be completely superfluous because the cognition of the first object would be sufficient to refute idealism. To avoid this absurdity, we have two alternative readings (also suggested by Hoyos Jaramillo): (1) we can take 'phenomena' as 'given' – that is, as objects of sensibility or 'appearances' in the sense in which Kant uses this term in the Aesthetic, leaving indeterminate whether the 'object' these phenomena witness is a noumenon or an object of experience (which would be the object of sensibility no longer as such, but as organized by the intellectual forms); or (2) if we want to take 'phenomena' in the sense of objects of experience, then in order to avoid the tautology that objects of experience bear witness to objects of experience, we must interpret 'object' as noumenon.

But even these two alternatives are not satisfactory. While the latter alternative again makes the reference to the witnessed object superfluous, the former alternative makes it impossible for phenomena to witness anything at all. Indeed, if we take phenomena as 'given' or 'appearances' in the sense of the Aesthetic – that is, as one of the contributing factors eventually resulting in an object of experience – then we cannot take them as something of which we are aware. Notoriously, Kant's point is not that we are conscious first of 'appearances' and that we then organize them through the intellectual forms. It follows that appearances (in the specified sense) cannot bear witness to anything. Thus it seems that we are left with the following reading: 'phenomena' in our passage are mental entities, modifications of our mind of which we are conscious because they are the objects of our experience. Moreover, in being caused (*causata*), they witness the presence of their cause – that is, of an object. Since we have identified the sensible world with the mental, it follows that this object, in order to be an extra-mental entity and thus refute idealism, must be a noumenon.

This suggests, *pace* Guyer, that in 1770 Kant was still far from the form of realism (and correlatively of transcendental idealism) that he would hold in the *Critique*. The analysis of the passage at hand indicates that Kant was tempted – at least when faced with the idealist challenge – to interpret phenomena as mental entities and to ascribe real, mind-independent existence only to noumena, in turn interpreted as a separate set of objects and as causes of these mental entities. Thus in his confrontation with idealism, Kant tended to slip into a form of metaphysical realism (which he would later call transcendental realism). This does not mean that he accepted with full awaremess a two-sets-of-objects interpretation of the phenomena/noumena distinction. It seems, rather that he himself was still unclear as to precisely how that distinction was to be interpreted. When faced with the sceptical challenge, however, he found the dogmatic interpretation highly appealing, thinking, mistakenly, that this would help the cause of realism. Certainly, he was still very far from the clear intuition of the Fourth Paralogism that the objects whose existence must be proven against idealism are not the alleged supersensible causes of phenomena, but rather the phenomena themselves, understood as genuine empirical objects.

If we accept this reading of Kant's position in 1770, then we can also shed some light on the mystery of the restoration of the causal argument after the powerful objections of Metaphysics Herder. We saw that the crucial problem with that argument was that it rested on an a priori definition of the substance/mind. Only by ruling out (through questionable abstract reasoning) the possibility of the mind's self-affection, could Kant conclude that some external cause was required to explain the inner changes of the mind. That argument was easily rebutted by the sceptic in two steps: (1) experience teaches us that the mind *is* capable of self-affection (for example, dreams and products of the imagination); and (2) whether we experience a genuine object or 'see' a mere product of the imagination, we are always entertaining a representation (or 'idea,' in the Cartesian-Lockean sense). In other words, the immediate objects of our experience are representations. Therefore, we are never in the position to know whether there is something beyond these representations.

Let us now recall that in 1770, Kant was operating with the sensibility/understanding distinction, which he had not possessed before. Moreover, we have seen that he had now a tendency to reduce phenomena to mental entities. By doing so, he was incorporating the sceptical assumption that our knowledge is limited to 'apprehensions,' so that no empirical proof can really succeed against idealism. Kant had already learned this lesson by the time of the Metaphysics Herder. Idealism is right in claiming that our (sensible) knowledge is limited to 'representations.' Idealism, however, overlooks the point that something unknown underlies our apprehensions and that, to a certain extent, we have access to it through our understanding.

It is important to notice that this is certainly a causal argument, albeit one very different from the argument we saw in the *Nova Dilucidatio*. The latter did not even consider the problem of going beyond the inner alterations of our mind – it considered it impossible for them to be self-produced. The new argument does not rest on this assumption; it even concedes to the sceptic that there is no way to *experience* the object whose existence we want to prove. Nonetheless, it insists that *something* underlies our representations that we do not *experience*, but rather cognize through pure intellectual means. Thus Kant believed he had found a way to incorporate the sceptical position and at the same time surpass it. The *Dissertation* – at least as far as the argument against idealism is concerned – does not constitute an unexplainable return to a position that Kant had abandoned during his sceptical period. It is, rather, a second attempt – one that starts from very different premises.

This reconstruction, obviously, is not to suggest that the new causal argument, unlike the early one, constitutes a satisfactory refutation of the sceptic. It is quite clear that the force of this argument is bound both to a dogmatic interpretation of the phenomena/noumena distinction and to an equally dogmatic assumption about the knowability of the intellectual world. When Kant reconsidered the possibility of pure intellectual cognition, he was forced to abandon his new causal argument and to rethink the whole problem of idealism from the beginning. More importantly, when Kant saw that no causal argument whatsoever could succeed against idealism, he was compelled to rethink the appearances/things in themselves distinction – that is, the foundation of his philosophy.

As we can see if we turn to the texts on idealism from the silent decade, Kant realizes that no appeal to a supersensible cause can silence the sceptic. However, he still does not grasp that the only way out is to reject consciously and systematically the identification of phenomena with mental entities. Only when Kant achieves this crucial insight does he *at once* solve the idealism problem and reshape his general philosophical position. It is no accident that the Fourth Paralogism of 1781 contains both the critical solution to the problem of idealism and one of the few standard definitions of transcendental idealism,[32] together with the crucial distinction between transcendental and empirical realism. As we shall see in later chapters, Kant's refutation of the sceptic and his clear definition of the kind of realism that his position entails are inseparable intellectual achievements. At least after 1770, the question of idealism is one of the driving forces behind Kant's general philosophical development.

The Letter to Herz (1772): The Definitive Abandonment of the Causal Argument

The letter to Herz of 21 July 1772 contains a passage – extremely interesting for our purposes – inserted in the context of Kant's attempt to reply to Lambert's criticism of the *Dissertation*. Lambert contended that the ideality of time puts at risk the reality of change. Indeed, change presupposes time. If time is ideal, then change must be ideal as well.[33] Kant rephrases Lambert's critique as follows: 'Changes are something real (according to the testimony of inner sense). Now, they are possible only on the assumption of time; therefore time is something real that is involved in the determination of the things in themselves.' Having rephrased Lambert's challenge in this way, Kant replies by pointing out that a parallel argument is not used for the reality of spatial objects. The argument would go as follows: 'Bodies are real (according to the testimony of outer sense). Now, bodies are possible only under the condition of space; therefore space is something objective and real that inheres in the things themselves.'

Kant wants to emphasize the contrast between the two premises: 'changes are something real (according to the testimony of inner sense)'; and 'bodies are real (according to the testimony of outer sense).' Since the reality of bodies is not guaranteed by the testimony of outer sense, whereas the reality of changes is guaranteed by the testimony of inner sense, we tend to accept the first argument and to consider the second as at best dubious. As Kant puts it, the fundamental reason why we accept only the first argument is this: 'It is obvious, in regard to outer things, that one cannot infer the reality of the object from the reality of the representation, though in the case of inner sense the thinking or the existence of thought and the existence of my own self are one and the same.'[34]

Given these premises, Kant's answer to Lambert is the following: I experience the changes in my inner state through time, which is the form of my inner sensibility. This, however, does not make them unreal. Quite the contrary – they are certain because my inner sense is infallible. But the reason for the infallibility of inner sense is not that inner sense is not subject to a form, whereas outer sense is. The reason is simply that 'in inner sense the thinking or the existence of thought and the existence of my own self are one and the same.'[35] In other words, inner sense is more reliable not because it is not subject to a form, but because there is no gap between the representation and the thing represented. It follows that one can affirm both that inner sense is subject to a form – that is, that time is transcendentally ideal – and that changes are empirically real. Analogously, the reason why we do *not* infer the reality of the spatial thing from the reality of its representation has nothing to do with the fact that space is the form of outer sense. Rather, the reason is that unlike in the case of inner sense, spatial objects are not the same as their representations. In sum, the fact that changes and spatial objects are experienced through forms of sensibility does not take away anything of their reality. Thus Kant concludes: 'I do not deny that changes are real any more than I deny that bodies are real, even though by *real* I only mean that something real corresponds to the appearance.'

Quite independently of the force of Kant's reply to Lambert, there are at least three aspects of it that are highly relevant to our purposes. To begin with, although Kant does not put the point in causal terms, it is clear that he is denying a kind of inference from the reality of the effect (the representation) to the reality of the cause (the alleged object). The reason for this denial seems to be the familiar consideration that no spatial object might correspond to the representation, as happens with hallucinations or dreams. We have seen that Kant was aware of these considerations by the early 1760s. The novelty here is that he sees that the same considerations apply even when we distinguish between phenomena and noumena – in other words, the crucial distinction in the *Dissertation* does not remove the difficulties underlying this invalid inference.

Second, the text shows that in 1772 Kant still thinks that inner sense and outer sense enjoy completely different degrees of certainty. And although he claims that he believes in the reality of change as much as he believes in the existence of external objects ('I do not deny that changes are real any more than I deny that bodies are real'), he also insists that inner sense and outer sense do not have equal epistemic status. He believes that both change and external objects are 'real,' but his own argument presupposes that the existence of external objects, unlike that of change, cannot be held with certainty. Note that it is highly unlikely that Kant is merely introducing a hypothetical counter-argument to Lambert without embracing it. Kant's language suggests that he is taking as self-evident the fact that outer sense, unlike inner sense, suffers from a deficiency of epistemic reliability ('*it is obvious*, in regard to the reality of outer things, that one cannot infer the reality of the object from the reality of the representation'[36]).

Third, and most importantly, note that Kant has begun to see that external objects are always 'real' in an empirical sense and never in the sense in which a thing in itself is real. Part of his reply to Lambert turns on the idea that change and external objects can be ascertained as real precisely through a form of sensibility. Indeed, the question of whether change is real in itself ('objectively or in itself') is dismissed by Kant as a sort of category mistake: it presupposes that things in themselves are in time. Things in themselves are neither changeable nor unchangeable in the sense in which the things we experience are. Indeed, Kant seems to think that even to say that things in themselves are unchangeable would be to presuppose time as a background against which we could experience this lack of change.[37] It is a mistake to try to look into things in themselves to ground the reality of time and change. Analogously, we could add – although Kant does not say it explicitly – it is a mistake to look into things in themselves to ground the reality of space and spatial things in it.

Kant has begun to see that all doubts about the reality of what we experience (be that change or external objects) cannot be answered by an appeal to the supersensible; yet the formula through which he expresses this new and crucial insight is still hopelessly vague and risks encouraging precisely the mistake he has warned us against. Kant's definition of what is real is indeed: 'By *real* I only mean that something real corresponds to the appearance.'[38] Obviously, the very idea that what is real 'corresponds' to the appearance can be taken again in the sense that what is real is what goes beyond the appearances – that is, beyond the sensible world – which is exactly what Kant wanted to avoid.[39]

Thus we can summarize the main point of our analysis of the letter to Herz. Its relevance for our purposes lies in the fact that it points to Kant's initial awareness of the impossibility of grounding the existence of external objects on *any* inference from a representation, understood as a mental entity, to its object, understood as its alleged cause. Moreover, Kant begins to see the necessity of attributing a sensible (not a super-sensible) kind of reality to external things, though this insight is not firm and has not found a full and convincing formula. Finally, Kant seems to lack a convincing argument that could replace the causal argument he has implicitly rejected. The situation does not seem to change as we move on to the mid-1770s – that is, to what Kant says about idealism in the lectures known as Metaphysics L_1.

Metaphysics L_1 (late 1770s): Idealism Remains as Problematic in Philosophy

The dating of Metaphysics Herder is uncontroversial because we know the year in which Herder matriculated at the University of Königsberg (1762) and the year in which he left (1764). The dating of Metaphysics L_1 is far more difficult because we lack a comparably decisive indication. In fact, Kant scholars have been disputing this dating since the end of the last century. For our purposes, it is sufficient to note that there is a general agreement that these notes cannot be dated earlier than 1775-6 and that they precede the first edition of the *Critique* (1781). Only Arnold proposes an *ante quem* date later than 1781. But this suggestion is highly suspect for many reasons already pointed out by others, as well as for the fact (surprisingly overlooked in the debate) that Metaphysics L_1 presents a striking agreement with rational psychology, which can hardly be consistent with the hypothesis that Kant gave these lectures after writing the Paralogism chapter of the first *Critique*.[40] It follows that we can place these notes in the second half of the 1770s. They are Kant's only treatment of the problem of idealism between his letter to Herz and the first *Critique*.

It seems that by the second half of the 1770s Kant had not yet found a convincing reply to the sceptical challenge. In Metaphysics L_1 he reiterates the absolute superiority of inner sense over outer sense:

> The first thing that is entirely certain is this: that I am; I feel myself, I know for certain that I am; but with just such certainty I do not know that other beings are outside me. I do see appearances (phenomena); but I am not certain that the same thing underlies these appearances; for in dreams I also have representations and appearances, and were the dreams only orderly, so that one would always begin to dream where one has left off, then one could always maintain that one was in the other world. (28:206)[41]

This passage strongly suggests that phenomena or appearances – which are here clearly used interchangeably – are identified with mental entities. Moreover, the vague formula we saw in the letter is echoed in the way in which Kant formulates the uncertainty from which our outer knowledge suffers: 'I am not certain that the same thing underlies these appearances.' Kant seems to fall back on the idea that the question of realism is to be solved by an appeal to what goes beyond appearances/phenomena. Given this, it comes as no surprise that Kant is still unable to find an answer to idealism. He himself seems to admit as much in the rest of the passage.

First, Kant introduces the distinction – which he will later use in the *Critique* – between the problematic and the dogmatic versions of the doctrine. Both egoism – the position that I am the only one who exists – and idealism – only thinking beings like me exist – can be taken either problematically or dogmatically. In the first case, it is doubted that there are other beings or that there are material beings besides the subject. In the second case, both claims are not doubted; rather they are denied apodictically. Again, prefiguring the *Critique*, Kant attributes a positive value only to the problematic version, which has the virtue of clarifying that outer sense and inner sense are not equally reliable. He argues: 'The reliability of inner sense is certain. I am, I feel that and I intuit myself immediately. This proposition thus has a reliability of experience. But that something is *outside me*, of that the senses can provide no reliability; for the appearances can indeed be a play of my power of imagination. Further the senses also cannot provide any reliability against idealism' (28:205–6).

As often happens in the Lectures, it is unclear whether Kant is here expressing his opinion or whether he is presenting someone else's. Certainly, as in the case of Metaphysics Herder, this exposition of problematic idealism and egoism is not a mere repetition of Baumgarten because the corresponding sections in Baumgarten's *Metaphysica* contain only a definition of the egoist. Quite the contrary – it seems that here Kant wants to criticize Leibniz and thus indirectly also Baumgarten, who follows Leibniz in considering the world as an aggregate of monads – that is, spiritual entities.[42] Kant criticizes this position by showing that it is a form of dogmatic idealism. Indeed, it asserts that only spiritual substances exist, and it presupposes a sort of intellectual intuition which would reveal that the bodies we experience are actually entities with representative power (*vis representativa*) – that is, monads. But since we do not have this intellectual intuition, it follows that unlike problematic idealism, Leibniz's and Baumgarten's dogmatic idealism is of no use and must be 'banned from philosophy.'[43] Consequently, there is no doubt that Kant is not merely repeating Baumgarten.

This, however, is not sufficient to conclude that Kant embraces the sceptical claims he is making. Indeed, it is still possible that he is merely presenting the sceptical challenge without embracing the considerations on which it rests. There are, however, two reasons to believe that he does subscribe to some of the tenets of problematic idealism. To begin with, he clearly agrees with the idea that the senses cannot give any proof; after all, he comments in passing that 'this [idea] is very good in philosophy.' Second, he ends the exposition of problematic egoism and idealism with a comment that seems to reflect his final assessment of the whole issue: since the senses cannot give any proof, 'egoism and idealism remain as problematic in philosophy.'[44] This means that unlike dogmatic idealism, which 'is of no use,' problematic idealism cannot be simply dismissed. It remains in philosophy as a meaningful problem. We still lack an argument to refute it.

To be sure, Kant points out that the understanding 'can indeed add something to the reliability of the senses, for if things are altered, then there must be a ground of the alteration.' This passage is quite obscure as it stands. If by the things that are altered one understands our mental states, then this remark echoes the causal argument that we have seen in the *Dissertation* and that we thought Kant had completely and definitively abandoned. There is, however, no indication that the alterations Kant is talking about are mental ones. It seems, rather, that he has in mind the following: We observe that (all) things are altered. Since we take these alterations (for example, ice melting) as in general independent of our will, we can hardly explain why they occur unless we postulate a factor beyond our causal power – that is, something outside us. Since it is our understanding that introduces causality as 'rule of synthesis' among phenomena, it is our understanding that 'can ... add something to the reliability of the senses.' This reading is confirmed by Kant's emphasis – which is lost in Ameriks's translation, that the ground of the alteration is 'in the things' (*in ihnen*). It would hardly makes sense to say that the ground of the alteration of things is in them, if we take those things which are altered as inner modifications. The whole point of the causal argument is, indeed, that the ground of the inner alterations is *not* 'in them.' It follows that, contrary to appearances, Kant is not rehabilitating the causal argument of the *Dissertation*.

Kant himself, however, does not seem to consider his argument to be a straightforward refutation of the sceptic. The very cautious language he uses suggests as much: our understanding adds 'something' to the reliability of the senses, which seems to suggest that their inability to produce a proof is not *completely* rescued by our understanding. More importantly, even if Kant took his argument as conclusive, it is quite clear that it is not. The fact that we take the alterations around us as independent of our will does not rule out the possibility that both the altering and the altered things are nothing but a mere play of representations in our mind.

Reflexion 5400 (late 1770s): The Bridge to the Critical Period

That Kant himself was not very happy with his argument in the Lectures is confirmed by a Reflexion, which, if Adickes's dating is correct, is roughly contemporaneous with these notes. Here Kant adopts a completely new argument: 'We are certainly not aware that [phenomena] are external, namely that they are not mere products of the imagination and dreams, but we do know that they are the original of all possible products of the imagination and thus that they are not products of the imagination.'[45]

Thus, phenomena must be real because they are what provides the imagination with the material ('the original') that it requires in order to operate. This is the first appearance of an argument that Kant will also use in the critical period, both in the Fourth Paralogism and in the Refutation of Idealism, but that interpreters almost unanimously consider unsatisfactory. We will discuss this argument and its weaknesses in chapter 3. For the moment, it is far more important to note how in this attempt to answer the sceptic, Kant is once again called on to redefine and clarify the concept of phenomenon. Right before the quoted passage, he points out that when we ask whether something exists outside me, this question is legitimate only if we do not ask for something that exists in itself. The legitimate question is, therefore, 'whether there be external phenomena.' The question of scepticism can be neither posed nor answered with reference to something that has an 'absolute existence,' that is, with reference to the things in themselves. The objects we must prove against the sceptic are phenomena. And Kant takes these as genuine objects, not as mental entities, as it is evident from his characterization of them as a source of the material of the imagination in the quoted passage. If phenomena were mental entities, obviously they could not serve as the external source of the material on which the imagination operates.

Thus, in this crucial Reflexion, which can be rightly considered the bridge to the critical period, Kant is securing the progress he had already made in the letter to Herz: the objects whose existence must be proven are phenomena, which, precisely because they have to perform this antisceptical function, cannot be understood as mental entities. The *formula* that Kant uses for defining phenomena (as that to which 'objects correspond') is still open to misunderstanding and echoes the equally misleading expression of the letter to Herz, yet it is undeniable that Kant finally sees with full clarity that no reference to things in themselves is needed (nor is it legitimate) to answer the sceptic and that all our efforts must focus on grounding the existence of phenomena, which can no longer be understood as mental entities precisely because of the antisceptical function that is attributed to them. The weakness of Kant's proof does not undermine in the least the enormous value of the transformation of the notion of phenomena – a transformation to which Kant is led in his attempt to counter the sceptic.

Let us now evaluate Kant's stance towards the sceptical challenge on the threshold of the critical period. To begin with, the idea that only inner sense is certain because it enjoys an immediate relation with its object, whereas outer sense inevitably suffers the lack of immediate contact, contradicts one of the main tenets of the Fourth Paralogism, which, as we shall see, centres on the attempt to re-establish *some sort* of epistemic parity between the two senses.[46] Second, the thesis (which rests on the preceding one) that the senses cannot prove the existence of external objects is reminiscent of the line of thought in the 1772 letter and also stands in flat contradiction with the Fourth Paralogism's idea that 'the immediate perception (consciousness) of [external objects] is at the same time a sufficient proof of their reality.'[47] Third, we have seen that in Metaphysics L_1 Kant still tends to identify phenomena/appearances with mental entities – which constitutes the greatest obstacle he has placed in the path of a refutation of the sceptic.

We have also seen that there have been improvements in Kant's anti-sceptical tactic, but these have led mostly to negative results. Specifically, Kant has progressively learned that no causal argument will be ever able to silence the sceptic; that the phenomena/noumena distinction does not rescue the causal argument; and that the identification of phenomena and mental entities with the related reference to an unknown cause (or causes) of them is no help. But precisely these failures were pointing him in a completely new direction. If scepticism is to be refuted, then the objects whose existence is to be shown can no longer be what remains 'behind' phenomena. Rather, they must be exactly these phenomena, no longer identified with mental entities, but rather with genuine, mind-independent objects. This is the line of thought we have seen advanced in the letter to Herz and repeated in R5400. In other words, the phenomena/noumena distinction had to receive a new sense. The Fourth Paralogism, to which we now turn, must be seen as the full realization of these improvements resulting from a thirty-year confrontation with the problem of idealism.

2 The Nature of Transcendental Idealism and Its Foundations

In the preceding chapter we saw how the precritical reflection on the problem of idealism led Kant to reinterpret the distinction between appearances and things in themselves. If in 1770, in the attempt to solve the problem of scepticism, he took appearances as mental entities and things in themselves as the genuine mind-independent objects that cause those mental entities, in the silent decade he began to see that no successful refutation of scepticism could be mounted on this interpretation of the transcendental distinction. Thus he came more and more to assign to appearances the role of those objects whose existence must be proven against the sceptic. Obviously, this presupposed the reinterpretation of appearances, no longer as mental entities, but rather as genuine objects existing outside the mind, and of things in themselves as the same objects viewed in abstraction from the forms of our sensibility. The new antisceptical argument and the definition of the truly critical sense of the transcendental distinction were reached conjointly.

In the first edition of the *Critique*, this double intellectual achievement is definitively established. In the Fourth Paralogism, Kant explicitly denies that the sceptic can be refuted through reference to things in themselves. The sceptic must be countered by appealing to appearances, because even if we can admit that some extra-sensible object 'causes' our intuitions, pointing to this alleged cause will never ground realism. Rather, the new refutation must rest within the limits of possible experience and take advantage of two crucial ideas that arise from the proper understanding of the transcendental distinction: (1) We know nothing about the extra-sensible cause of our intuitions; it could very well be some spiritual entity similar to the Evil Genius, but this need not concern us because it is not the existence of this object that must be proven in order to refute the sceptic. (2) The objects of our experience are genuine objects that we grasp immediately – that is, without the mediation of an 'idea' or mental representative state.

Both of the above points depend on transcendental idealism (specifically, on transcendental idealism properly understood in the new critical sense), which Kant in fact sees as the only perspective from which scepticism can be countered – 'the only refuge,' as he puts it.[1] This suggests that an analysis of transcendental idealism is preliminary to any discussion of the specific antisceptical argument of the Fourth Paralogism. That analysis, to which this entire chapter is devoted, is carried out in three main parts.

To begin with, we must show that transcendental idealism, despite its identification of empirical objects with 'mere representations,' does not entail the reduction of spatio-temporal objects to mental entities. If this were the case, the Fourth Paralogism – where that identification is often repeated – would amount to a refutation of Descartes's idealism through a rehabilitation of Berkeley's *esse est percipi*, something that can hardly be viewed as a foundation of the independent existence of the external world.[2] The focus of the first part is thus on the nature of transcendental idealism per se. We attempt to show that Kant's idealism can and should be distinguished carefully from phenomenalism. Many contemporary interpreters today reject the phenomenalistic view of Kant that was standard in the Anglo-American world until a few decades ago. In fact, interpretations as diverse as those of Collins, Hanna, Langton, Melnick, Matthews, Pippin, and Allison's can be placed in the same non-phenomenalistic camp.[3] Nonetheless, other interpreters – Guyer and, more recently, Van Cleve – are still outspokenly attached to the phenomenalistic reading.[4] This suggests that the debate is still open and that a fresh reconsideration of the issue might be in order, quite independently of our antisceptical purposes.

As will become clear, everything turns on two different senses in which both Kant and a phenomenalist would call the empirical object a 'representation.' In exploiting this distinction we shall come close to Allison's specific form of non-phenomenalism. The novelty of our approach stems from the historical perspective – largely ignored by Allison – in which our argument is embedded. The results of the preceding chapter, in which we analysed the importance of the antisceptical challenge for the mature definition of transcendental idealism, will help us mount new evidence in favour of the non-phenomenalistic reading.

In the second part, I shall apply the results of the first part to show that, contrary to what the overwhelming majority of interpreters assume, even the Fourth Paralogism should not be read as a profession of phenomenalism. This is undoutably a result more difficult to achieve than arguing generally in favour of a non-phenomenalistic reading. In fact, while even Guyer implicitly recognizes that the Refutation of Idealism in the Second Edition is not infected by phenomenalism, the First Edition of the *Critique* – in particular the Fourth Paralogism – is generally viewed as helplessly committed to that view.

Even if transcendental idealism were convincingly distinguished from phenomenalism, this would still be insufficient for our purposes. If transcendental idealism is to serve as the main premise of our antisceptical argument, something must be said about its *truth*. Obviously, it is extremely difficult (if not impossible) to defend an interpretation of transcendental idealism and an account of Kant's arguments for it in such a short space, since the topic is so large and since countless objections have been given to Kant's arguments. This holds both for the the direct argument of the Aesthetic, in which Kant argues from the a priori and intuitive nature of the representations of space and time (a result established in the Metaphysical Exposition) to the ideality of space and time; as well as for the indirect argument of the Dialectic, in which Kant argues from the reductio ad absurdum of transcendental realism (considered as the common assumption underlying the antinomical conflict) to the truth of its opposite – that is, transcendental idealism. Nonetheless, we can at least focus on one of the two main foundational arguments – namely, the direct argument of the Aesthetic – to show that Kant's idealism has the resources to rebut powerful criticisms that have recently been levelled against it. Readers should view this analysis, which occupies the third part of the present chapter, as a modest attempt to shake the widespread confidence with which the condemnation of Kant's idealism is generally uttered, with final assessments that range from a charge of sheer inconsistency to a charge that imputes that it is dependent on heavy metaphysical assumptions. It is not my ambition to offer a full-scale defence of transcendental idealism. Rather, I will be satisfied if my analysis convinces readers that questions about the soundness of transcendental idealism are at least still open and that for this reason it is not absurd to use them to underpin my antisceptical argument.

The Formal Nature of Kant's Idealism

One way to determine the nature of Kant's idealism, and to distinguish it from phenomenalism, is to focus on Kant's reply to his reviewers

Garve and Feder, who took his position precisely as a form of phenomenalism. In that reply Kant proposes to replace 'transcendental' with 'formal' or 'critical,' as a means of qualifying his idealism in order 'to distinguish it from the dogmatic Idealism of Berkeley, and from the sceptical Idealism of Descartes.'[5] But what does formal or critical idealism mean, and how is a formal or critical idealism different from Berkeley's and Descartes'?

Misleading Accounts

Unfortunately Kant's own explanation of this difference is not as useful as one might expect. In the Appendix to the *Prolegomena*, which contains Kant's reaction to the superficial reading by Garve and Feder, he starts with the suggestion that the real difference between him and Berkeley relates to the status of the representation of space and to the consequent ability to explain a priori knowledge. For Berkeley the representation of space is a posteriori; thus he cannot explain the a priori features of our cognition of space geometry. The problem with this account is that even if true, it is perfectly compatible with the possibility that for Kant space is a mere (innate) idea in the mind and that all spatial objects in it are likewise devoid of any ontological independence. To insist merely on the a priori nature of our representation of space does not say anything about the ontological status of spatial objects. In fact, an a priori representation of space could even be an innate idea in our mind that orders the other mental entities our experience consists of, as in the Berkeleyan world view. Rather, the crucial difference is that for Berkeley, the ideality of space and of all the objects contained therein means that they exist only insofar as a mind (either finite or infinite) perceives them; whereas for Kant this ideality means that space is the subjective form through which we perceive objects as distinct from ourselves, while these objects exist even if no mind perceives them. Thus Kant's claim that he is 'one in confession with the above idealists' as to the fact that space is a property not of the things in themselves, but only of appearances, becomes in this context quite misleading.

Another unsuccessful attempt to pinpoint the difference between his notion of ideality of space and Berkeley's is found in the *Critique*. Kant is aware that his idea that space is a subjective form that cannot be predicated of the objects considered as they are in themselves might be interpreted as a straightforward reduction of the status of space to that of a secondary quality. Now, if extension is identified with a secondary quality, it follows that objects as they appear to us merely *seem* to be external. Hence the ideality of space would threaten the genuine existence of the external world. In order to block this misunderstanding, Kant draws a distinction between the ideality that characterizes space (and time) and the subjectivity of secondary qualities. Kant argues that while secondary qualities 'may, indeed, be different for different men' (A29/B45), supposedly all human beings agree about the spatial features of an object. On this ground, he contends that his doctrine teaches the (empirical) '*reality*, that is, the objective validity of space, in respect of whatever can be presented to us outwardly as object' (A28/B44). In this way he contrasts the objective validity of space with the subjective validity of secondary qualities. Note, however, that to emphasize that all of us represent things other than ourselves as spatial and that spatial properties do not leave room for disagreement (geometry is universally valid) is not sufficient to remove the false impression that Kant is denying the genuine existence of spatial things outside the mind. The objective validity could simply be understood in the following sense: (a) the (innate) idea of space is always attached to the representation of objects other than ourselves, and (b) for some kind of pre-established harmony the representations of each human being agree with those of all others concerning the spatial features of 'objects.' Put simply, it should not be too difficult for God (or an Evil Genius) to coordinate the ideas in our minds in such a way as to produce agreements regarding the spatial properties of what we take to be genuine objects. Kant actually seems to encourage this interpretation when he claims that besides this lack of objective validity, secondary qualities 'agree with the representation of space in this respect, that they belong to the subjective constitution of our manner is sensibility' (A28/B44).

The same false impression is given when Kant considers colours, tastes, and the like as 'insufficient' examples to illustrate the ideality of space. They are 'insufficient' because when we say that the redness of a rose is 'ideal,' we mean that the colour cannot be taken as a property of the thing itself, but we still take the spatial features of the rose (regardless its colour) as features of the rose itself. Kant presents his position as a 'critical reminder' that even spatial features are not properties of the thing in itself (see A30/B45, and also A45 B62). Kant is even more misleading in the *Prolegomena* when he states explicitly that he goes further than Locke 'and for weighty reasons rank as mere appearances the remaining qualities of bodies also, which are called primary, such as extension, place, and in general space' (see *Prolegomena*, 43–4). By arguing in this way, Kant leads us to think that the ideality of space is simply the final step in the reinterpretation of the object as a collection of 'ideas' à la Berkeley.

To underscore the real difference between secondary qualities and space, Kant should have said something like the following. Space and secondary qualities are mind-dependent in two different ways. Space 'depends on us' in the sense that it is the form through which our mind represents things distinct from us. Although space cannot be predicated of things as they are in themselves, it can certainly be predicated of things qua represented by us. In other words, space is an *objective* feature of appearances. Secondary qualities, by contrast, are not even objective features of appearances. Unlike spatial features, they depend on the subject in the sense that they merely 'seem' to be objective features (of appearances), whereas they only exist in the mind of the subject.[6] Although to my knowledge Kant never puts the difference in these terms, it is quite clear that this is what he should have said in order to avoid a great deal of confusion for readers.[7]

Alternative Accounts

Fortunately there are texts in which Kant states the difference with Berkeley in clearer terms. For example, he tells us that the formal (and critical) nature of transcendental idealism must be contrasted with the 'material' idealism of Berkeley and Descartes (as Kant in a quite different context characterizes it).[8] Their idealism is 'material' because it focuses on the contents of consciousness: they think that the immediate objects of our experience, the *matter* of cognition, are 'ideas' or 'mental representations.' By contrast, Kant's idealism is *formal* because he holds that the objects of our cognition (mental items and external objects) are known through subjective forms that cannot be attributed to the objects as they are in themselves. This is the result achieved in the Transcendental Aesthetic, in which Kant discovers that space and time are not properties of the objects considered in themselves, but rather are forms of our intuition of objects. Since our knowledge is bound to these subjective forms – it is not a knowledge *sub specie aeternitatis* – this idealism is also *critical*: it determines the limits, the scope of validity of our knowledge, and it curbs any pretensions we might have to take our knowledge as knowledge of how things are in themselves. To emphasize the formal and critical nature of transcendental idealism, in the sense just spelled out, means to focus on the crucial difference between Kant and Berkeley: the idealism of the former amounts to an awareness of the limits of our knowledge; the idealism of the latter turns on the assertion of a new ontology in which all objects of our knowledge become mental entities. Hence we must take the form–matter distinction in this context as an alternative approach to expressing the fundamental difference between an epistemological and an ontological project.

Another way to clarify the nature of Kant's idealism is, as I have already said, to pay attention to the development of Kant's thought between 1770 and 1781. We saw that in 1770 Kant tended to interpret the distinction between appearances and things in themselves as a distinction between two sets of objects: mental entities (appearances), and genuine mind-independent objects (things in themselves). We also saw that Kant's critical period began precisely when he consciously and firmly abandoned this interpretation and instead began to regard external appearances as genuine, mind-independent objects. This was a decisive step towards interpreting the transcendental distinction as one between two perspectives from which the same set of objects can be viewed. Many interpreters ignore or misunderstand this development in Kant's thought, and continue to take the transcendental distinction in precisely the precritical sense. Accordingly, notwithstanding Kant's protests, they tend to interpret critical idealism as a dreadful combination of two theses: (1) our knowledge does not reach beyond the mental, and (2) things in themselves exist as genuine mind-independent objects, although we supposedly know nothing about them. One can hardly imagine something worse than this mix of phenomenalism, dogmatism, and sheer inconsistency.

This reading of transcendental idealism runs counter to the actual development of Kant's thought; furthermore, the *Critique* contains rather strong indications against it. In the Preface to the Second Edition, Kant contends that his distinction is 'between things as objects of experience and those *same* things as things in themselves.'[9] In this context he also contends that according to his teaching, 'the object is to be taken in a twofold sense, namely as appearance and as thing in itself' and that things in themselves are merely 'those same objects [appearances] taken in another sense.'[10] In a different passage, in which he introduces the distinction between his idealism and the material variety we have already mentioned, Kant writes that appearance 'always has two sides, the one by which the object is viewed in and by itself (without regard to the mode of intuiting it – its nature therefore remaining always problematic), the other by which the form of the intuition of this object is taken into account. This form is not to be looked for in the object in itself, but in the subject to which the object appears; nevertheless, it belongs really and necessarily to the appearance of this object' (A38/B55).

Thus the same set of objects can be regarded from two different points of view: the forms through which we are bound to represent objects can be taken into account, or abstraction can be made thereof. Those objects are appearances if such forms are taken into consideration. Things in themselves are merely the same objects that we intuit as appearances if we abstract from the mode in which we intuit them. Kant makes the same point in the third of the General Observations that conclude the Aesthetic. Here he is concerned about distinguishing appearance from illusion:

> When I say that the intuition of outer objects and the self-intuition of the mind alike represent the objects and the mind, in space and in time, as they affect our senses, that is, as they appear, I do not mean to say that these objects are a mere *illusion*. For in the appearance the objects, nay even the properties that we ascribe to them, are always regarded as something actually given. Since, however, in the relation of the given object to the subject, such properties depend upon the mode of intuition of the subject, this object as *appearance* is to be distinguished from itself as object *in itself*. Thus when I maintain that the quality of space and time, in conformity with which, as a condition of their existence, I posit both bodies and my own soul, lies in the mode of intuition and not in those objects in themselves, I am not saying that bodies merely *seem* to be outside me, or that my own soul only *seems* to be given in my self-consciousness. It would be my own fault, if out of that which I ought to reckon appearance, I made mere illusion.[11]

Kant makes here three highly instructive points: (1) He suggests – and this is a reaffirmation of the two-perspective interpretation – that when we factor in the sensible conditions of the representation of an object, we are constrained to distinguish the way in which the object appears from the way in which *the same object* is in itself. (2) As a corollary of the first point, he rejects the idea that the ideality of space makes it merely *seem* that spatial objects are outside me. And (3), he emphasizes that the ideality of space and time does not make objects in space and time mere illusions.

Kant could not make it any clearer that the ideality of space takes nothing away from the existence of such objects outside the mind. Affirming the ontological mind-independence of these objects is obviously compatible with affirming that they are mind-dependent for the way in which they appear to us. Indeed, this reflects the forms of our sensible representing. When we combine this idea with the two-perspective interpretation, we see that Kant can quite legitimately call the genuine objects we experience in space 'representations' without thereby reducing them to mental entities. Indeed, 'to avoid all misapprehension' of his doctrine, at the beginning of the General Observations on the Transcendental Aesthetic, Kant identifies appearances and representations, but he explicitly considers them as *things*: 'What we have meant to say is that all our representation is nothing but the representation of appearance; that the *things* are not in themselves what we intuit them to be.'[12]

To grasp the non-phenomenalistic meaning of identifying appearance as representation is crucial if we are to correctly interpret the two most common definitions of transcendental idealism contained in the *Critique*. One is from the Fourth Paralogism:

> By *transcendental idealism* I mean the doctrine that appearances are to be regarded as being, one and all, representations only, not things in themselves, and that time and space are therefore only sensible forms of our intuition, not determinations given as existing by themselves, nor conditions of objects viewed as things in themselves. To this idealism there is opposed a *transcendental realism* which regards time and space as something given in themselves, independently of our sensibility. The transcendental realist thus interprets [*vorstellt*] outer appearances (their reality being taken as granted) as things in themselves, which exist independently of us and our sensibility, and which would be therefore outside us – the phrase 'outside us' being interpreted in conformity with pure concepts of the understanding. It is in fact this transcendental realist who afterwards plays the part of empirical idealist. After wrongly supposing that objects of the senses, if they are to be external, must have an existence by themselves, and independently of the senses, he finds that, judged from this point of view, all our sensuous representations are inadequate to establish their reality. (A369)

Thus in the very definition of transcendental idealism we find the idea that 'appearances are to be regarded as being, one and all, representations only.' Given the preceding analysis, it should be clear that Kant is not advocating a Berkeleyan reduction of external objects to 'ideas' or 'representations.' Rather, in order to clarify the contrast

Transcendental Idealism and Its Foundations   45

between his doctrine and transcendental realism, he is presenting the former as turning on the awareness that the object of experience is always structured by the forms through which we are bound to represent things. Given this, it is only natural that Kant refers to the genuine objects of our experience as 'representations.'

The non-phenomenalistic interpretation of the transcendental distinction is suggested even more clearly in Kant's other definition, from Section 6 of the Antinomy, in which he presents transcendental idealism as 'the key to the solution of the cosmological dialectic.'[13] He defines his position by contrasting it not only with transcendental realism, but also with empirical idealism, which he sees as an inevitable consequence of the former: 'All objects of any experience possible to us are nothing but appearances, that is, mere representations, which, in the manner in which they are represented, as extended beings, or as series of alterations, have no independent existence outside our thoughts. This doctrine I entitle *transcendental idealism*' (A490–1/B518–9).[14]

Taken in isolation, the identification between appearances and 'mere representations' and the denial that appearances have an 'independent existence outside our thoughts' could be taken as support for the phenomenalistic reading; however, the context points to something quite different. Kant is identifying appearances with things or objects insofar as they are sensibly intuited ('in the manner in which the are represented'). This emphasizes the role our sensibility plays in shaping genuine objects, not a reduction of these objects to mental entities.[15] That this is so can also be seen when we note that on the alternative reading, Kant would be saying that inner appearances – which are obviously mental entities – have no independent existence outside our thoughts, which is a sheer truism. This truism, however, disappears if we take Kant to be emphasizing that inner appearances have no independent existence outside our thoughts because, as much as outer appearances, they are shaped by a form of sensibility (time). That this is not a truism is readily conceded when we consider that this is the basis of the much discussed and controversial Kantian thesis that we do not know ourselves as we are, but only as we appear.

If Kant is merely emphasizing that outer (as well as inner) objects are represented through a form of sensibility, it is quite unproblematic for him to point out that as objects represented they are 'mere representations,' or even that they would not exist (as such) outside our thoughts. His identification between objects of experience and representations is just another way for him to say that the objects of our experience are subject to the forms of our sensible representing. Out of fairness to Kant – who, as we saw, is eager to keep his idealism sharply distinguished from 'material idealism' – this should be applied as a general hermeneutic rule for the correct interpretation of all problematic passages in the *Critique* in which he seems to identify external objects with mental entities. In the following section I will show that if this rule is respected, even the Fourth Paralogism will not seem committed to phenomenalism, as interpreters usually assume.

Before we move on to the Fourth Paralogism, however, I should mention that the Antinomy contains yet another indication of the non-phenomenalistic nature of Kant's idealism. This time we need not focus on the definition of transcendental idealism, but rather on the indirect foundation of it, which, Kant claims, the Antinomy is able to provide. In order to appreciate this point we need to introduce in barest outline the structure of this indirect foundation.

In the Antinomy Kant lists valid arguments proving that the world is finite in its spatio-temporal extent, that it is composed of simple, indivisible items, that there are uncaused causes and that there is a necessary being. Yet there are also valid arguments which indicate precisely the opposite – that the world is infinite in its spatio-temporal extent, that it is composed of infinitely divisible parts, that every cause is caused by yet another cause, and that no necessary being exists. Thus reason – the faculty that generated the two sets of arguments – seems to be in contradiction with itself.

Kant views the antinomical conflict as the result of a common assumption shared by the finitistic and infinitistic positions. The assumption is that the world as a whole (or as the complete sum of events) exists in itself, which is identical with transcendental realism. Given this assumption, the finitistic and infinitistic positions are the only two possibilities. However, each position can reject its opposite with a valid argument; from this, it follows that either we leave reason in contradiction with itself – a condition that Kant calls suggestively the 'euthanasia of pure reason' (A407/B434) – or we consider the apparently contradictory conclusions as arising from the fact that the two sides share a false premise.

This conflict can be removed simply by discarding the false premise that the arguments share – namely, the idea of the world as a whole existing in itself. Since this is identical with transcendental realism, its opposite – transcendental idealism – is indirectly proved. As Kant puts it: 'If the world is a whole existing in itself, it is either finite or infinite.

But both alternatives are false (as shown in the proofs of the antithesis and the thesis respectively). It is therefore also false that the world (the sum of all appearances) is a whole existing in itself. From this it then follows that appearances in general are nothing outside our representations – which is just what is meant by their transcendental ideality' (A506–7/B534–5).

For the sake of clarity, let me formalize this argument. Given the following definitions – R = 'the world is a whole existing in itself' (identical to transcendental realism), A = 'appearances in general are nothing outside our representations' (identical to transcendental idealism), F = the world is finite, and I = the world is infinite – and using v to indicate exclusive disjunction, the argument can be formalized in sentential logic as follows:

(1) $R \, v \, A$ Premise
(2) $R > (F \, v \, I)$ Premise
(3) $-I$ Conclusion of the proof of the thesis
(4) $-F$ Conclusion of the proof of the antithesis
(5) $-F \, \& -I$ Conjunction; 3, 4
(6) $-(F \, v \, I)$ De Morgan; 5
(7) $-R$ Modus Tollens; 2, 6
∴ A Disjunctive Syllogism; 1, 7

As this formalization clearly indicates, the conclusion can be drawn only if (1) holds. But (1) asserts that transcendental realism and transcendental idealism are two mutually exclusive options. This means that transcendental realism is supposed to cover nothing less than all philosophies except Kant's. If this were not so, then from the rejection of transcendental realism, the truth of transcendental idealism would not follow. Very simply, some other philosophical stance could be inferred with equal right from the falsity of transcendental realism. Thus Kant considers transcendental realism as a common mistake that infects all philosophies preceding the *Critique*. This is confirmed by his contentions that 'until the critical philosophy all philosophies are not distinguished in their essential [character],'[16] and that the confusion between appearances and things in themselves (the essence of transcendental realism) is a 'common prejudice,'[17] in the history of philosophy.

The significance of this for the purpose of grounding a non-phenomenalistic reading of Kant's idealism is twofold. To begin with, even philosophies such as Berkeley's and Hume's that do identify the objects of our experience with mental entities ('ideas' broadly construed) are considered varieties of transcendental realism – something that already suggests that Kant takes his position to be quite different from phenomenalism. More importantly, however, the fact that all philosophies preceding Kant are viewed as infected by transcendental realism indicates that the distinction between appearances and things in themselves cannot be identical with the distinction between mental entities and objects corresponding them. Otherwise, Locke (for example) would count not as a transcendental realist, but as a transcendental idealist. Thus the transcendental distinction should be taken as an awareness (completely new in the history of philosophy) that our knowledge is subject to certain conditions whose existence imposes the need to distinguish between the way in which we, human beings, are constrained to represent things and the way in which things could be seen from a perspective that abstracts from such conditions. Once again, we find the same difference between an epistemological and an ontological concern that we emphasized before as the essence of the difference between Kant and Berkeley.

Let us now apply the results of this analysis to the difficult case of the Fourth Paralogism.

How to Avoid a Phenomenalistic Reading of the Fourth Paralogism

To read the Fourth Paralogism without seeing in it a straightforward profession of phenomenalism is certainly not an easy task. The text has long been considered the touchstone for those interpreters who tend to reduce Kantian appearances to Berkeleyan ideas.[18] This tradition began with Jacobi, who found in the First Edition of the *Critique* eleven passages in which Kant allegedly identifies appearances with 'representations' (in the sense of mental entities). Three of these are from the Fourth Paralogism. Kemp Smith took up this hermeneutical tradition by explicitly identifying Kant's position in the Fourth Paralogism with that of Berkeley and thus dismissing it as a pointless attempt to counter Cartesian doubts about the existence of external objects with plain denial of them. As Kemp Smith puts it: '[The Fourth Paralogism] refutes the position of Descartes only by virtually accepting the still more extreme position of Berkeley. Outer objects, Kant argues, are immediately known because they are ideas merely. There is no need for inference, because there is no transcendence of the domain of our inner consciousness. In other words, Kant refutes the problematic idealism of Descartes, by means of the more subjective idealism of Berkeley.'[19]

Turbayne has presented a similarly extreme assessment of the Fourth Paralogism. According to him, in our text Kant consciously – albeit not explicitly – embraces Berkeley's stance.[20] Recently, in the article 'Two Perspectives on Kant's Appearances and Things in Themselves,' Robinson has listed thirty-three passages from both editions of the *Critique* and the *Prolegomena* in which the identification between appearances and mental entities is 'clear and unequivocal.'[21] Five are from the Fourth Paralogism, and, interestingly, four of these are different from those cited by Jacobi. This leaves us with seven passages, to which we can add five more that are cited neither by Jacobi nor by Robinson, but that could be used as well to support the phenomenalistic reading of our text.[22]

We can organize the passages into three groups: first, those (by far the majority) in which Kant claims that external objects are 'mere representations,' or 'representations in us'; second, those which state that matter (or external objects), if separated from our sensibility, is nothing; and third, those in which the real in space is identified with the perception of it. I intend to show that none of these passages need be taken in a phenomenalistic sense and that another reading is possible. Given this preliminary result, I will argue that an alternative interpretation – one at least equally compatible with the text – is to be preferred on the grounds that it enables us avoid attributing sheer nonsense to Kant.

Starting with the first group, besides the already discussed definition of transcendental idealism, perhaps the two passages that most strongly suggest the phenomenalistic reading are the following:

> External objects (bodies) ... are mere appearances, and are therefore nothing but a species of my representations, the objects of which are something only through these representations. Apart from them they are nothing. (A370)

> These external things, namely matter, are in all their configurations and alterations nothing but mere appearances, that is representations in us, of the reality [*Wirklichkeit*] of which we are immediately conscious. (A371–2)

Here, Kant is contrasting his stance (transcendental idealism) with that of Descartes (transcendental realism). Descartes is a transcendental realist because, on Kant's reconstruction, he takes space and time and the things contained in them as things in themselves, whereas for Kant things appear to us with spatio-temporal properties precisely because they are represented by the mind as such. This is why he underscores the difference by calling the objects of experience 'representations.' As we noted, the mere fact that Kant characterizes appearances in this way is insufficient to commit him to the claim that these appearances/representations are mental entities. To this we can now add that the adjective 'mere,' which modifies 'representations,' need not be taken emphatically as though we were talking about 'mere' mental entities to be contrasted with the genuine and robust existence of external objects. It can instead be taken as further emphasizing on the fact that these things we are talking about are not things in themselves, but 'mere' appearances – namely, things as we intuit them from our particular and limited perspective.

To be sure, Kant does not just say that external objects are 'mere representations'; he also qualifies this already sufficiently problematic expression by adding the puzzling phrase 'in us.' This phrase is perhaps what suggests most clearly the phenomenalistic reading. However, it can be dealt with by means of considerations similar to those already used. If the objects that we experience are not things in themselves, but appearances, which owe some of their features (spatiality and temporality) to the way in which our sensibility intuits them, then they can meaningfully be said to be 'in us' – that is, within the sphere of the representing power of the mind. More precisely, since anything we represent has already been 'shaped' by the forms of our sensibility, it certainly can be said to be 'in us' in the sense of falling within the scope of our sensible representing. Appearances are thus nothing 'outside us' because a reference to our sensibility is built into the very notion of them. In this sense, they can certainly be said to be 'in us' without implying that they exist as mere mental entities.[23]

The main support for this reading is Kant's discussion of two ways in which objects can be said to be outside us: the empirical and the transcendental.[24] Given the result of the Aesthetic, the spacial things we experience must be considered 'outside us' in the empirical but not in the transcendental sense. To claim the latter would be to imply that they were completely independent of our sensibility. Conversely, they are 'in us' in the transcendental but not in the empirical sense. To claim the latter would be to reduce them to mental entities.[25] It is perhaps useful to illustrate this crucial point (see table 2.1).

Although table 2.1 proves quite clearly the existence of a logical space in which an appearance can be predicated as 'in us' and at the same time as a genuine external object with full independent ontological status, some might still be unclear as to the precise meaning of such

Table 2.1

	Things in us	Things outside us
In the empirical sense	Mental entities	Spatial objects
In the transcendental sense	Outer/inner appearances*	Things in themselves

* Notice that things in us in the transcendental sense can be outside us in the empirical whereas things outside us in the transcendental sense are not in us in the empirical sense.

a concept. What, after all, does it mean when we say that our forms of intuiting shape an object X and that precisely through that 'shaping' X becomes an appearance? While it is common among Kant commentators to explain his metaphorical language through further metaphors (here the metaphor of shaping), it is usually not especially helpful. Hence it is perhaps necessary to give some more intuitive content to the concept of an object that is in us transcendentally but outside us empirically. As a starting point, we might pick up the rather unproblematic idea that the objects of our experience owe some of their properties to the perceiving subject. This model is common to virtually all epistemological stances, with the possible exception of naive realism. For example, all modern philosophers insist that secondary qualities cannot be attributed (at least as such) to the objects of cognition per se. The crucial reform that Kant introduces in this model is best understood not by saying that he considers also primary qualities as the subject's contribution (something quite true, but unhelpful or misleading if not properly qualified). Rather, the idea is that the arguments of the Aesthetic indicate that those features which render the object precisely as an object for a finite mind like ours (space and time) cannot be attributed to the object itself; rather, they are the subject's own contribution to the constitution of the sensible object.

We shall turn to these arguments soon. For the moment, as a first approximation to the main thrust of the Aesthetic, a simple example might help. Take an object that is in front of you right now. I focus on my computer screen because this is what I have before my eyes. For Kant it is my sensibility that creates the 'here and there' respectively of me (the intuiting subject) and of the screen (the intuited object). The human sensibility is what introduces *fractures*, the 'here and there' determinations, without which no distinction between subject and object, as well as between objects, could take place. Without such fractures, there would be no *here* and *there* and the world would be an uninterrupted continuum. While other sensible beings might introduce these fractures through a form other than space (for example, ticks detect hosts by reacting to certain biochemicals), the human mind is committed – as a matter of simple fact – precisely to this form. This does not mean, of course, that the *specific* spatial location of the object is my own contribution. The fact that the screen is right in front of me, and not behind me or to my left or right, is for Kant quite independent of the subject. It does not fall in any possible sense in her power. This is why space for Kant, unlike Leibniz, is not a relational property. On my interpretation, the subject contributes to the constitution of a spacialized world by introducing the distinction between here and there, by introducing fractures in an otherwise undifferentiated world, but exactly where the now discrete objects find themselves is determined just by where things are placed (so to speak) by God or Fate.

Coming back to our chart, to claim that objects are transcendentally in us but empirically outside us is to assert that they have been rendered discrete and identifiable by the intuitive power of the human mind (they fall within the scope of the differentiating mind), and that their specific location is outside the subject itself. Conversely, objects that are transcendentally outside us can be thought to be beyond that differentiating power, and not subject to the fractures-creating power of the human mind. More on this crucial point will be said when we analyse the arguments of the Transcendental Aesthetic on which – as should have become evident by now – everything turns. In the hope that this first approximation has helped clarify things enough for the present purposes, I now return to the analysis of the other two groups of phenomenalistic-sounding passages.

In the passages listed in the second group, Kant claims that matter independently of sensibility is nothing.[26] This seems identical with Berkeley's idea that the notion of material substance – taken in the usual sense of something existing independently of the perceiving mind – is absurd or inconsistent.[27] We have just seen, however, that, from the perspective of the transcendental idealist, there is a clear, non-phenomenalistic sense in which one can state that matter is nothing 'independently of sensibility.' Matter, as we know it – namely, with the spatio-temporal features that characterize it and that are given by the forms of sensibility – is nothing if one abstracts from these forms. This spatio-temporal matter simply would not be such, and in this sense it would be nothing. Evidently, it all turns on an ambiguity in the sense in which matter is 'nothing independently of sensibility.' Berkeley means that the perception of a subject is necessary for the very existence of the object. Kant means that the object exists outside the mind independently of any perception. The forms through which human cognizers perceive matter, however, contribute to determining how it appears in such a way that independently of them, the object as it appears to us would be nothing. Kant's claim, properly understood, boils down to the idea that if X determines how Y appears to us, once X is removed, Y can no longer appear to us as such, and thus can be nothing for us. Clearly, there is nothing phenomenalistic in this.

Moving to the third and final group, we will find that Kant even identifies the reality of the object with the perception of it: 'All outer perception, therefore, yields immediate proof of something real in space, or rather is the real itself [*das Wirkliche selbst*]' (A375). And also: 'Reality [*Wirklichkeit*] in space, being the reality of a mere representation, is nothing other than perception itself.'[28] There is probably nothing closer to the Berkeleyan *esse est percipi* in the entire *Critique*. Even interpreters (such as Rousset) whose main concern is to oppose the tendency to interpret Kant's philosophy as a kind of absolute idealism, wherein the object of experience is entirely determined by 'thought' broadly construed, have given up hope of defending Kant when he goes so far as to identify the object of perception with the perception itself.[29] But do we really have to concede this partial victory to the phenomenalistic reading? Is there not a way to take the identification of the object of experience with its perception in a non-phenomenalistic sense?

The key to a solution lies again in the idea that, for Kant, the perception of the object contributes to the determination of what the object is for us. The fact that the object appears to us as occupying a location in space is the result of the object being perceived (or, as we have seen before, represented). Therefore, in this sense, the object's reality, understood as its being represented as a spatial object existing outside the subject, is the perception of it. This, however, does not mean that the ontological place of the object of experience is in the mind. It is rather that the object would not appear in the way it does – namely, with its spatial features – if the mind did not perceive it. Once again, it is crucial to bear in mind that there is a way in which we can let features of a given object of our experience depend on our perception of it, without making that object a mental entity.

Kant himself invites us to resist any phenomenalistic interpretation of his identification between the object and our perception of it. Immediately after claiming that 'all outer perception [...] is the real itself,' he adds: 'In this sense empirical realism is beyond question; that is, there corresponds to our outer intuitions something real [*Wirkliches*] in space' (A375). It is important here to appreciate Kant's effort to differentiate between 'perceptions' (here evidently considered as equivalent to matter, real objects, appearances) and 'intuitions,' that is, the mental states to which these 'perceptions' correspond. By calling 'intuitions' the mental states that correspond to 'perceptions,' Kant is inviting us to take the latter as genuine objects rather than as mental entities.

Also recall that this identification between perception and things perceived is not a novelty of the Fourth Paralogism. Kant is here merely repeating the definition of 'actuality' that he offers in the Second Postulate of Empirical Thought. For an object to be actual, the postulate requires 'the connection of the object with some actual perception, in accordance with the analogies of experience, which define all real connection in an experience in general' (A225/B272). This connection between actuality and what is perceived in accordance with the analogies is the gist of Kant's criterion – in the Fourth Paralogism (and elsewhere) – for distinguishing actual experience from dreams or hallucinations. We shall analyse this criterion in the next chapter. For the moment, suffice it to note that the correlation or even identification between actuality and perception is not an unfortunate peculiarity of the Fourth Paralogism. In fact, it plays a crucial role in Kant's entire theory.

This concludes our analysis of the three groups of passages. It is perhaps important to clarify that I have not tried to prove it impossible to take them in a phenomenalistic sense. My goal instead has been to find a non-phenomenalistic reading that is at least as plausible as the phenomenalistic one. If there is such a reading – and I think I have shown that there is – the principle of charity requires us to prefer it over one that attributes to Kant the absurdity of removing scepticism about the empirical world by introducing dogmatism – to use Kant's characterization of Berkeley's idealism – about its non-existence (Kemp Smith's position). This is in fact the conclusion to which any phenomenalistic reading of the Fourth Paralogism is committed. Note that it is not possible to avoid this result by claiming that, although Kant endorses Berkeley's phenomenalism, he can still appeal to the thing in itself to ground realism. This is precisely the kind of argument that Kant was still embracing in the silent decade, but that he clearly and explicitly rejects in the Fourth Paralogism. One of the great advances beyond the early view is the clear recognition that this dogmatic form of realism is unsatisfactory and capable only of promoting scepticism rather than refuting it. In a crucial passage, Kant notes that if appearances are reduced to mental entities, and if things in themselves are taken as the causes of these mental entities, then skepticism is unavoidable: 'If we regard outer appearances as representations produced in us by their objects, and if these objects be things existing in themselves outside us, it is impossible to see how we can come to know the existence of the objects otherwise than by inference from the effect to the cause; and being so, it must always remain doubtful whether the cause in question be in us or outside us' (A372).

Moreover, Kant adds that neither can the sceptic ask for a proof of what is behind the world that we experience through the senses; nor can we provide one: 'Even the most rigid idealist cannot, therefore, require a proof that the object outside us (taking 'outside' in the strict [transcendental] sense) corresponds to our perception. For if there were such an object, it could not be represented and intuited as outside us' (A375–6). It is precisely when we assume that a supersensible object should do the job of grounding realism that we become vulnerable to scepticism: 'Transcendental realism ... inevitably falls into difficulties, and finds itself obliged to give way to empirical idealism' (A371).

If we combine the denial of the possibility of grounding realism in things in themselves with the main thrust of the phenomenalistic reading – namely, that appearances are mental entities – we end up reducing Kant's attempt to ground realism to a twofold denial of realism: on the one hand, a denial that sensible objects exist outside the mind, and on the other, a denial that it is possible to rely on the existence of supersensible objects. This suggests that if an alternative to the phenomenalistic reading is allowed by the text – and we have seen that it is – this should be preferred over one that commits Kant to plain nonsense.

At this point, I think that enough has been said to ground the formal, non-phenomenalistic nature of transcendental idealism in general and of the Fourth Paralogism in particular. This amounts to the removal of one of the preliminary obstacles we face in our attempt to rehabilitate the antiskeptical argument of the Fourth Paralogism. As noted, the second and more difficult obstacle is represented by the fact that Kant's foundation of transcendental idealism has received fierce criticism from different philosophical perspectives. We now turn to an analysis of this foundation in the Aesthetic and to the main criticisms of it.

The Foundation for Transcendental Idealism in the Aesthetic

In the Aesthetic we can identify four distinct arguments for the thesis that space and time are forms of our sensibility and are neither objects existing in themselves nor determinations of such objects: (1) a transcendental argument that turns on an analysis of the status of the representation of space and time in the Metaphysical Exposition combined with an argument by elimination that infers what space and time must be, given the results of the Metaphysical Exposition; (2) an epistemological argument based on the idea that transcendental idealism is the only theory that can account for the synthetic a priori status of Euclidean geometry (and more in general of any synthetic a priori science); (3) a metaphysical argument that rests on the characterization of space and time as mere relations and on the idea – more or less explicitly borrowed from the tradition – that 'a thing in itself cannot be known through mere relations' (B67); and (4) a theological argument turning on the idea that if space and time are 'conditions of all existence in general, they must also be conditions of the existence of God,' (B71) – a notion considered as self-evidently absurd.[30] Since even interpreters who favour transcendental idealism doubt (for good reasons) that the last three arguments have any chance at succeeding, we shall focus on the first argument only.[31]

The structure of this argument is as follows. First, with the two apriority arguments and the two intuition arguments in the Metaphysical Exposition, Kant proves that representations of space and time are a priori intuitions as well as necessary conditions of the possibility for objects to be given to the mind. Arguing by elimination, he infers in the 'Conclusions from the above concepts' that the fact that representations of space and time have these features can be explained only if the contents – or more precisely, the referents – of these representations, space and time themselves, are neither objects nor objective features of things, but rather forms of our sensibility. Kant expresses the principle that supposedly justifies this inference in the Transcendental Exposition, in the context of his argument from the status of Euclidean geometry: 'How, then, can there exist in the mind an outer intuition which precedes the objects themselves, and in which the concept of these objects can be determined *a priori*? Manifestly, not otherwise than in so far as the intuition has its seat in the subject only, as the formal character of the subject, in virtue of which, in being affected by objects, it obtains *immediate representation*, that is, *intuition*, of them; and only insofar, therefore, as it is merely the form of outer *sense* in general' (B41).

Evidently, a necessary – although, as we shall see, insufficient – condition of the success of the entire argument is that representations of space and time are a priori intuitions. In the Metaphysical Exposition,

Kant presents two arguments for the apriority and two arguments for the intuitive nature of representations of space and time. Next we discuss and defend these very controversial arguments.

The Metaphysical Exposition

The first argument for the apriority of the representation of space goes as follows:

> 1. Space is not an empirical concept which has been derived from outer experiences. For in order that certain sensations be referred to something outside me [*ausser mir*] (that is, to something in another region of space from that in which I find myself) and similarly in order that I may be able to represent them as outside and alongside one another [*ausser und nebeneinander*], and accordingly as not only different but as in different places, the representation of space must be presupposed. The representation of space cannot, therefore, be empirically obtained from the relations of outer appearance. On the contrary, this outer experience is itself possible at all only through that representation. (A23/B38)

The precise determination of the thesis that Kant is presenting here has become the object of some dispute among Kant scholars. According to Allison, Kant is saying that the representation of space is a necessary condition for the experience of objects as distinct from ourselves and from one another. This representation makes possible the attribution of certain sensations to a determinate place, and in this sense contributes to the very constitution of an object of experience. Since this representation is necessary for the very experience of these outer objects, it cannot be derived from the same objects. It is therefore a priori. To claim otherwise would be to claim that what has been shown to be a necessary condition of experience can be derived from experience itself – something that apparently involves a contradiction.[32]

An important point that Allison makes in his interpretation is that the *ausser mir* and the *ausser und nebeneinander* must not be taken in a spatial sense; if it were, Kant's claim would reduce itself to a tautology – namely, that the representation of space is necessary for the representation of the different places that the objects occupy. Despite their spatial connotation, argues Allison, *ausser mir* and *ausser und nebeneinander* should be taken as referring to objects that are supposed to be distinct from us and from one another in some way that is not necessarily spatial. Since we can think of other beings who represent objects distinct from themselves and from one another in a non-spatial way, Kant's claim is not tautologous. Thus the point is that the way in which we, human cognizers, represent objects distinct from us and from one another is through the representation of space. In this sense, space functions as a necessary condition of our experience of objects.

Recently, Warren has raised doubts of a textual and systematic nature as to the validity of this interpretation. He argues that Kant *does* take *ausser mir* and *ausser und nebeneinander* in a spatial sense, as is clearly indicated by the text. 'Something outside me [*ausser mir*]' is explicitly identified with 'something in another region of space from that in which I find myself,' and 'outside and alongside one another [*ausser und nebeneinander*]' with 'not only different but as in different places.' Thus Kant seems to be saying that the representation of space is necessary for representing objects as occupying a region of space distinct from mine and for representing objects as occupying different regions of space. For Warren, not only is this non-tautologous, but it also contains a very important truth about the specificity of the representation of space compared to other features of our experience. The claim is not tautologous because, on Warren's interpretation, Kant means that 'when we represent objects as bearing a spatial relation to one another (for example being outside one another), we presuppose a representation of the space these objects are in.'[33] In other words, in order to represent spatial relations, I need to represent the spatially related objects as occupying parts or regions of space that are distinct from the objects themselves. And this is the ground for the further claim that in order to represent spatially related objects, we require the representation of space, understood as the framework that encompasses these parts or regions.[34]

Contrast this with relations such as 'being brighter than.' In order to represent one object as brighter than another, I do not need to represent also a brightness space that the related objects occupy. Obviously, we can order the degree of brightness of each of the related objects in a brightness-space, but we do not need to. We can have the experience of one object being brighter than another without also representing the brightness-space that encompasses the degrees of brightness of the two related objects. To the contrary, we must represent the space that encompasses the regions occupied by the spatially related objects. This is far from being trivial; by arguing that the representation of space is necessary for the representation of spatial relations, Kant is revealing a distinctive feature of the representation of space.

Moreover, on this interpretation, the foundation of the apriority of the representation of space becomes straightforward. As Warren aptly puts it: 'Given that the representation of 'brighter than' relations does not presuppose the representation of brightness-space, we can form the latter representation from the former. By contrast, in the case of spatial (or temporal) relations, we *cannot* proceed in an analogous fashion, forming the representation of space (or of time) from a concept of spatial (or temporal) relations which has been independently acquired, and more specifically, which has been independently acquired from experience.'[35] This is so because, unlike with 'brighter than' relations, the representation of spatial relations presupposes the representation of regions of space and the representation of space itself. Therefore, this representation cannot be acquired from the experience of these relations. It is a priori.

Another important difference between Allison and Warren is that the latter denies that the representation of space is a necessary condition of objects as distinct from myself and from one another. Instead, Warren thinks that to identify an object as distinct from another, we need not rely on the fact that the two objects at hand occupy different spatial locations. The example that Warren gives is a distinction based on a difference of colour (pink and not-pink). Now, if I can represent two objects as distinct from each other on the basis of a feature other than space, it follows that space is not a 'necessary condition of the possibility of distinguishing objects from one another,' which is what Allison contends. Certainly, if two objects are identical in all other respects, I can still focus on the different places they occupy. But this makes space a sufficient, not a *necessary* condition of the distinction (or individuation) of objects.

It is not clear whether Warren is willing to infer from all this that the representation of space is not a necessary condition of our experience in any possible sense. If this is his thesis, we cannot agree with him. In fact, it may be true that one can focus on a feature other than space in order to distinguish or individuate objects, but the occupation of a certain region of space is at most something that can be ignored in favour of some other distinguishing property; it is not something that can be removed. Warren himself seems to admit as much when he acknowledges that 'if a and b are to [be] considered with respect to their colors properties, they must be regarded as extended and so the representation of space does enter after all.'[36] It is quite evident that there would be no object to represent if we abstracted from space. Thus, space is perhaps not a necessary condition for the representation *of distinctions among objects*, but it still is a necessary condition for the representation of objects in the first place.

One might think it possible to concede to Warren that the first apriority argument centres on the minimal thesis that he identifies (henceforth, Warren's Thesis), whereas the establishment of the stronger thesis that space is a necessary condition of the representations of objects (henceforth Allison's Thesis) is left to the second argument. But even this concession would be too generous, because already in the first argument, Kant has himself introduced Allison's Thesis. In fact, he concludes his argument by saying that 'this outer experience is itself possible at all only through that representation [the representation of space].' In other words, outer experience in general – not merely the representation of spatial relations – is possible only through the representation of space. This claim is identical with the second argument, in which Kant's focus on determining the conditions for the possibility of outer experience in general is abundantly clear. In fact, the second argument has it that 'space must therefore be regarded as the condition of the possibility of appearances.' It thus seems that the most we can concede to Warren is that his thesis is the main focus of the first apriority argument, whereas Allison's Thesis is merely stated, and not argued for – something that would be left to the second argument.[37]

The determination of the two theses (Allison's and Warren's) that Kant seems to convey in the first apriority argument positions us to deal with a recent criticism of the same argument by Greenwood, who denies Kant's fundamental tenet that 'if the having of the representation of space is a necessary condition of the possibility of experiencing objects, then the representation of space cannot be empirically derived from the experience of objects in space.' For Greenwood, the fact that the representation of space is a necessary condition of the experience of objects is compatible with the possibility that we acquire the representation of space empirically. As he puts it: 'The fact that in any possible world human representation of objects is spatial representation, is perfectly compatible with the claim that in the actual world, humans acquire the concept of space, or spatial concepts, by observing objects in spatial relation to each other.'[38]

The fact that Greenwood identifies the thesis that the representation of space is a necessary condition with the thesis that 'in all possible words, human representation of objects is spatial representation' is highly instructive. The latter is a mere descriptive claim, which is certainly compatible with the possibility that we acquire the representation of space empirically. In fact, it might be that because of some mysterious psychological mechanism, the representation of space invariably arises from the representation of objects and their relations in such a way that it always accompanies (as opposed to enables) our representation of external objects. However, we have seen that the essence of Kant's position is rather that the representation of space functions as a condition that, if not satisfied, makes the very experience of objects other than ourselves impossible. And this is clearly incompatible with the possibility that we derive the representation of space from outer objects.[39] At least, one cannot claim this without showing that the principle on which this impossibility rests – that something that has been stipulated as a condition of the possibility of experience cannot be derived from experience – is fallacious.

To be sure, Greenwood attempts to do precisely this:

> To be able to represent a property of O as it is in itself is to be able to represent a property of O *as O is, or would be, apart from such a representation*, and hence, of course, as it is apart from any conditions of such a representation. But this is not at all the same thing as to represent that property *apart from any condition of representing O*, which, given there are such conditions, is obviously impossible. Nothing, however, follows from that impossibility about the first thing: the representability or non- representability of properties of O as it is in itself.[40]

Greenwood's point, if I understand him correctly, is that we might be able to represent a property of an object as it is in itself independently of our representing it, and, therefore, independently also of the conditions of our representing it, even if we have stipulated that our representing is subject to certain conditions. This is so, presumably, because it could be the case that the representation that is subject to the conditions we have stipulated as necessary for our representing by happenstance 'maps onto' characteristics of things as they are in themselves. Thus, by representing objects under our conditions – that is, spatio-temporally – we might end up representing characteristics of objects as they are in themselves. If this is a fair reconstruction of Greenwood's rather obscure claim, his criticism is nothing but the old 'neglected alternative' objection that Trendelenburg had already raised against Kant – that even if we grant that space and time are forms of our sensibility, how do we know that space and time are not also properties of the things in themselves?

This is a perfectly legitimate question, which we shall discuss soon, but note that it has no bearing on our problem. In fact, we were discussing whether the representation of space could be derived from an outer experience, not whether things in themselves might be spatio-temporal. In other words, the apriority thesis centres on the origin of the representation of space (it claims that it cannot be experience) and on the fundamental, enabling role it plays in our experience. As such, it is untouched by the possibility that things in themselves might have the property of space, *as long as this property is not assumed to be the source of our representation of space*. All that the apriority argument establishes is that it is contradictory to claim that the representation of space is a condition of the representation of external objects and that the same representation could be derived from the experience of these objects, quite independently of whether these objects have or do not have the property of space.

Obviously, if the apriority thesis holds (understood as grounding the status of space as a necessary condition in the correct sense), then Greenwood's general criticism of transcendental idealism falls. In fact, he denies the apriority thesis in order to remove the ground on which the thesis of the ideality of space and time rests.[41] But as we have seen, his rejection of the apriority thesis depends on a misunderstanding of the very thesis that Kant tries to establish. To be sure, one could argue against this thesis – namely, that the representation of space functions precisely in the way we indicated (as a necessary condition in the proper sense). But this is not what Greenwood does.

In any event, it seems that further evidence in favour of Kant's thesis is required. As we have seen, in the first apriority argument Kant does not do much more than *state* the thesis, thus provoking much of the perplexity that interpreters have expressed ever since. In light of this, it becomes crucial to analyse carefully the second apriority argument, in which Kant uses the representability of empty space as further evidence in favour of the apriority of the spatial representation. The argument runs:

2. Space is a necessary *a priori* representation, which underlies all outer intuitions. We can never represent to ourselves the absence of space, though we can quite well think it as empty of objects. It must therefore be regarded as the condition of the possibility of appearances, and not as a

determination dependent upon them. It is an *a priori* representation, which necessarily underlies outer appearances. (A24–B38–9)

As we have already noted, in this argument the status of the representation of space as a necessary condition of outer experience is very explicit. The hermeneutical difficulty has long revolved around the sense in which we must take the impossibility of representing the absence of space and around the possibility of representing space as void of objects. Starting with the first half of the claim, it is obvious that Kant cannot be talking about a logical impossibility, because in his own system things in themselves must be represented (although obviously not intuited) as not in space. Also, it cannot be a mere psychological impossibility – at least, if by that is meant a contingent fact about our mental constitution rather than a fact about our very faculties, which, as Kant assumes throughout the *Critique*, are not changing or contingent. Rather, as Parsons points out, the claim is that although the thought of the absence of space is logically consistent and therefore not vacuous, 'we can't give content to that thought in the sense that matters: relation to intuition.'[42] In other words, we cannot remove space and still have something to intuit. This is so because the spatial properties of an object – as the first argument also contends – are those which are responsible for the very 'giveness' of the set of empirical predicates constituting an object. For this reason we assign priority to extension over other predicates (such as colours). This is what Kant means both in the *Critique* and in the *Prolegomena* when he claims that we can remove from the content of an object its colour, its impenetrability, and other predicates arising from sensation, along with intellectual forms (substance, force, divisibility), and still have something to intuit: extension and figure.[43]

All of this helps us with the second part of the argument. The possibility of representing space as void of object is not to be understood in the sense that we can represent the object 'space.'[44] It is, rather, that the representation of space has a content irreducible to that of the things *in* space. This becomes quite clear when we recall Warren's interpretation of the first argument. We saw that Warren emphasized the fact that when we represent objects as bearing spatial properties, we must represent them as occupying parts or regions of a broader space. It is precisely the representation of this broader space, logically independent and irreducible to the objects in space, that Kant thinks stands in our experience even if space is devoid of objects.

This also positions us to reply to an objection that Parsons and Greenwood have raised against the second argument's ability to refute a relational account of space. They claim that even granting that we can represent space as void of objects (which Greenwood tends to take in the sense of void or empty space), it could still be the case that the thought of space without objects 'is just the thought of space with objects about which nothing is assumed'[45] or, even more clearly: 'At the extreme, the notion of a complete void would have to be construed in terms of some merely hypothetical framework of objects.'[46] Thus Leibniz's idea that ultimately the representation of space is dependent on the representation of the objects in space would be salvaged.

This objection, however, can be dismissed if we keep in mind that Kant's claim is not that we can represent empty space; nor is it that on Leibniz's relational view, the very notion of empty space would be impossible. As Warren clarifies for us, at least part of Kant's thesis, already in the first argument, is that spatially related objects can be represented only if one also represents two 'things' distinct from the objects themselves: a) the regions occupied by the objects, and (b) the space that encompasses those regions.[47] Instead of arguing that we can represent empty space, in the second argument Kant is rather imagining that we abstract from the objects and represent the regions that the objects occupy and the space that encompasses them. Unlike an abstraction that would remove space and leave empirical properties, such abstraction is possible by virtue of the fact that the representation of the regions (and of the encompassing space) is distinct from the objects that occupy them. There remains something to intuit even if we abstract from all the empirical objects and their properties. Moreover, since we can represent the encompassing space independently of the objects that occupy it whereas we cannot represent the objects without this framework, it is pointless to argue that the representation of this framework ultimately depends on hypothetical objects. Rather, the representation of hypothetical (or real) objects presupposes this.

Warren's point that the representation of space is necessary for the representation of spatial relations is also important when it comes to understanding the first intuition argument. Kant's basic claim is that there is a fundamental contrast between the way in which a concept relates to its extension (the sum of the objects falling under the concept) or to its intension (the sum of the marks that define the concept) and the way in which space relates to particular spaces. Kant writes: 'In the first place, we can represent to ourselves only one [*einigen*] space; and if we speak of diverse spaces, we mean thereby only parts of one and the same unique space. Secondly, these parts cannot precede the one all-embracing space, as being, as it were, constituents out of which it can be composed; on the contrary, they can be thought only as *in* it. Space is essentially one [*einig*].'

In the first part of the argument, Kant alludes to the contrast between the many things that can fall under a concept and the fact that we represent only one space. Since a concept can have only one thing as its referent (say, the concept of God), it is the second part of the argument, in which Kant emphasizes the contrast between the intension of a concept and the parts of space, that is crucial for establishing the desired result. Here Kant points out that the parts of space are dependent on the whole. We can represent them only if we also represent the whole that encompasses them. Contrast this with the way in which the marks of a concept relate to the concept itself. The marks can be thought about independently of the whole. Evidence of this is that they can form new concepts if combined with other marks. While in the case of the representation of space the whole has priority over the parts, in the case of the intension of a concept the parts have priority over the whole. It follows that the representation of space is not a concept; and since Kant takes the concept–intuition distinction as exhaustive, it also follows that the representation of space is an intuition.

Note that the peculiarity of the representation of space on which the contrast rests – its being prior over its parts – is the same that Warren identified in the first apriority argument. The only difference is that Kant now uses it to infer, not that the representation of space is a priori, but that it is an intuition. Actually, Kant also infers in the conclusion that the representation is a priori; he even misleads us as to the real focus of the argument by emphasizing more the apriority than the intuitive character: 'Hence it follows that an a priori, and not an empirical, intuition underlies all concepts of space' (A25/B39). As indicated, however, this is the result of the fact that Kant uses roughly the same fundamental premise (priority of space over its parts or irreducibility of space to its parts) to ground both the apriority and the intuitive nature of the representation of space.

In the last sentence of his argument, Kant finds a confirmation of the intuitive nature of the representation of space in the fact that in order to know that the sum of two sides of a triangle is greater than the third, we need to appeal to intuition (or construction in intuition, to be precise): 'For kindred reasons, geometrical propositions, that is, for instance, in a triangle two sides together are greater than the third, can never be derived from the general concepts of line and triangle, but only from intuition, and this is indeed *a priori*, with apodeictic certainty.' (A25/B39).

The mere analysis of the concept of line and triangle cannot yield the result that the sum of the two sides of a triangle is greater than the third. Note that Kant is not appealing to Euclidean geometry in order to say that only on his interpretation of the representation of space as intuitive (and a priori), can the necessary and universal status of Euclidean geometry be explained. This is his strategy in the Transcendental Exposition. Here Kant is focusing, rather, on the condition of possibility of determining a geometrical truth *in general*. The fact that this is a truth of Euclidean geometry is a mere accident. His point is that unless we appeal to intuition – that is, if we merely investigate the concepts at stake – we can never establish that truth. And this is taken as evidence for the fact that although we can have very elaborate concepts of space, the original content of the representation of space must arise from intuition. The difference between the structure of the Transcendental Exposition and the present claim is perhaps the reason why Kant in the Second Edition left this claim in the Metaphysical Exposition and did not place it in the Transcendental Exposition, as he did with argument 3 of the First Edition. Finally, note that, unlike the first part of the argument, emphasis is clearly not on the apriority, but rather on the intuitive nature of the representation of space.[48]

The second intuition argument, in its First and Second Edition versions, goes as follows:

> Space is represented as an infinite given magnitude. A general concept of space, which is found alike in a foot and in an ell, cannot determine anything in regard to magnitude. If there were no limitlessness in the progression of intuition, no concept of relations could yield a principle of their infinitude. (A25)

> Space is represented as an infinite *given* magnitude. Now every concept must be thought as a representation which is contained in an infinite number of different possible representations (as their common character), and which therefore contains these *under* itself; but no concept, as such, can be thought as containing an infinite number of representations *within* itself. It is in this latter way, however, that space is thought; for all the parts of space coexist *ad infinitum*. Consequently, the original representation of space is an *a priori* intuition. (B39/40)

The First Edition argument seems to contend that space is given to us with a determination of its magnitude (infinity) that could not be known merely by analysing the 'general concept of space.' As Allison points out, this is true, but irrelevant, as becomes clear when we think of the way in which we represent, not space, but the world. We represent the world as an infinite magnitude (at least if we believe that the world is infinite), but we do not infer from this that the representation of the world is an intuition.[49] Thus, from the fact that we represent space as an infinite magnitude, we cannot infer that the representation of space is an intuition.

This criticism, however, seems to miss the force of the argument. Kant's point is not merely that space is 'thought' or 'represented' as an infinite magnitude, but that it is *given* as such. By this, Kant means that space is immediately present to the mind with that feature (infinity or unboundedness of its extension). In other words, Kant is appealing to a brute phenomenological fact: the manner in which the magnitude of space (which happens to be infinite) is given to us is different from the manner in which we think the content of a concept (say, the infinity contained in the concept of the world).

Evidence in favour of this interpretation is that Kant keeps the first sentence of the old argument in the Second Edition, but amends it by emphasizing precisely the givenness of space. The problem with the First Edition argument is not that it asserts an irrelevant truth, as Allison thinks, but that it comes very close to a *petitio principii*; this is because in order to ground the intuitive nature of the representation of space, it does no more than state the allegedly obvious phenomenological fact that space (better, its determinate magnitude) is given to us in a way different from the way in which the content of a concept is thought.

The Second Edition argument can be read as an attempt to correct this defect. Now Kant tries to *ground* the idea that space is given in a manner different from the manner in which the content of a concept is thought.[50] As in the first intuition argument, the proof turns on the idea that the relation between a concept and its content (intension) is radically different from the relation between the representation of space and its content (the various spatial regions). Space, Kant contends, is represented 'as containing an infinite number of representations within itself.' This means that the parts of space, no matter how large and how many, are always thought as a delimitation of the all-encompassing space, which is therefore represented as an infinite (better, unlimited), singular entity.

By contrast, what falls 'within' a concept – that is, the marks that define that very concept (its intension) – cannot be infinite. The basis of this claim is simply that a concept with an infinite number of marks could not be grasped by the human mind. Thus there is a fundamental contrast between the possibility of conceiving infinity by looking 'within' the representation of space (in its content) and the impossibility of conceiving infinity by examining the concept's intension.

The second intuition argument, like the preceding ones, has been subjected to interesting and powerful criticisms turning on the allegedly implausible psychological assumptions on which it rests. One of the most recent critical analyses comes from Parsons,[51] who points out that we conceive of the concept of God as a concept with an infinite number of marks. Kant is correct when he states that we cannot grasp them all. But then, does the contrast that Kant has in mind require that we grasp all of the infinite parts of space or even an infinite entity that contains within itself the possibly infinite parts of space? If so, it seems that conceiving of an infinite number of marks is no more difficult for us than conceiving of an infinite number of spatial parts or even an infinite singular entity.

To reply to this objection, it is crucial for us to introduce the distinction between infinite (numerically infinite) and unbounded. The point is not that we are supposed to be able to represent an infinity of parts within space or, so to speak, the infinity of an infinite entity. The point is rather that no matter how greatly we enlarge our intuition of space by adding new regions to our original representation, the resulting representation will never be conceived as the extreme limit of space – namely, as capable of exhausting the possibility of 'going beyond.' Thus unboundedness, and not numerical infinity, is the hallmark of our representation of space. But in the case of the infinite marks of God, it is precisely a numerical infinity that is at stake. Thus the real contrast on which Kant's argument rests is that in the case of the representation of space, we have the possibility of grasping a particular kind of infinity (unboundedness); whereas in the case of a concept whose intention is infinite, there is no way of 'getting our mind around' the infinity that pertains to such content (numerical infinity).

These are Kant's arguments aimed at showing that the representation of space is an a priori intuition. As we have seen, Kant draws from this claim the conclusion that space is just a form of human sensibility – a thesis that is equivalent to the transcendental ideality of space. To this conclusion we now turn.

The Conclusions from the Above Concepts

Kant draws two conclusions from the preceding proof of the a priori and intuitive nature of the representation of space. Before dealing with these conclusions, however, it might be helpful to introduce two reminders. One is that the logic of Kant's entire argument is to ask how the very existence of an a priori intuition such as that of space can be explained. This is equivalent to the question of how such a priori intuition can be possible. The other is that the thesis of the apriority of the intuition of space should not be reduced to the affirmation of the non-empirical origin of such representation. In fact, the latter is compatible, among other things, with the possibility that we have an innate idea of space. Kant's thesis, established in the Metaphysical Exposition, is rather that the representation of space functions as a means through which we can represent objects as distinct from ourselves. This transcendental function is actually the basis *from which* the apriority of the representation of space is affirmed.

Having this in mind, we can move to an analysis of the two 'Conclusions.' These are as follows:

> (a) Space does not represent any property of things in themselves, nor does it represent them in their relation to one another. That is to say, space does not represent any determination that attaches to the objects themselves, and which remains even when abstraction has been made of all the subjective conditions of intuition. For no determinations, whether absolute or relative, can be intuited prior to the existence of the things to which they belong, and none, therefore, can be intuited *a priori*.
>
> (b) Space is nothing but the form of all appearances of outer sense. It is the subjective condition of sensibility, under which alone outer intuition is possible for us. Since, then, the receptivity of the subject, its capacity to be affected by objects, must necessarily precede all intuitions of these objects, it can readily be understood how the form of all appearances can be given prior to all actual perceptions, and so exist in the mind *a priori*, and how, as a pure intuition, in which all objects must be determined, it can contain, prior to all experience, principles which determine the relations of these objects. (A26/B42)

In both passages, Kant first gives the conclusion – 'Space does not represent any property of things in themselves, nor does it represent them in their relation to one another,' and 'Space is nothing but the form of all appearances of outer sense' – and then provides the justification for this claim. Thus in the first passage he points out that 'no determinations, whether absolute or relative, can be intuited prior to the existence of the things to which they belong, and none, therefore, can be intuited *a priori*' – that is, since we have learned that space can be intuited prior to the existence of the things in space, it cannot be a property of such things. In fact, no property of an object can be intuited prior to the existence of an object. In the second passage he contends that we can easily understand how the spatiality of things can be given to the mind prior to the intuition of such things if we assume that this spatiality is the form through which our sensibility is affected by objects other than ourselves. In other words, the very existence of an a priori intuition can be explained if we assume that the content of this intuition is a feature that the objects have by virtue of the formal structure of the mind that intuits them. In fact, such intuition would be universal and necessary for all individuals equipped with that formal structure; it would also be independent of sensation – that is, it would present the two criteria of apriority.

Kant clearly thinks that the two rival accounts – the Newtonian, broadly understood as encompassing any absolutistic account of space, and the Leibnizian, broadly understood as encompassing all relational views – are incompatible with that fact. Indeed, he begins his Conclusions with the affirmation that 'space does not represent any property of things in themselves, nor does it represent them in their relation to one another.' Arguing by elimination, he infers from this that his account is the only possible explanation. In the literature it has been noted that the incompatibility of the Leibnizian view is rather evident: if space is nothing but relations among things, then it is incomprehensible how space is not cancelled out even if we abstract from all things in space. However, the incompatibility with the Newtonian view is less evident. It seems that Kant has said nothing in the Metaphysical Exposition to rule out the possibility that space is an objective property. Certainly, given the apriority of the representation of space, the content of this representation could not come from an experience of such a property. But there remains the possibility that space is an innate idea that we infallibly attach to all external intuitions of things that are themselves spatial. If so, both the apriority of our representation and the status of space as absolute/objective property would be preserved. In other words, the proponent of this alternative would insist that all Kant is capable of ruling out is that the objective space is the source of our representation of space. But to the extent that the apriority of the representation of space can explained as the result of our having an innate idea of space, this would still be insufficient to show that there cannot be a correspondence between such innate idea of space and the object 'space' pertaining to the objects themselves.

Kant does not ignore this difficulty. In paragraph 27 of the Transcendental Deduction he discusses whether it is possible to adopt a 'middle course' between his idealistic stance and a straightforward empiricism that interprets the conditions of knowledge as simply products of the mind's exposure to the world. This middle course would describe categories (but clearly, the claim could be extended to sensible forms) as 'subjective dispositions of thought, implanted in us from the first moment of our existence, and so ordered by our Creator that their employment is in complete harmony with the laws of nature in accordance with which experience proceeds – a kind of preformation-system of pure reason'[52] (B167). Kant rejects this middle course – which is strikingly similar to the model assumed by the objection – by arguing that besides being strongly dogmatic, it would leave the necessity of the forms unexplained. In fact, if the representation of space is simply an innate idea that, presumably, we can apply at our discretion just as we can any other idea we possess, then we cannot say that such representation functions as a necessary means through which we become aware of objects as distinct from ourselves. But this is precisely what Kant establishes in the Metaphysical Exposition. This is why in the preceding reminder I was very careful to distinguish between mere apriority and the transcendental status of the representation of space.

If both accounts – the Leibnizian and the Newtonian – are incompatible with the conclusions of the Metaphysical Exposition, then it appears that Kant's thesis that space is a form of sensibility is the only explanation left. As Kant puts it: 'It is, therefore, solely from the human standpoint that we can speak of space, of extended things, etc. If we depart from the subjective condition under which alone we can have outer intuition, namely, liability to be affected by objects, the representation of space stands for nothing whatsoever.' Obviously, since he is arguing by elimination, we can never rule out the possibility of other explanations. Remember, however, that our analysis applies not just to Leibniz and Newton, but to any relational or absolutistic account of space. And since it is even difficult to imagine what 'middle ground,' other than the innate ideas option, there could be between these two alternatives, I believe that the inference by elimination to Kant's thesis is safe.

Note at this point that since the 'middle ground' just examined raises the possibility that our 'subjective, innate space' perfectly and fortunately maps onto the objective space, space would result as a form of real things rather than of objects insofar as we represent them (that is, rather than of appearances). In other words, this third way denies that space is a *form* of our experience (in the proper sense); in this way is removed the need to distinguish between objects as they appear and objects as they are in themselves. A quite distinct objection that has been raised against Kant, known as the 'neglected alternative' – acknowledges that space is such a form, and consequently recognizes the need for the transcendental distinction, but also points out that space could be a property both of appearances and of things in themselves. In other words, the objection acknowledges that space is a form of sensibility, and therefore that we must distinguish between appearances and things in themselves – but denies that space is *nothing but that*. To this objection we now turn.

The Neglected Alternative Objection

In replying to such an objection, it is pointless to appeal to the status of the representation of space established in the Metaphysical Exposition, simply because the objection concedes that space is a form of appearances. This is the crucial difference with regard to the previous objection. The attack against transcendental idealism turns now on the supposed fact that Kant has no right to affirm – as he explicitly does – that 'space does not represent any property of things in themselves.' To affirm that much means to go beyond the limits, drawn by Kant himself, on what we can know. In fact, to know that things in themselves are not in space is already to know *something*.

The neglected alternative has attracted the attention of Kantian scholars since the first appearance of the *Critique*, and in recent years they have developed interesting replies to it. In *Kant's Transcendental Idealism*, Allison attempted to explain how Kant is entitled to rule out the possibility that things in themselves are in space. He did this by heeding the significance of Kant's thesis that space is a form of sensibility. This thesis, which is granted by the objection, implies (according to Allison) that the empirical space is essentially different from the putative transcendental space (the space that should pertain to things in themselves), because the former presents the feature of being dependent on the subject, whereas the latter is *ex hypothesi* independent of it. If the spatial relations holding among appearances are the result of the mind's organization or 'imposition' of a spatial order, then the transcendental space must be numerically and qualitatively different: numerically, because we are certainly talking about two distinct spaces; and qualitatively, because the transcendental space, unlike the empirical one, is not in any way dependent on the human mind.

The obvious problem with this analysis is that even if well grounded, the two differences (numerical and qualitative) do not seem to trouble the basis on which the objection rests. In fact, regarding the qualitative difference, it is not so crucial for the transcendental space to lack the feature of mind-dependence. After all, this is compatible with a scenario in which spatial relations among appearances map perfectly onto spatial relations among things in themselves. Thus, ten centimetres between two objects considered as they appear could be identical to the ten centimetres between those two objects considered as they are in themselves. This seems to be the main point of the objection. A fortiori, it is difficult to see how the objection could be shackled by the (true) consideration that the two spaces are numerically distinct. Once again, the sole crucial point for the objection is that the spatial organization that our mind imposes could map onto the spatial organization holding among things in themselves, not that the empirical space is numerically identical with the transcendental space. Actually, since the objection acknowledges that Kant identifies the empirical space with the form of outer sense, it is reasonable to assume that the objection itself *presupposes* that empirical and transcendental spaces are numerically distinct.

Falkenstein, in the most detailed and recent analysis of the matter so far, has pointed out that Allison's thesis does not succeed in ruling out the possibility of a strong analogy between the two spaces.[53] In order to rule out this possibility, it is necessary to focus, not generically on the mind-dependence of empirical space, but on the peculiar nature of spatial properties relative to 'objective' properties. Thus Falkenstein distinguishes between a 'comparative order' and a 'presentational order.'[54] The former is the order in which objects can be organized according to their intrinsic features; the latter is the order in which objects can be organized according to features that depend on the way in which they are given (or presented) to our intuition. An organization of objects according to their colours is a comparative order because colour is considered a property intrinsic to the object (how much light it absorbs). A spatial organization of objects is a presentational order, because the relations among objects are constituted by the way in which the same objects are presented to our intuition (remember that the objection concedes the ideality of empirical space). Since the transcendental space is not a presentational order (*ex hypothesi* it does not depend on our intuition but pertains to the objects themselves), it is irreparably and significantly different from empirical space. According to Falkenstein, this difference is sufficient to remove any significant analogy between the two spaces and therefore the basis on which the neglected alternative objection rests.

As Falkenstein himself recognizes, this is still not enough to deny *any* possible sense in which things in themselves could be in space. For example, spatial properties of things in themselves could be intrinsic properties of those things (something like the characteristics of monads, which for Leibniz ground the spatial properties *as they appear to us*, according to the metaphysical principle that relational properties must be grounded on substantial properties). Nonetheless, the distinction between the two orders at least clarifies that the two spaces cannot even be significantly similar – a point that the objection implicitly assumes. Moreover, the same distinction gives weight to Allison's intuition that the mind-dependence of empirical space, contrasted with the mind-independence of transcendental space, constitutes the best reply to the objection. It does so by showing precisely how this mind-dependence renders empirical space different from the putative transcendental space.[55]

This concludes our analysis of Kant's foundation of transcendental idealism in the Aesthetic. Let us now turn to one of the most informed and powerful criticisms of it.

Guyer's Non Sequitur

Guyer seems to concede that at least some of Kant's arguments in the Metaphysical Exposition are sound. Such is the case with the apriority arguments, which he recognizes as 'obviously intended as purely epistemological arguments about the conditions under which particulars can be recognized for any possible inductions or empirical concepts-acquisitions at all and are not meant as psychological observations about the genesis of representations.'[56] He is willing to concede the soundness of these arguments and, for the sake of argument, of the entire Metaphysical Exposition, yet he also insists – and this is really the main thrust of his critique – that from the proof that the representations of space and time are a priori intuitions and play the role of conditions of the possibility of experience (what he calls the 'indispensability of space and time'), it does not follow that the referents of these representations must be only forms of sensibility. They could be both forms of sensibility and objective features.[57]

Guyer explains how these two claims are compatible in the following way. The fact that we have a priori representations of space and time is explained in terms of our acquaintance with a sort of innate 'form' of our mind. This acquaintance is what makes possible the representation of space devoid of objects. Since we do not need to derive this representation from the objects, the representation is a priori. The fact that this representation serves the fundamental purpose of making the representation of an external object possible – the other claim established by the apriority argument – is explained by Guyer in the following manner: the form of the mind with which we are acquainted 'restricts us to the experience of objects which are themselves spatial and temporal.'[58] Thus we cannot have representations of objects unless they are spatio-temporal. On this reading, the apriority of the representation of space is compatible with the transcendental reality of space and time, and furthermore, the latter is actually what explains how the a priori representations of space and time function as necessary conditions for objects to be given to the mind. The spatio-temporal features of the objects are precisely what satisfy these a priori restricting features of our mind, thus making a representation of the same objects possible.

Obviously, according to this reading the apriority of the representation of space and time does not entail the idealism that Kant advocates. This indeed entails that the data the mind receives are shaped by subjective forms – that is, they are given a structure that otherwise they would not have. The mind does not simply select a certain type of data that have certain features. Only when we assume that the mind 'shapes' the objects does the need arise to distinguish between things as they appear to this 'shaping' mind and things as they are in themselves. On Guyer's reading, however, the mind certainly plays a role in the cognitive process but this role is limited to the selecting of certain data that remain completely untouched by the mind. It follows that no idealism whatsoever is involved.

Moving to the criticism of this kind of non sequitur reading of the main argument of the Aesthetic, we notice that Guyer's position suffers a consequence that we can hardly accept. According to his interpretation of how the a priori forms work, knowledge becomes completely contingent. If knowledge arises only if the objects have the characteristics (spatiality and temporality) necessary to satisfy the a priori forms, it clearly follows that, if it happened that these objects lacked such characteristics, knowledge would not arise. We would exist with these a priori forms in our mind, but they would remain systematically unsatisfied, thus leaving us with nothing to intuit, in some sort of total 'blindness.' Note that the problem does not arise only in the case of a priori knowledge. The point is not that, on this model, we would not have a priori knowledge of the world, or that we would have it only contingently, as Guyer holds.[59] Even a posteriori knowledge would be completely contingent, obviously not in the sense that a posteriori knowledge is not universal and necessary (this is just what a posteriori knowledge is), but in the sense that it would happen only because of the fortunate agreement between the world and the restricting a priori forms of the mind.[60]

But the problem is not simply that, on Guyer's reading, we could exist and still have no world to intuit – admittedly a scenario already quite unsatisfactory. Since the forms of sensibility are also forms or conditions of self-knowledge, it turns out that on Guyer's interpretation even self-knowledge is completely contingent. If the data that are supposed to bring information about the contents of my consciousness were actually not temporal, we would be unable to experience them. In other words, we would exist but we would have no access whatsoever to ourselves or, equivalently, no knowledge whatsoever that we exist. Insofar as this possibility is not ruled out, it seems that Guyer is committed to a form of scepticism even more radical than that of Descartes. Descartes took the fact that we have some contents in our mind (at least our own thoughts) as beyond doubt; Guyer places at risk even this fact. Indeed, Guyer ends up in a position similar to that of the transcendental realists, whom Kant ridiculed for doubting the reality of our self-knowledge. As Kant puts it, this is 'an absurdity of which no one has yet been guilty' (B71).

Note that a standard realist – by which I mean someone who rejects Kant's proof that the representations of space and time function as necessary conditions of the possibility of experience – does *not* suffer this consequence. For such a realist, the mind takes on whatever forms the objects have. Basically, our mind is bound to reproduce (more or less accurately) the features of the objects. Various accounts of this principle are capable of covering realistic positions as different as Aristotle's and Locke's. On this model, the problem of a possible 'disagreement' between mind and object that would leave us with nothing to intuit cannot possibly arise. But it does arise for Guyer who accepts Kant's proof that representations of space and time function as necessary conditions of the possibility of experience. When that much is granted, but the mind's 'shaping' is denied, the possibility of a systematic mismatch between mind and world is unavoidable.

Another way of expressing the dissatisfaction with the consequence to which Guyer's model is bound is to say that it rehabilitates some form of pre-established harmony between *ordo rerum* and *ordo idearum*. Once again, on his model knowledge arises only if there is harmony between subjective forms and objective features. But since this harmony cannot be explained as the result of the causal influence of the objects on our mind – this sort of imprinting from outside would contradict the apriority thesis – it follows that the only possible way in which this harmony could happen (and remain valid in time) is through some kind of divine intervention or completely fortunate (and mysterious) harmony between 'ideas' and 'things.' Thus it seems that Guyer's criticism leads us to the following alternative: either Kant's idealism, with its strong notion of structuring or objectifying conditions of knowledge, or a (transcendentally) realistic position that describes knowledge in terms of something like a happy, fortunate, and completely fortuitous encounter between the world and our mind's own constraints. I think that, if this is the alternative, one is hardly tempted to discard transcendental idealism.

Note finally that Guyer's account – in fact, any account that accepts the proof of the Metaphysical Exposition regarding representations of space and time as necessary conditions of experience – is bound to such a conclusion. All accounts that take Kant's conditions as objective features of the mind that in some sense 'select without structuring' the data of experience are bound to the idea that knowledge arises in a completely accidental way, or to some sort of pre-established harmony. Kant himself was strongly aware that his conditions of experience could be interpreted in this way, and he was concerned enough to delineate the problems of this position. We have already discussed the crucial paragraph 27, in which Kant lists the reasons why that 'preformation system of pure reason' cannot be accepted. Here it is interesting to mention a supplementary reason we have not yet cited. This middle course – which is strikingly similar to Guyer's model – would reduce our knowledge (a priori as well as a posteriori) to 'sheer illusion' (B168). This is so because, on this reading, all we can legitimately claim is that we see 'spatio-temporal things' – or 'causal connections,' to use Kant's own example – but it would still take some deus ex machina for these features to have a correspondence in the objects. And Kant, interestingly, comments that 'this is exactly what the sceptic most desires' (B168).

With little adaptation, we can apply this Kantian critique to Guyer. He stipulates that knowledge arises only if the raw data contain the required spatio-temporal features, in such a way that it seems that if knowledge happens, then we can be assured that the objects that correspond to it do have spatio-temporal features. Yet it is quite easy to imagine some Evil Genius affecting us in such a way that the conditions/filters in our mind are satisfied even if no actual external object exists. It would simply be a question of reproducing the way in which a real spatial object affects us – something that a mighty Evil Genius should not find too difficult to do. Moreover, as we saw, since the very same thing can be affirmed about inner knowledge, we could say that Guyer's model is even 'more than what the skeptic desires.'

This result is hardly surprising. On Guyer's reading – just to limit ourselves to outer knowledge – the thesis of the immediacy of outer perception on which much of Kant's antisceptical argument rests (see the next chapter) is seriously weakened. There is certainly a sense in which Guyer could say that according to his model, by the very fact that I see a spatial object, I know that the object is really 'spatial' – otherwise it would not have been allowed into my mind. But the discrepancy remains between the objective feature (spatiality) and the condition that is supposed to be satisfied by that objective feature. Thus the possibility that an Evil Genius affects me in precisely the same way that a spatial object would is not ruled out. Indeed, it seems that one could go as far as to claim that for Guyer, I need to perform an inference from the fact that something has entered my mind to the existence of the required objective element. And this is the exact opposite of immediacy, as Kant construes it.

Compare this with Kant's idealism. For Kant, anything transcendentally external that affects me receives from me the feature of spatiality.

To use the usual metaphor, the mind shapes the transcendentally external object into a spatial object. Built into the very notion of shaping there is the denial of any possible gap between the shaping mind and the shaped object. For Kant, the object is 'construed' as spatial and thus the very question as to whether the representation is adequate to the object cannot even arise. This is a delicate point, which we shall address in depth in the next chapter. For the moment, suffice it to grasp intuitively the clear superiority of Kant's idealism over Guyer's realistic model with respect to the ability to refute scepticism.[61]

This concludes our analysis of the foundation of transcendental idealism in the Aesthetic. To sum up the main points, we focused on the epistemological argument of the Aesthetic that runs from the result of the Metaphysical Exposition (the representations of space and time are a priori intuitions) to the Conclusion (the representations of space and time can be a priori intuitions only if space and time are forms of our sensibility). Then we dealt with some old and new objections mounted against the Conclusion. Our discussion, to be sure, won't be sufficient to remove the profound and widespread scepticism that surrounds transcendental idealism. Our analysis, however, did not dare to set such a high standard for itself. The goal was more modest: to clarify the logical structure of Kant's argument. Once this logical structure is clear, it becomes evident that much of Kant's proof rests on the Metaphysical Exposition. Kant there shows that the representations of space and time are of a peculiar nature that distinguishes them from all other representations of our cognition. Then he asks the crucial question: How are these representations possible? This is a serious question whose absolutely central role in the economy of the entire foundational argument of the Aesthetic still escapes the attention of many. But if *this* is the challenge that sceptics are ready to meet (as Guyer courageously does), then the same is not as easily won by the sceptic as one might think. In the case of Guyer, for example, we saw that his alternative explanation of the peculiar nature of the representations of space and time end up in a philosophical stance that is profoundly less appealing than Kant's idealism itself. This, of course, does rule out the possibility of other, more satisfactory accounts. In the wait for such alternatives, however, we hope to have convinced our readers that Kant's challenge is a fascinating one and that, after all, his own solution – transcendental idealism – properly understood, is less flawed and hopelessly outdated than what many think.

3 The Antisceptical Argument of the Fourth Paralogism

In the preceding chapters we saw that the *Critique* in general and the Fourth Paralogism in particular, if read with the appropriate hermeneutical tools, are committed to a kind of idealism that despite appearances can and should be sharply distinguished from phenomenalism. We saw that Kant's idealism has the resources to rebut standard criticisms regarding its nature and its foundations that aim at threatening its plausibility. In this sense, transcendental idealism can support the weight of being the fundamental premise of the antisceptical argument of the Fourth Paralogism. The present chapter spells out this argument. The key lies in reinterpreting the sceptic's challenge from the perspective of transcendental idealism (properly understood). From this standpoint, the sceptic's hypothesis – the world could be a consistent systematic hallucination – becomes a metaphysical question that can be ruled out as illegitimate. Specifically, it can be treated as a vain inquiry into the nature of the thing in itself.

On my reading, the Fourth Paralogism establishes this result through the following steps. To begin with, by placing the critique of Descartes in the Paralogism chapter, Kant is implicitly suggesting that there is a connection between Descartes's scepticism and transcendental illusion, the force that motivates the drive towards the unconditioned that is critically analysed in the Transcendental Dialectic. In an attempt to determine this connection – which Kant never spells out – I will argue that the thesis of the epistemic superiority of inner over outer knowledge – the crucial premise of Descartes's scepticism – rests largely on the mistake that infects rational psychology, namely, it misinterprets a subjective condition of thought as a characteristic of an object (the subject, understood as a particular determinate entity).[1] Second, the same thesis of the superiority of inner over outer knowledge is further weakened through Kant's proof that not only the perception of our mental states and of our existence, but also the perception of external objects, is immediate. Thirdly, Kant deals with the crucial problem of hallucinations or delusions caused by the imagination. On the one hand, he introduces a criterion for detecting these forms of delusions and thereby distinguishing them from genuine experience. This criterion turns on the idea that a particular hallucination can be detected by its failure to harmonize with the laws of experience in general. Yet on the other hand, he dismisses the possibility that the entire world could be a kind of systematic or lawful hallucination (a kind of hallucination that obviously would not be detected by using the criterion) with the argument that the very functioning of the imagination (the faculty that would produce this systematic hallucination) presupposes the existence of external objects as the sources of the material on which the imagination exercises itself.

For good reasons, this last step has been rejected by virtually all interpreters. So I will propose replacing it with a reflection on the very meaning of this systematic hallucination hypothesis – which I take as identical with the Evil Genius hypothesis – within the framework of transcendental idealism. Using materials that Kant himself suggests in the Fourth Paralogism and elsewhere, I will show that wondering whether the cause of all our representations of external objects is itself external or merely internal amounts to wondering about the nature of the thing in itself. This wonder – which is the essence of the sceptic's hypothesis – is illegitimate in the context of transcendental idealism; furthermore, the possibility that this thing is some spiritual entity such as the Evil Genius can even be granted by Kant because it is not the existence of this 'thing' that a transcendental idealist wants to secure. Whatever that 'thing' is that affects us, be it a spiritual or a material entity, we represent it as a world in space through the form of outer sense. The existence of this empirical world is all that concerns the transcendental idealist.

Thus my answer to scepticism will not rest on detecting contradictions in the sceptic's position. Nor will I attempt to identify a premise to which the sceptic is committed (such as the reality of inner experience) in order to show that it presupposes something that the sceptic denies or doubts (such as the reality of outer experience). In the proof I offer, the 'game of idealism' will *not* be 'turned against itself' as Kant thought he was able to do with his 1787 Refutation of Idealism. I will not even be arguing, as Carnap did, that empirical idealism is meaningless because it falls outside what can be verified. My opinion – which I believe also would have been Kant's – is that empirical idealism is a philosophical stance with a legitimate and clear meaning. My strategy, then, will be to uncover the metaphysical nature of the sceptical hypothesis, which is obscured by its arising from a seemingly innocent generalization of normal cases of hallucinations. In particular, my argument will revolve around reducing scepticism to an inquiry into the nature of the thing in itself.

The steps to my argument dictate the structure of this chapter. In the first section, I explain why Kant views Descartes's scepticism as a particular case of transcendental illusion. In the second section, I focus on the thesis of the immediacy of outer perception, which is the first ingredient in Kant's overall refutation. Since this thesis depends largely on the arguments of the Metaphysical Exposition in the Transcendental Aesthetic, I will presuppose the result of my analysis in the preceding chapter. So that readers will be able to appreciate the strength and originality of Kant's position, I will be proposing a comparison with Reid's affirmation of the same thesis (our outer experience is not mediated by 'ideas'). In the third section, having introduced Kant's criterion for distinguishing hallucinations from real experience, I present the antisceptical argument; then in the fourth section I rebut what I consider to be a crucial but also last-resort counter-objection open to the sceptic. The chapter closes with some remarks on Kant's supposed abandonment of the Fourth Paralogism argument in the Second Edition.

The Fourth Paralogism and Transcendental Illusion

The first question the interpreter confronts in dealing with the Fourth Paralogism is, quite simply, its location. Why does Kant place the critique of scepticism among the Paralogisms? Given the architectonic of the *Critique*, the Fourth Paralogism corresponds to the modal categories and these 'have the peculiarity that, in determining an object they do not in the least enlarge the concept to which they are attached as predicates. They only express the relation of the concept to the faculty of knowledge'(A219/B266). This means that they assert whether an object – whose concept they do nothing to determine – is existent, or necessary, or merely possible. Since the Cartesian sceptic does not doubt the appropriateness of our concepts of things, but rather whether (external) things exist, the placement of the critique of this kind of scepticism in the Paralogisms seems to be rather natural. Moreover, rational psychology – the science that is under attack in this section of the *Critique* – is in the main a Cartesian project, and this by itself would justify such placement. Besides these two reasons, however, I think there is a more profound one, which has to do with the connection between transcendental illusion and a basic premise of scepticism – namely, the superiority of inner over outer knowledge.

At the end of the 1781 Paralogisms chapter, Kant offers us one of the general definitions of transcendental illusion contained in the Dialectic.[2] He contends that 'all *illusion* may be said to consist in treating the *subjective* condition of thinking as being knowledge of the *object*' (A396). In the Paralogisms this means taking the logical predicates contained in the notion of a thinking subject as features of a particular, determined object (the subject understood as a determinate entity). Kant states this very clearly in the Second Edition: 'The logical exposition of thought in general has been mistaken for a metaphysical exposition of the object' (B409). In the first three Paralogisms the logical features of the thinking subject in general that are mistaken for objective features are substantiality, simplicity, and personality. But what, precisely, is the logical feature that rational psychology mistakes for an objective feature in the Fourth Paralogism?

The Fourth Paralogism corresponds to the modal group of categories – in particular, to the category of existence.[3] So one would expect that the feature in question is the very existence of the subject. Since a subjective condition of thinking is, obviously, that the thinking subject exists, the logical feature mistaken for an objective feature should be the very existence of the subject. At first glance, however, the existence of the subject is not the feature that Kant seems to have in mind. In the introductory 'topic' of rational psychology, where, in correspondence with the four groups of categories, he lists the logical features of the thinking subject that rational psychology mistakes for objective features, he characterizes the feature corresponding to the modal group of categories as follows: 'It [the soul] is in relation to *possible* objects in space' (A344/B402). As the reader discovers in the Fourth Paralogism, the objects with which the soul is in relation are merely *possible* because their existence, ascertained through an inference from effect to cause, is doubtful.

Although Kant attempts to present this attribute as a feature of the soul (how it relates itself to objects in space), it prima facie seems to be a feature that concerns more the objects and the way in which they exist rather than the soul itself. However, this impression would be mistaken. The existence of objects is merely possible because of the particular way in which the soul ascertains their existence; just as importantly Kant contrasts this way with the way in which the soul ascertains its own existence. Indeed, the absolutely certain access that the soul has to its own existence seems to be the background against which he contrasts and evaluates the merely possible existence of external objects. Thus to say that the soul is in relation to objects in space that are merely *possible* because their existence is inferred is an indirect way of emphasizing the immediacy and certainty through which the existence of the soul can be ascertained.

This is confirmed, in the final section of the First Edition version of the Paralogism chapter, by the approach Kant takes to characterizing the feature of the soul corresponding to the Fourth Paralogism. He states that the thinking 'I' regards itself 'as the correlate of all existence, from which all other existence must be inferred' (A402), and adds that the thinking subject knows '*the unconditioned unity of existence in space, i.e.* that it is not the consciousness of many things outside it, but the consciousness *of the existence of itself* only, and of other things merely as its *representations*' (A404). These expressions are quite obscure, yet Kant's point is clear enough: what the rational psychologist assumes he is able to determine through merely logical means – that is, on the basis of the mere 'I think' – is '*the existence of itself* [the subject] only.' Access to the existence of other beings occupies an inferior epistemic level because those beings' existence is inferred from the representations that lie within the subject. The existence of the subject, or 'unconditioned unity of existence,' is thus the real feature at stake in the Fourth Paralogism. This feature serves as the reference point – as the paradigm of the unity enjoyed by possible objects in space. This explains why Kant characterizes it as the unconditioned unity of existence '*in space.*'

Thus the original error analysed in the Fourth Paralogism is not that the soul regards outer objects as merely possible. This is a mere consequence. The original error lies in taking one's existence in that paradigmatic manner, which, in turn, is a consequence of assuming that one's existence can be ascertained through merely logical means. In the Fourth Paralogism, transcendental illusion is precisely the force driving the inference from this particular condition of thinking (existence of the subject) to the existence of the subject as an objective fact. Since this existence is analytically inferred from the 'I think,' it is absolutely certain and, as such, is in contrast to the doubtful (or possible) existence of external objects. The analytic nature of the inference that leads to the existence of the subject engenders an enormous epistemic gap between the affirmation of the existence of the subject and that of external objects. Indeed, if we concede that our existence as subjects can be ascertained in this analytical way, knowledge of our existence will differ from knowledge of the existence of outer objects in *kind*, not just in degree of certainty. The former enjoys a priori status; the latter can only be a synthetic a posteriori claim.

By placing the refutation of scepticism in the Fourth Paralogism chapter, Kant is suggesting that the first step in refuting the sceptic entails showing that this difference in kind is merely apparent. More precisely, by revealing how the idea of an analytical inference from the logical description of the subject of thought to the existence of the subject is merely illusory, Kant is removing one of the grounds on which the superiority of inner over outer knowledge rests. Once the mistake that lies at the heart of this inference is detected and it turns out that even the cognition of my existence presupposes an empirical intuition (perception), inner and outer knowledge are no longer considered different in kind.

Note that Kant, on my reading, does not establish this point through his actual discussion of the Fourth Paralogism, but merely through the placement of his criticism within his general treatment of rational psychology. This placement suggests – albeit implicitly – that the same ipostatization of the features of a merely logical subject (the 'I' of apperception) into a noumenal subject that Kant detected in the first three Paralogisms is also key to the criticism of the fourth. Once the idea of an intellectual access to the existence of a subject is replaced with the idea of an empirical access to ourselves, Kant can introduce his crucial idea – which he explicitly presents in his discussion of the Fourth Paralogism – that both the existence of myself and that of an external object are 'proved in the same manner' (A370) and that 'the only difference is that the representation of myself, as the thinking subject, belongs to inner sense only, while the representations which mark extended beings belong also to outer sense.' (A371) In fact, the critique of the Fourth Paralogism *assumes* that our existence must be *perceived* in inner sense. Indeed, the first premise of the Fourth Paralogism is that 'my own existence is the sole object of a mere perception' (A367), or, equivalently, that Descartes was justified in limiting 'all perception' to the proposition 'I, as a thinking being, exist'.' (A367). Since it is hardly trivial that Descartes took the cogito as resting on a perception, Kant is here presenting the Cartesian position as already reinterpreted and criticized. And the criticism is precisely that there is no access to my existence without empirical intuition – specifically, the perception of my thoughts in inner sense.[4]

If this analysis explains why Kant placed his critique of scepticism in the Fourth Paralogism and what the connection is between scepticism and transcendental illusion, it opens up a new twofold problem. On the one hand, the very idea that we become aware of our existence necessarily through a perception is ambiguous. In the *Critique* Kant presents two different modes of self-consciousness – one through inner sense, the other through apperception. Each is based on a 'perception,' but in a very different way. The problem for us is simply to ascertain which mode Kant is assuming in the Fourth Paralogism.

For Kant, through apperception we can become aware of our spontaneity – that is, our activity as thinkers. But this activity cannot be captured by an intuition. Indeed, any intuition would give us only a *thought* and not the very activity of *thinking*. As Kant puts it in a footnote in the Transcendental Deduction: 'Since I do not have another self-intuition which gives me the determining in me (I am conscious only of the spontaneity of it) prior to the act of *determination*, as time does in case of the determinable, I cannot determine my existence as that of a self-active being; all I can do is to represent to myself the spontaneity of my thought, that is, of the determination' (B158n).

Moreover, according to Kant, in this non-sensible consciousness of the activity of thinking one can also find an awareness of existence: 'In the synthetic original unity of apperception, I am conscious of myself, not as I appear to myself, but only that I am. This *representation* is a *thought*, not an *intuition*'[5] (B157). The content of this 'pure' self-consciousness cannot be provided by an (empirical) intuition, yet perception is still necessary for it. As Kant clarifies in the Second Edition version of the Paralogism, I need an empirical material (what perception provides) for the very exercise of the faculty of thinking. But this material functions merely as the *occasion* of the act of thinking. In fact, the object of the perception that is necessary for this act need not even be the subject itself or one of its inner states. It could be anything, because independently of its object, any perception can play the role of occasioning the activity of thinking. Once this activity is occasioned, although we can really *know* only the products of this activity, we can be *aware* of the activity itself that generated those products. In turn, once we become conscious of this activity, we can also become aware of the existence of an agent that does the activity. In this sense, we are aware of the existence of the subject as thinking agent.

Self-knowledge through inner sense is based on perception in a manner very different from self-consciousness through apperception. In the former case, perception is not a mere occasion, as we perceive the mental states that are successively given in inner sense. It follows that perception is what provides the very content of our cognition. Since we will be dealing with the details of this kind of empirical self-knowledge in the following chapter, we can limit ourselves here to clarifying the role that perception and inner sense play in this kind of cognition.

This in itself is sufficient to solve our problem of determining the mode of self-knowledge with which Kant is operating in the Fourth Paralogism. Kant's explicit reference to inner sense tells us that he is operating in the Fourth Paralogism with the first, 'thick' mode of self-knowledge – that is, inner experience. So, for example, he claims: 'External things as well as myself exist upon the immediate witness of my self-consciousness. The only difference is that the representation of myself, as the thinking subject *belongs to inner sense* only, while the representations which mark extended beings belong also to other sense' (A371, my emphasis).

But if it is clear which notion of self-consciousness Kant is operating with, it is less clear whether his main point holds true – that both the existence of myself and that of external objects are 'proved in the same manner,' (A370) – considering that he himself acknowledges the other, non-sensible mode of becoming aware of our existence. In fact, the idea that in apperception the existence of the subject is already given (and given in a non-sensible manner) seems to contradict the presupposition that we thought Kant wanted to rule out by placing his critique of scepticism among the Paralogisms. The idea of a non-sensible access to our existence seems to make self-consciousness again different *in kind* (rather than in degree of certainty) than the consciousness of outer objects.[6]

One way to solve the problem is to understand that the 'I' whose existence is contained in apperception is not what Descartes (and the rational psychologist of the Fourth Paralogism) thought he was able to infer from the consciousness of thinking. The 'I' that arises from the radical doubt is a *res cogitans*. As we have seen, however, through apperception we become conscious of an activity, not of a thing. The thought of this activity obviously includes also the thought of an agent. But by no means can we take this as cognition of a determined entity or (more simply) of a thing. It is nothing but the pure thought of the subject of this activity. Through this thought, the number of the 'items' of which the world is composed is by no means increased. In order to come to know the existence of myself as one of the 'things' that constitute the world, I require a perception, no longer as mere occasion but as the *vehicle* that provides the determinations of that particular 'thing' (the empirical 'I'). It follows that for Kant, notwithstanding his misleading expressions, the only way to ascertain the existence of ourselves as actual 'things' is through inner experience. And this tells us that the result established by positioning the refutation in the Paralogism – that is, no intellectual access to our existence, and therefore no difference in kind between inner and outer experience – is not undermined by Kant's doctrine of apperception as a mode of self-consciousness.

A last point needs to be clarified. By showing that we cannot analytically ascertain our existence, as the rational psychologist contends, Kant is not saying that access to our existence is dubious. The fact that we know the existence of ourselves as 'objects' through inner sense does not mean that my existence becomes dubious because it is open to the delusion of the imagination. In criticizing the cogito, Kant never meant to refute Descartes's point that inner experience is immune to the kinds of delusion to which outer experience is vulnerable. The point is simply that this undeniable advantage of inner knowledge need not be taken as the result of a presumed 'intellectual' access to our own existence. Indeed, what the actual discussion of the Fourth Paralogism (as opposed to its placement) is meant to convey is that the *immediate* relation between the mind and the object that is rightly predicated in the case of inner knowledge should *also* be predicated on outer knowledge, notwithstanding the undeniable delusion that it suffers. Briefly put, the point is not to lower inner knowledge to the level of outer knowledge, but rather to elevate (as much as possible) outer knowledge to the level of inner knowledge. This result can never be achieved if we first do not free ourselves of the mistake (motivated by transcendental illusion) that inner knowledge enjoys a kind of *'intellectual* immediacy' denied to outer knowledge. Once it is shown that the access we have to our own existence, albeit certainly immediate, is still of a sensible kind, a preliminary obstacle on the way to re-establishing a certain parity between inner and outer knowledge is removed. The next antisceptical step is precisely to show that outer knowledge enjoys the same kind of (sensible) immediacy as does inner knowledge.

The Immediacy of Outer Perception

Before asking how Kant manages to ground the immediacy of outer perception, we must confront a preliminary problem, one that hinges on the fact that the very notion of an 'immediate perception' (be it inner or outer) is problematic within Kant's system. For Kant, only intuitions are immediate whereas concepts and judgments entertain a mediate relation with the object. Kant makes this point quite clearly in the section of the Analytic devoted to the logical employment of the understanding: 'Since no representation, save when it is an intuition, is in immediate relation to an object, no concept is ever related to an object immediately, but to some other representations of it, be that other representation an intuition, or itself a concept. Judgment is therefore the mediate knowledge of an object, that is, the representation of a representation of it' (A68/B93).

The problem with the notion of immediate perception is that in many places in which Kant defines perception, he takes it as involving a kind of judgment. In fact, what distinguishes a perception from a mere sensation is that only the former contains a conceptual synthesis. For example, in the B version of the Metaphysical Deduction, Kant writes that 'all synthesis, therefore, even that which renders perception possible, is subject to the categories' (B161). But perception does not involve only pure concepts. In general, perception is presented as a sensation to which a concept is applied, be it pure or empirical. An objective perception, as opposed to a merely subjective one (that is, to a sensation), is even identified with knowledge.[7] Since knowledge obviously requires the application of empirical concepts as well as pure ones, and since this application is nothing but an act of the faculty of judgment, it turns out that a perception is a judgment in which some (pure or empirical) concepts are applied to sensible data. But if a perception is a kind of judgment, and if a judgment is a 'mediate knowledge of an object,' how can Kant consistently talk of an *immediate* perception?[8]

The solution to this difficulty turns on the precise determination of Kant's notion of immediacy. In the context of the Fourth Paralogism, immediacy means that a temporal or spatio-temporal *indeterminate* object is given to the mind without the medium of a third thing. The understanding (taken here as what synthesizes the sensible material through pure and empirical concepts) is presented with an object that is already given to the mind as either temporal or spatio-temporal. The presentation of this indeterminate temporal or spatio-temporal object, which is the autonomous contribution of sensibility, is what informs me about the existence of 'something' in space or in time. As Kant puts it in the body of the Fourth Paralogism: 'It is sensation ... that indicates a reality in space or in time, according as it is related to the one or to the other mode of sensible intuition'(A373–4). Judgment – determinative judgment, to be precise – enters the picture when this already either temporal or spatio-temporal indeterminate 'something' has to be brought under a concept. In this way, what used to be merely a temporal or spatio-temporal indeterminate 'something' becomes a determinate object. By subsuming this object under a concept, judgment relates a representation (the concept) not to the object itself, but to the object that is already organized according to the forms of sensibility. For this reason it is in a mediate relation to the object. But the existence of an indeterminate object was already given through the apprehension of this temporal or spatio-temporal material, and it was given immediately. Thus the mediacy through which the material is organized under pure and empirical concepts does not contradict the immediacy through which the not yet determined object is given to sensibility. It follows that Kant can consistently talk of an immediate perception even if the latter involves judgment.

Moving to the *foundation* of the immediacy of outer perception, the question becomes this: How is the existence of an (indeterminate) object given to my sensibility *immediately*? The minor premise of the Fourth Paralogism reads: 'All outer appearances are of such a nature that their existence is not immediately perceived, and that we can only infer them as a cause of a given perception' (A367). Much of the anti-sceptical argument of the Fourth Paralogism turns on whether Kant succeeds in refuting this claim.

Kant uses for this refutation two basic tools. One is the result established in the Transcendental Aesthetic, in which space is reduced to the form of our outer sense – a form that presents itself to the mind as a pure intuition. Implicit in all this is the standard definition of intuition as what 'refers immediately to its objects' (A320/B377). The other is the criticism of the transcendental realist's model of perception.

Starting with the last point, Kant contends that the idea cherished by the sceptic – that the existence of outer things is *not* immediately perceived – is a direct and perverse outcome of transcendental realism.[9] As he puts it: 'Transcendental realism ... inevitably falls into difficulties, and finds itself obliged to give way to empirical idealism, in that it regards the objects of outer sense as something distinct from the senses themselves, treating mere appearances as self-subsistent beings, existing outside us. On such a view as this, however clearly we may be conscious of our representation of these things, it is still far from certain that, if the representation exists, there exist also the object corresponding to it' (A371).

Transcendental realism assumes that the objects of our experience are things in themselves. As such, they are what they are independently of our senses. There is nothing in the objects of our experience that they have by virtue of our intuition of them. Given this model of the mind/object relation, Kant argues that scepticism is unavoidable.[10] What is presented immediately to the mind is *never* the object, but always a copy or representation of it. In sharp contrast, for a transcendental idealist space is not an objective property that must be 'picked up' (somehow) by the mind; rather, it is a form through which we first become aware of objects other than ourselves. The problem of scepticism arises precisely when some sort of 'picking up' is introduced as the model of a cognitive act. Kant's idealism can be construed precisely as a denial of this idea.

Once again, everything turns on the status attributed to space in the Transcendental Aesthetic. Recall, there it was shown that the way in which objects are what they are is *not* independent of our sensibility. For the transcendental idealist, space is not an objective property, but the form that makes possible the very representation of something other than myself. As such, space infallibly enters the constitution of an object of experience other than the knowing subject. The immediacy through which objects other than myself are given is thus guaranteed by the fact that space, rather than being a feature among others that must be derived from experience, is in fact the subject's insufficient yet necessary contribution towards the constitution of an external object. To use the (too) common metaphor, on Kant's account the immediacy of outer perception is guaranteed by the fact that the mind 'shapes' whatever affects my outer sense.[11] To perceive an object means to constitute it as spatial, and obviously there is no room for mediacy here.

Perhaps this crucial idea of the immediacy of outer perception can be clarified further by concentrating no longer on the status of space as *form of intuition*, but rather on the status of the representation of space as *formal intuition*. Kant argues that 'space and time are represented *a priori* not merely as forms of sensible intuition, but as themselves *intuitions* which contain a manifold [of their own]' (B160). Moreover, this manifold has priority over the representations of particular objects contained in it.¹² As Kant puts it: 'We can never represent to ourselves the absence of space, though we can quite well think it as empty of objects' (A24/B38–9). Even if there were no objects, we would still intuit an external framework. Although we cannot intuit the object 'space' as an infinite container devoid of determinate objects, we can intuit an external horizon – let us call it an externality – that is waiting to be filled with determinate objects. There can be no question that this external framework is given to us immediately. In fact, the Transcendental Aesthetic shows that it is given to us as an a priori intuition, and any intuition – let alone an a priori intuition – is by definition the cognitive act that allows the mind to make direct contact with the object.¹³

Obviously, all of this merely shows that the pure, formal intuition of space is given immediately. What can we say about the spatial *objects*, with all their empirical determinations? If space, as a pure horizon, is given immediately, and if external objects are determinations of this external horizon, they are themselves immediately given. In occupying parts of this horizon, empirical objects borrow the immediacy through which the horizon itself is given. How could something that merely delimits a horizon immediately given be itself not given in the very same way? Hence there is no inference in our perceiving an external object. Its presence is immediately grasped because space, being an intuition with its own (pure) manifold, is immediately given in our cognition, and the object itself is simply a determination of this given.¹⁴

A quite paradoxical, but I think helpful, way of expressing the same point is to say that on Kant's account, the mind 'reaches' or 'touches' the external object. The reason is again that external objects occupy a place on a horizon that is pre-given to the mind. It is as if the subject, thanks to the pure intuition of space, could consider each spatial object as something that, as determination of its horizon, acquires a 'closeness' to itself. This obviously does not mean that the object ends up being 'in' the mind as a mental entity. The idea is quite the opposite. The pure intuition of space allows the subject, as it were, to go outside of itself and be in direct contact with everything that occupies a determined place in its spatial horizon.¹⁵

Reid's Realism

There is, of course, a lot of contention over Kant's certainty that a transcendental realist is committed to an indirect model of perception. Kant seems to operate with the model of classical empiricism, yet he offers no explanation why, for example, direct realism is not even a possibility. One would think that there is nothing incoherent in the position according to which (1) we know things as they are in themselves, and (2) we have direct access to them – that is, access not mediated by a third entity such as a mental entity of some sort. So it seems that a transcendental realist is by no means committed to the gap between mind and object that Kant confidently assumes.

In order to fully appreciate the strength and originality of Kant's defence of the immediacy thesis, and to ground his assessment of transcendental realism as necessarily committed to the sceptical threat, it would be instructive to discuss briefly Reid's theory of perception. Through his attack on the theory of ideas, Reid attempts to reach roughly the same result as Kant: the relation between the mind and external objects is *not* mediated by a mental entity. Interestingly, Reid's argument rests on an intuition very similar to the one exploited by Kant: he considers space a necessary component of our outer perception *without being derived from outer perception itself*. In this way he champions the direct realism that we introduced earlier as a possible counter-example to Kant's general characterization of the transcendental realist.

In his critique of Berkeley and Hume, Reid sets up an *experimentum crucis* to test the soundness of scepticism: either space is an 'idea of sensation,' by which he means something that can be derived from the experience of objects, or it is not. If it is, then skepticism is unavoidable because every experience of a spatial object is mediated by an idea that is supposed to resemble the spatiality of things. If it is not, space turns out to be an irreducible brute datum of our experience that is immediately given to us *and that cannot be put at risk out of the supposed necessity that we bring it to our consciousness through a representation*. Any attempt to show that this idea is derived by the senses (Reid deals specifically with Locke's attempt to derive the idea of space from the sense of touch) is actually circular because the 'externality' of these experiences is always presupposed.[16] It follows that space and the things in it are not given through an idea in the mind, but immediately.[17]

There are similarities between Kant and Reid regarding the non-empirical origin of the representation of space, but there is also a crucial difference: Reid does not explain the surprising fact that space is not derived from experience and yet is a necessary component of each outer perception. He seems to lack the resources to explain how an affection, which supposedly only brings what is in the affecting thing – can make us conceive immediately something that, *ex hypothesi*, is not in the thing itself, namely, its spatial location. He admits as much in a revealing passage: 'How a sensation should instantly make us conceive and believe the existence of an external thing altogether unlike to it, I do not pretend to know.' All Reid is willing to say is that, by a quite mysterious law of nature, 'such a conception or belief [space] constantly and immediately follows the sensation.'

From a Kantian perspective, Reid's position fails to recognize that space is a 'form of sensibility' and that it functions as a condition for the representation of objects other than ourselves. Lacking this insight, Reid is open to the charge that even if we admit his point that no sensation can originate the representation of space, two options are still open to the sceptic. One is to say that the idea of space is an innate idea, which is obviously compatible with the point that all we actually perceive are ideas (innate and non-innate). The other is simply to blame Reid for asking us to accept this mysterious mechanism according to which the idea of space arises from an affection, whereas the object that affects our sensibility is not supposed to provide the feature of spatiality. Why should the sceptic accept the immediacy of outer experience if it ultimately rests on a mechanism that Reid himself considers 'utterly inexplicable'?[18]

These two objections are inevitable consequences for the peculiar kind of realism Reid champions. If we lack the fundamental idea that objects are organized by the forms of our sensibility, but at the same time want to deny the empirical origin of some objective properties, we can only conclude either that we have an innate idea of space or that we are confronted with an inexplicable mystery. An idealist, conversely, suffers neither of these consequences. To begin with, the idea that space is a form of our sensibility has very little to do with the notion that it is an innate idea. As we saw in our critique of Guyer in the preceding chapter, Kant's notion of a condition of the possibility of experience is very different from that of an innate idea (as well as less vulnerable to the skeptical threat). Moreover, the idea of space as a form of sensibility at least explains the peculiar status of the representation of space. All of this suggests that Kant's idealism manages to ground the immediacy thesis in a much more convincing way than any realist approach, regardless of its good intentions.

Is the significance of this result really limited to the peculiarities of Reid's version of realism, or we can rather generalize our findings to all forms of realism, including direct realism? In order to avoid the difficulties Reid confronts, the direct realist could hold that space *is* a property derived from the external objects, but insist that the mind perceive the spatiality of things without any mediation. On this reading, the mind would be presented directly with space, which would therefore be considered along with all other properties of external objects. As I have said, there is nothing inherently incoherent in this position, but the realist needs to show that the arguments of the Transcendental Aesthetic are flawed. There Kant proved that the representation of space is not an 'empirical concept' (A23/B38), mainly because any external representation presupposes it. Thus even if we were to concede to the direct realist that the whole of our perception functions as he suggests – that is, through some sort of unmediated access to the property of things – the property 'space' would nonetheless constitute an important exception, as long as the first two arguments of the Metaphysical Exposition hold. Thus, either the direct realist convinces us that these arguments are incorrect, or Kant's characterization remains valid regarding the close relation – as inevitable as undesired – between realism (of all kinds) and scepticism. Needless to say, this shifts the burden of the proof onto the Transcendental Aesthetic, and we can here simply refer to our defence in the preceding chapter.

We now move on from the foundation of the immediacy thesis to its significance. The obvious consequence of the immediacy thesis is that the superiority of inner experience over outer experience is weakened (although, as we shall see, not completely erased). The intuition of my inner states (and thus the consciousness of my existence) and the intuition of outer objects are both immediate: 'External things exist as well as I myself, and both, indeed, upon the immediate witness of my self-consciousness' (A371). As Kant puts it: 'In order to arrive at the reality of outer objects I have just as little need to resort to inference as I have in regard to the reality of the object of my inner sense, that is, in regard to the reality of my thoughts. For in both cases alike the objects are nothing but representations, the immediate perception (consciousness) of which is at the same time a sufficient proof of their reality' (A371).

The sheer superiority of inner sense, to which Kant was still ready to subscribe in the late 1770s, is at last denied. The parity on which he insists, however, is open to an obvious objection. Even if we accept the idea that when I see a genuine external object, this object is perceived immediately, it is still the case that sometimes I merely *seem* to see such an object, but I am actually hallucinating. It is a fact about human nature that we sometimes see things that on closer scrutiny do not exist. But these epistemic failures seem to affect only outer knowledge and leave inner knowledge completely untouched. Here Descartes's famous considerations in the Second Meditation hold. If I am conscious of a certain mental state (seeing the table), then, by that very fact, that mental state exists. Briefly put, the existence of a mental state coincides with its being represented. More importantly, *I* must exist in order to have that representation. Whereas in outer knowledge I may be wrong about the very existence of the object of my perception, the mere appearance of a representation in my mind assures me of the existence of myself as the being that entertains or thinks that representation. It follows that despite the immediacy of outer perception, inner knowledge still enjoys a certain degree of epistemic superiority over outer knowledge.

It is important to realize that Kant never meant to deny *this* superiority. When he contends that matter is 'proved in the same manner as the existence of myself as a thinking being is proved,' he only means to deny that there is a special kind of *intellectual* access to my existence (the mistake at the basis of the Fourth Paralogism of rational psychology). But this is perfectly compatible with the idea that our *sensible* access to ourselves and to our states is infallible. In other words, the cogito, if properly understood as based on the perception of my mental states leading to the knowledge of the empirical 'I,' is perfectly correct for Kant. The idea of denying the existence of this empirical 'I' is indeed for Kant simply 'an absurdity' (B71). Even merely doubting such existence is out of the question. As he points out in the Fourth Paralogism: 'There can be no question that I am conscious of my representations; these representations and I myself, who have these representations, therefore exist' (A370).

But if Kant holds both that the access to my representations and to myself is infallible and that the access to outer things is open to 'delusion of the imagination' such as hallucinations, it seems that the very notion of immediacy of outer perception is again put at risk. For one is tempted to infer from the existence of hallucinations that the normal relation between the mind and an outer object is mediated by a mental representation. The only difference between hallucinations and normal cases of perception would be that only in the latter case does an object actually correspond to the representation. This is indeed the reasoning on which scepticism is based. But this reasoning is clearly based on a non sequitur. The existence of hallucinations says nothing about how I perceive genuine external objects. Indeed, all that the immediacy thesis establishes is that *if I ever perceive a genuine external object*, I perceive it immediately. This is clearly compatible not only with the existence of sporadic hallucinations, but also with the possibility that the entire world is a systematic hallucination. In that case, our ability to perceive genuine external objects immediately would simply never be actualized.

The result of this analysis is that the immediacy thesis *by itself* is not sufficient to refute the Cartesian sceptic. In fact, the immediacy thesis and the Evil Genius hypothesis seem compatible. Nonetheless, the immediacy thesis establishes the apparently minimal but (as we shall see) ultimately crucial point that if we were ever to perceive a genuine external object, it would be immediately. Indeed, to make this point is already sufficient to refute the sceptic's idea that even in cases of genuine experience, we perceive them mediately (through a mental entity). In the following sections we shall see that only if this idea is rejected can the refutation of the sceptic get off the ground. Though modest, the immediacy thesis plays precisely this dialectical role in the overall refutation.

The Refutation of the Sceptic: The Official Strategy

Kant's standard attempt to move beyond the immediacy thesis is found in a passage in which he acknowledges clearly the possibility of illusory representations to which no objects correspond, as in hallucinations or dreams: 'From perceptions knowledge of objects can be generated, either by mere play of imagination or by way of experience; and in the process there may no doubt arise illusory representations to which the objects do not correspond, the deception being attributable sometimes to a delusion of imagination (in dreams) and sometimes to an error of judgment (in so-called sense-deception)' (A376).

Now if notwithstanding the immediacy thesis, delusions of imagination are possible, it seems that the sceptic can easily raise his usual question: how do you know that what you have just acknowledged can happen occasionally does not happen systematically? To be sure, Kant provides a criterion for distinguishing such delusions from experience. But as he himself seems to realize, this criterion will turn out to be at best superfluous.

The criterion for recognizing delusions is the following: 'To avoid such deceptive illusion, we have to proceed according to the rule: '*Whatever is connected with a perception according to empirical laws, is actual.*'[19] Perhaps an example will help elucidate Kant's point. Let us assume that, being particularly afraid of the dark and finding ourselves in a dark room, we are so overwhelmed by fear that we believe we see a threatening individual. However, we are lucky enough to find a light switch while we are still 'seeing' this individual. When the light goes on, we find that our room contains no dangerous company. We are led to consider our past 'perception' as a hallucination because to take it otherwise would commit us to giving up the empirical law (actually an application of it to this particular situation) that declares that bodies cannot 'go out of existence' or 'disappear' from our sight with such rapidity. In other words, we take our vision as a hallucination because it does not cohere with the rest of our well-tested and usually reliable empirical laws.

Interestingly, Kant considers the deception in question and the 'provision against it' – the criterion we have just seen – to affect both dualism and idealism. By these two terms he means respectively his position and the position of his opponent.[20] One might wonder why Kant argues that idealism should be affected by this provision. Why should the sceptical idealist be interested in distinguishing between real experience and hallucinations, if part of his point is that there is no certain way to distinguish between the two?

The answer is that even the sceptic must account for the regularity and coherence of experience. In other words, even if our entire experience is 'really' just a trick of the imagination or of some Evil Genius, it is just a fact that we do distinguish between hallucinations and normal cases of experience. Indeed, as we have seen, we usually detect these deceptions by seeing how much our particular experiences cohere with the empirical laws that regulate the whole of our experience. The assumption that all of our experience is actually nothing but a trick of some Evil Genius does not mean that the above criterion cannot be applied. Actually, it is *part* of the sceptical hypothesis that nothing would change in our 'experience' if nothing corresponded to our representations. Even if nothing corresponded to our representations, we would be drawing the distinction between bits of normal 'experience' and deviant cases. Since the latter do not cohere with the rest, we would take them as 'hallucinations,' obviously not realizing that they are simply deviant hallucinations within the general 'big hallucination' to which our experience actually amounts.

The fact that even the sceptic is committed to the lawfulness of what appears to us is obviously still not enough to refute the sceptic. All we have achieved is the concession that, if the entire external world were a trick of some Evil Genius, we would experience it with the same regularities to which we are accustomed. But Descartes would readily concede that much, and Kant is perfectly aware of this. In fact, he seems to hold that his criterion is at best superfluous with regard to refuting the sceptic because empirical idealism is 'already' refuted through different considerations:

> Empirical idealism, and its mistaken questionings as to the objective reality of our outer perceptions, is already sufficiently refuted, when it has been shown that outer perception yields immediate proof of something actual in space, and that this space, although in itself only a mere form of representations, has objective reality in relation to all outer appearances, which also are nothing else than mere representations; and when it has likewise been shown that in the absence of perception even imagining and dreaming are not possible, and that our outer senses, as regards the data from which experience can arise, have therefore their actual corresponding objects in space. (A376–7)

Thus Kant's strategy for removing the spectre that our experience may be, *systematically* and not just on certain occasions, a mere product of the imagination, does not rest on the criterion introduced for detecting *particular* hallucinations. Rather, it rests on the following two claims, each of which Kant seems to take as sufficient to refute the sceptic: (a) the immediacy thesis, and (b) the thesis that the imagination is dependent on outer sense (and thus that the reality of the latter cannot be denied without also removing the very possibility of the former).[21] We have already seen why the immediacy thesis, although sound, by itself is not sufficient for the refutation. Can we then complete the argument by relying on the other thesis?

Unfortunately, as critics have largely recognized, the thesis of the imagination's dependence on outer sense is highly unsatisfactory.[22] It rests on a bold limitation of our imaginative power that, without clear justification, is assumed to be unable *by itself* to produce outer representations. Moreover, as Allison has pointed out, even if one concedes for the sake of argument that the faculty of imagination, *as we know it*, suffers this limitation, 'the possibility still remains that our representations of outer things are the results of some unknown "hidden faculty."'[23] Descartes himself mentions this possibility in the Third Meditation when he addresses the problem of the source of ideas that seem to come from outside us. According to Descartes, the observation that these ideas are independent of our will is not sufficient reason to consider them as externally caused. He bases this claim on the following consideration: 'Perhaps there is in me some faculty or power adequate to produce these ideas without the aid of any external objects, even though it is not known to me.'[24] Finally, this line of thought seems to ignore the central idea that underpins the Cartesian hypothesis of the Evil Genius. In fact, Descartes's intention is precisely to raise the possibility of a power that goes well beyond the power of the imagination as we know it.[25] Thus Kant's strategy in the Fourth Paralogism suffers a serious difficulty. Its failure, at least as it stands, leads us to wonder whether the problem raised by the possibility of a 'super-imaginative power,' can be dealt with differently.

The Refutation of the Sceptic: The Alternative Strategy

I suggest that an alternative refutation can be mounted by combining two points, both of which depend on transcendental idealism: (1) the abandonment of the transcendental realist's picture of perception (the result achieved in the proof of the immediacy of outer perception), and (2) a reflection on the meaning, within a transcendental idealistic perspective, of the very possibility of a super-imaginative power that generates our *entire* experience, even in its lawfulness (which distinguishes the 'big hallucination' from occasional and thus non-problematic hallucinations).

To begin with, the sceptic assumes that both in the case of normal experience and in the case of hallucinations we perceive an 'idea' (with a spatial content), and that the difference between them is that in the latter case no object corresponds to the 'idea.' The immediacy thesis refutes this fundamental premise of the sceptical argument by establishing that whenever I perceive an external object, I do it immediately. As we saw, the existence of (particular) hallucinations is not sufficient grounds for inferring that what I normally see is an 'idea' in my mind. Now, my entire experience teaches me that the world is constituted by two distinct sets of objects: merely temporal inner states (and myself as the owner of these states), and spatio-temporal objects. Particular hallucinations certainly exist, but they are easily detectable through the above-mentioned criterion. Since they can be recognized only against the background of experience, their existence does not change in the least the general picture that my entire experience gives me of the world. It follows that when the sceptic asks the fatidic question, 'How do you know that what happens in the particular cases of hallucinations is not the general rule?' we need not confess ignorance, as we would do if we accepted the assumption that all my experience concerns is 'ideas.' On the contrary – we can start replying (and this is crucial) that what my entire experience teaches me is that there are external things, mental entities, and hallucinations.

Now, to wonder whether the world is different from the one my entire experience informs me about obviously means to wonder how the world is from a perspective external to experience itself. The fact that we are talking about our *entire* experience or about *all* we know is crucial. When the sceptic asks us to wonder whether our entire experience could be illusory, he is really asking us to see the world from a point of view external to experience – that is, from an absolute standpoint. From the perspective of transcendental idealism, however, this means wondering how the world is in itself – namely, how it is from a point of view that abstracts from the way in which my sensibility makes things appear – that is, in space and time. But it is clear that if this is what the Cartesian sceptic is asking us, his challenge – the possibility that one's entire external experience is an illusion – turns out to be an illegitimate concern. It turns out to be a vain inquiry into the nature of the thing in itself.

We can reach the same result if we construe the sceptical challenge as raising the possibility that the world is a product of some super-imagination.[26] To say that spatial objects could be systematically just a product of an unknown faculty or super-imagination is to raise a question the answer to which *by definition* falls outside the sphere of possible experience. It means wondering about the nature of what affects my senses, before they organize the material resulting from the affection into a spatio-temporal object. But it is not this unknown X whose existence we need to prove in order to ground an empirical kind of realism. As Kant puts it: 'We can indeed admit that something, which may be (in the transcendental sense) outside us, is the cause of our intuitions, but this is not the object we are thinking in the representations of matter and of corporeal things' (A372). If we stay within the limits of possible experience and do not attempt to determine what matter (or the soul) in itself is, the question as to whether what we immediately perceive as an external, spatial world is different from the way it appears, becomes absurd: 'If, as the critical argument compels us to do, we hold fast to the rule above mentioned [do not take matter and the soul as things in themselves], we shall never dream of seeking to inform ourselves about the objects of the senses as they are in themselves, that is, out of all relation to the senses.'[27]

In other words, it is quite possible that the cause of the affection that provides all the material of my experience is some sort of transcendent Ego endowed with an unknown (super)imagination. This transcendent Ego would play precisely the same role as does Descartes's Evil Genius. The problem is that once again the possibility of raising such a scenario presupposes that one can appeal to how things are independently of the organization of my senses. In the present case, it presupposes the possibility of appealing to the unknown cause of our intuitions. In some revealing passages found in the quite different context of the Second Paralogism, Kant provides the most explicit expression of the refutation/dismissal of the radical doubt that we are proposing. He writes: 'The something that underlies the outer appearances and which so affects our sense that it obtains the representations of space matter, shape, etc., may yet, when viewed as noumenon (or better, as transcendental object), be at the same time, the subject of our thoughts' (A358). Also: 'I may further assume that the substance which in relation to our outer sense possesses extension is in itself the possessor of thoughts' (A359). And finally: 'What, as thing in itself, underlies the appearances of matter, perhaps after all may not be so heterogeneous in character [compared to what underlies the appearance of the soul]' (B428). And he emphasizes the very same point at the end of the Fourth Paralogism: 'Though the "I," as represented through inner sense in time, and objects outside me, are specifically quite distinct appearances, they are not for that reason thought as being different things. Neither the *transcendental object* which underlies outer appearances nor that which underlies inner intuition, is in itself either matter or a thinking being, but a ground (to us unknown) of the appearances which supply to us the empirical concept of the former as well as the latter mode of existence' (A379–80).

Kant's point in these passages is clear enough. If we look at a thing from an absolute standpoint and not from the only one that is given to us – that is, sensible experience – then we can quite naturally concede to the empirical idealist that what appears as extended matter is 'in itself' the same thing as the subject – or, more precisely, merely an inner state of the (transcendental) subject. From such an absolute viewpoint, any kind of metaphysical speculation is allowed. Matter may be spirit in itself, or spirit may be matter in itself, or both matter in itself and spirit in itself may exist:

> If the psychologist takes appearances for things in themselves, and as existing in and by themselves, then whether he be a materialist who

admits into his system nothing but matter alone, or a spiritualist who admits only thinking beings (that is, beings with the form of our inner sense), or a dualist who accepts both, he will always, owing to this misunderstanding, be entangled in pseudo-rational speculations as to how that which is not a thing in itself, but only the appearance of a thing in general, can exist by itself.[28] (A380)

We are now in a position to see that once we have abandoned the idea that the immediate object of our knowledge is a mental entity, the hypothesis of an unknown super-imaginative power is equivalent to the possibility that the non-sensible cause of our representations – that is, the non-sensible correlate of appearances – is this imaginative superpower. This, however, simply gives a new name to what Kant calls an external (in the transcendental sense) cause of our representations. The hypothesis of the super-imagination is threatening for a transcendental realist (it would remove the objects that our knowledge is supposed to be about); yet the same hypothesis does not concern the transcendental idealist because it would boil down to substituting the term 'non-sensible cause of our representation' with the more suggestive 'super-power of imagination' or 'Evil Genius.' Once this super-imagination is shown to be necessarily confined to a non-sensible sphere, it becomes incapable of threatening empirical realism. We thus understand Kant's crucial remark that 'even the most rigid idealist cannot, therefore, require a proof that the object outside us (taking 'outside' in the strict [transcendental] sense) corresponds to our perception. For if there be such an object, it could not be represented and intuited as outside us' (A375–6).

Note how the argument I have just presented rests on a complete reversal of Kant's refutation in the *Dissertation*. While the 1770 argument turned on the affirmation of the genuine external existence of things in themselves, much of the present argument turns precisely on the possibility that things in themselves are not external and 'real,' but rather similar to some ideal cause such as the Evil Genius or an unknown imaginative power. Conversely, while the 1770 argument conceded to the sceptic that phenomena are merely mental entities, the present argument relies on the ontological mind-independence of phenomena. While the 1770 dogmatic interpretation of the things in themselves/phenomena distinction was the greatest obstacle put in Kant's way to refute the sceptic, the mature, truly *critical* interpretation of the same distinction constitutes the necessary background from which the new argument arises.

A Crucial Objection Answered

It should be clear by now that Kant's reply to the sceptic turns on reinterpreting the Evil Genius hypothesis in terms of a question that, systematically surpassing the *totality* of any possible experience, brings us into the field of the thing in itself. The success of this argument rests precisely on the legitimacy of this reinterpretation. One could object that Descartes's hypothesis arises from familiar cases of delusions of the imagination, such as hallucinations. As such, it certainly does not exceed the limits of ordinary experience. The sceptic needs only to affirm that unproblematic familiar cases of hallucinations could simply be the general rule. More precisely, particular hallucinations give us the opportunity to conceive of the possibility that – in analogy to what happens with these particular cases of delusion – our entire experience is a sort of 'big hallucination,' in which particular hallucinations would simply be deviant cases of the regular hallucinatory 'experience' in which we live. And it is not clear how, reasoning in this manner, the skeptic could arrive at the realm of the thing in itself. The possibility that he raises does not seem to have anything to do with the constitution of the noumenal world. Even if we assume transcendental idealism, it still seems that the possibility raised by the sceptic is perfectly legitimate. Doesn't the transcendental idealist acknowledge that hallucinations exist? How then can he deny the legitimacy of the hypothesis that our entire experience is nothing but a systematic hallucination?

At this point the immediacy thesis becomes crucial. As we saw, if we operate with the transcendental realist's model of perception, then the objects we experience (mental entities) are not those which we want to reach (objects external in the transcendental sense). Therefore, when we refer to our entire experience, we are always talking about a mental realm. It follows that the Cartesian hypothesis does not even become a question that surpasses the limits of our experience: it is simply a question about the possibility that our entire experience could lack its desired referent. But if we abandon the transcendental realist's model of perception – that is, if we accept the immediacy thesis – the only way to make sense of the idea that my entire external experience is a 'big hallucination' is to reject this experience and raise the possibility that the world, from a perspective other than the empirical one, could be different. In other words, the sceptical question can no longer be, 'Is there a correspondence between my entire experience (mental entities) and the desired objects?' The question *must* become, 'Could my entire experience, that is, the objects that I immediately perceive, be different from the way they appear?' This is, however, equivalent to saying that things in themselves could be (or simply are) different from the way in which the empirical objects appear. Strictly speaking, it is not that Kant could readily accept this, nor even that he could simply say we know nothing about this realm. It is rather that he would dismiss the question itself as illegitimate, exceeding the set of questions we can raise. As Kant puts it very clearly in a footnote in the Transcendental Dialectic: 'Although to the question, what is the constitution of a transcendental object, no answer can be given stating *what it is*, we can yet reply that the *question* itself is *nothing*, because there is no given object [corresponding] to it' (A479/B507n).

Clearly, this response is possible only from the standpoint of transcendental idealism because only from that standpoint does the question about the constitution of the transcendental object amount to nothing. To be sure, other philosophical standpoints can reject the sceptical hypothesis on the basis of the generic charge that it rests on a scenario that goes systematically beyond our experience. This is the case with Carnap's philosophy, which attempted to refute idealism precisely along these lines. Despite superficial similarities to Kant's refutation, however, Carnap's approach is profoundly different and open to serious difficulties precisely because it lacks a transcendental idealistic perspective. The analysis of Carnap's refutation – which we assume as paradigmatic of all refutations turning on a generic appeal to test within the limits of possible experience – should therefore help us see the force of Kant's idea that transcendental idealism is 'the only refuge.'

Transcendental Idealism as 'the Only Refuge'

Carnap dismisses idealism because in his view it is grounded in a metaphysical and therefore meaningless perspective. For Carnap, a question or a sentence is meaningful if and only if it describes a state of affairs that can be verified or falsified through experience. Since scepticism raises the possibility of a state of affairs (the world as a systematic hallucination) that *ex hypothesi* cannot be verified or falsified through experience, it is a meaningless position. Carnap's emphasis that we must remain within the domain of experience resembles the kind of Kantian argument we have proposed. But this resemblance has limits, and it is precisely the determination of these limits that will display at the same time the importance of transcendental idealism for our argument and its superiority over other refutations of the sceptic.

No matter how liberalized, the empirical verifiability principle of meaningfulness makes (as Carnap well knows) not only idealism but also realism meaningless. The issue between a realist and an idealist regarding the existence of any particular thing is merely a pseudo-dispute. The realist argues that the object exists independently of its being perceived, and the idealist argues for the coincidence of its existence and its being perceived. Thus 'there is complete unanimity so far as the empirical facts are concerned,'[29] as in principle there is no empirical fact that could settle the dispute between them. Moreover, what is true of the dispute over a particular object is true of the world in general. It follows that the dispute between idealism and realism – the world exists outside our mind versus the world is (or may be) identical with its being perceived – is a pseudo-issue as well.

Carnap's idea that between the idealist and the realist 'there is complete unanimity so far as the empirical facts are concerned' is highly instructive. It is not clear at all that by claiming that 'there is the object X out there,' a realist means the same thing of an idealist; the only way in which there could be unanimity is if the realist assumes that the immediate objects of his perception are mental entities. These are the 'empirical facts' (about which the idealist and the realist agree) that Carnap seems to have in mind. The disagreement between the idealist and the realist is merely over whether there is a corresponding object that exists independently of the mind. Thus the meaningless realist affirmation is that there is such an object, whereas the equally meaningless idealist affirmation is that there is no such object.

For Carnap, that we speak of external objects and therefore assume that they exist is merely the outcome of the fact that we have chosen a language that includes terms referring to abiding external objects. We choose this language simply because it is more efficient than a phenomenological language that includes only sense-data. But this efficiency is not to be taken as evidence in favour of the existence of external things. For Carnap, it is a merely practical advantage: it makes the verification or falsification of the sentences we utter easier. More precisely, a language that includes external things seems more efficient than any other for organizing and expressing our sense-data in such a way that our sentences can be verified or falsified. Thus the sense-data have priority.

Clearly, from a Kantian perspective Carnap is operating within a transcendental realist model. The immediate objects of our experience are mental entities. The only difference between the transcendental realist and Carnap is that the former wants to affirm the correspondence of objects to these mental entities as a matter of fact, independent of the language we choose, whereas Carnap judges the question as meaningful only within a certain language – specifically, the one that includes external things. It is also clear that the sceptic cannot be threatened by such an attempt to remove the meaningfulness of his position. The sceptic can be satisfied with the fact that on this account, his realist opponent also ends up in the same spot (his position turns out equally meaningless). He can even consider Carnap an ally, notwithstanding his tendency to reduce idealism to non-sense. Indeed, the freedom that Carnap gives us to choose between a language that includes external things and one that restricts itself to sense-data is really equivalent to the sceptical idealist's thesis that there is no way to determine whether a world corresponds to our sense-data. After all, that the realist and idealist positions are really indistinguishable is precisely what the *sceptical* idealist wants. Indeed, if there is a version of idealism that Carnap can be legitimately said to oppose, it is what Kant calls *dogmatic* idealism. The ability of Carnap's position to undermine sceptical idealism is another matter. Carnap's implicit acceptance of the priority of sense-data and his insistence on the merely practical nature of the choice of the language through which we express these data make his position strikingly similar to sceptical idealism.

Similar considerations apply to the case of contemporary versions of verificationism, such as that of Dummett. Notoriously, Dummett advocates the view that there is no truth (in any domain) *without evidence or at least the possibility of verification*. Unlike the early Carnap, however, Dummett denies that statements which are unverifiable, even in principle, are ipso facto meaningless. These statements, in his view, have meaning but possess no truth value. Since statements that at a certain point in time lack any direct or indirect evidence might later be attributed some evidential basis or even be proved, Dummett believes that certain statements are neither true nor false, but simply 'not true.' The class of the 'not true' statements is the class of propositions that lack evidence for their truth or their falsity. The proposition 'π is a transcendental number,' for example, was 'not true' until 1882, but became true when Ferdinand von Lindemann proved it.[30] For a realist, quite to the contrary, this proposition has been true all along and was 'merely' proved in 1882. This explains why Dummett rejects what he calls the principle of bivalence (at times considered equivalent to that of the excluded middle), whereby a proposition is always either true or false, and why he considers the acceptance of the same principle as what is 'integral' (read 'essential') to realism.

From this perspective, one might be tempted to argue that it is possible to mount a refutation of scepticism similar to the Kantian argument we have advocated. The argument would be roughly this: Scepticism, as we said, asks a question that systematically escapes any possible experience. It is difficult to imagine an experiential event that would falsify (or confirm) the thesis that at least one experience of external objects is not hallucinatory. While we can never know whether this particular experience is a hallucination, at the same time it is impossible to know whether this same experience is a trustworthy experience of a genuine external object. Hence, either there is a rational (as opposed to empirical) refutation of scepticism, such as Putnam's Brains in the Vat argument (on this more shortly), or scepticism must fall in the 'not true' category.

Now, in a Dummettian context, if there were such a rational argument, scepticism would no longer be 'not true' but simply false, and realism about the external world would move from the 'not true' category to the 'true' category. To find such an argument, however, would be to ground one kind of realism (the one regarding the material world) that Dummett apparently intends to attack. After all, his only quarrel with the phenomenalists seems to be their absent-minded acceptance of the principle of bivalence combined with their unnecessary attachment to strong reductionism (the translatability of a language that contains tables and chairs into a language of sense data). Therefore, Dummett cannot concede even the possibility of such a rational refutation. Now, if neither an experiential nor a rational refutation of scepticism is possible within Dummett's framework, we are perhaps authorized to conclude that the inclusion in the 'not true' category is precisely Dummett's way of dealing with scepticism.

There is, no doubt, a superficial resemblance between this line of thought and our argument. Both attempt to silence the sceptic, not through a direct refutation, but through a reconsideration of the very meaning of the sceptical challenge. Two things, however, make this argument essentially different from Kant's. To begin with, as we saw, realism about the external world turns out to be as 'not true' as scepticism is and for the very same reasons. Second, and consequently, scepticism on Dummett's reconstruction is by no means 'illegitimate'; again, it is simply 'not true' (like empirical realism). Therefore, to tackle the question of scepticism from a Dummettian perspective means to aim, at most, to show that scepticism and antiscepticism about the external world are on the same footing. While this seems to introduce a difference with Carnap – whose 'refutation' of scepticism paradoxically turned out to be a confirmation of dogmatic idealism – it is clearly insufficient for grounding that kind of independent existence of the external world which Kant (and any adversary of scepticism) was after. This result is hardly surprising: properly understood, in a Kantian context knowledge is about an ontologically independent realm (yet conditioned by our epistemic forms) – that is, the realm of appearances. The question of whether there is at least one non-hallucinatory experience has a very clear answer: yes. All experience that does not seem to violate the 'rules of experience' is about an objective realm that exists independently of the fact whether someone experiences it or not (although, obviously, *how* one experiences it depends on subjective forms). In Dummett, any reference to this independent realm would collide with his modified verificationism. Knowledge is not about an independent realm; rather, if the provocation is allowed, it is about our experience. From this perspective, any argument against scepticism can at most hope to tie the match with it.

The result of this analysis is that the mere appeal to the need to remain within the domain of experience is not sufficient to silence the sceptic and should not be confused with our antisceptical argument. If the idea that outer perception is immediate is not brought in, the mere appeal to what experience says is never going to be sufficient. Only if this appeal is combined with the immediacy thesis (and therefore with transcendental idealism) can scepticism be refuted. These were, in fact, just the two steps of our argument. We have already seen how the thesis of the immediacy of outer perception is by itself not sufficient. We now learn that the second step as well – at least, if it is taken as a generic suggestion to remain within the limits of experience – is by itself not sufficient. The appeal to experience as the framework within which questions are legitimate is not going to yield the desired result unless the experience we are referring to is sharply distinguished from the sense-data that Carnap assumes, or from a realm whose ontological independence is not affirmed by the epistemological framework we use, as in the case of Dummett. Only if we mean by 'experience' the world we immediately see, the spatial world given to us independently of the nature of the supersensible thing that affects us, can we really reinterpret and rule out the sceptical hypothesis as a illegitimate question. The idea of immediacy can be convincingly grounded only from a transcendentally idealist perspective, as we saw in our discussion of Reid. It follows that once again, transcendental idealism turns out to be the crucial and necessary premise of a successful refutation of the sceptic – or to repeat our favourite expression, the 'only refuge.'[31]

Kant and Putnam

The necessary role we have just assigned to transcendental idealism could be further questioned by referring to other apparently successful refutations that arise from a broadly construed Kantian framework, but that seem to bypass any appeal to idealistic premises. This is the case with Putnam's famous argument against the possibility that we are 'brains in a vat.' Putnam rephrases Descartes's hypothesis of the Evil Genius by imagining that we are brains placed in a vat containing a nutrient fluid and connected through a series of wires to a sort of supercomputer – the Matrix, we could say, after Hollywood's appropriation of this philosophical fantasy. The question obviously is this: How do we know that we are *not* brains in a vat?

Putnam thinks that a bit of reflection on how words refer to objects suffices to show that this scenario is a mere *logical* possibility, not a *real* one. To put it differently, it is a merely *consistent* story, but it cannot be the description of how things actually are. In particular, Putnam believes he can show that saying 'we are brains in a vat' is no different from saying 'I do not exist' or 'all general statements are false.' These two assertions are evidently self-refuting (albeit for different reasons). One approach to Putnam's argument is to see it as an attempt to show that the sentence 'we are brains in a vat,' whose inner logic does not seem to share any similarity with the two sentences just cited, turns out to be equally self-refuting. In other words, if Putnam's argument succeeds, then the sceptical position is refuted in a very straightforward way: it is built on a basic contradiction.

The argument goes as follows. Let us assume that we are in fact brains in a vat. When a brain in a vat thinks 'there is a tree in front of me,' he is not referring to a real tree (an external object as we understand it); by definition, if his thought refers at all, it refers to a 'tree in the image' – that is, to the image stimulated by the electrical impulses sent by the supercomputer. Something similar happens for any affirmation the brain might make about external objects, including the brain itself, understood as an external object in a way not different from the way in which we take our body as an external object. It follows that if the brain thinks (or says) 'I am a brain in a vat,' then it *must* mean 'I am a brain in a vat in the image.' Therefore, if we *are* brains in a vat, when we say 'we are brains in a vat', we are, so to speak, condemned to mean that we are 'brains in a vat in the image.' It was our intention to say something *not* about our internal sense data; yet the logic of our language – given the presupposition that we *are* brains in a vat – denies the possibility of reaching real things beyond them. This means, however, that if we are brains in a vat, then our sentence 'we are brains in a vat,' being part of a language that is forced to refer to inner sense data, affirms something false. Now, if the truth of a state of affairs described by a sentence removes the conditions of possibility of the sentence's being true, then the sentence is necessarily false. To quote Putnam's succinct conclusion to his argument: 'If we are brains in a vat, then "We are brains in a vat" is false. So it is (necessarily) false.'[32]

The 'vat-English' spoken by the brains has no chance of going beyond the level of sense data to which, by the very setting up of the experiment, those brains are condemned to remain confined. The rules that govern reference in vat-English exclude the possibility of reaching external objects. And when it comes to describing those few objects that constitute the poor furniture of the universe in the sceptical hypothesis, the self-refuting nature of the hypothesis itself becomes evident. This explains the self-refuting status of the affirmation 'we are brains in a vat.' A reflection of the conditions of the possibility of reference – as opposed to an appeal to transcendental idealism – has yielded a successful refutation.

In this ingenious argument, is there any appeal to transcendental idealism? Apparently not. All we have been given is a reflection on the logic of reference and on how this leads to the self-refutation of the sceptic. Note also that the impression that Putnam's argument is completely independent of transcendental idealism is strengthened by the fact that his argument is explicitly meant to be used, as an antisceptical tool, by what he calls the 'externalist' philosopher. In other words, the 'externalist' philosopher should be able to appeal to it in order to quash the sceptical challenge. Since such a philosopher believes that truth consists of correspondence between words (or thought signs) and objects *as completely independent of the system of description used* (in our language, completely independent of the mind), he is in fundamental disagreement with the transcendental idealist. In fact, what Putnam calls the 'externalist philosopher' is very close to what Kant calls the 'transcendental realist.' Now, if Putnam's argument is to be used by the externalist philosopher, then clearly no internalist (let alone idealist) premise can be assumed in the argument. In fact, Putnam believes he has shown that 'the very relation of correspondence on which truth and reference depend (on his [*the externalist's*] view) cannot logically be available to him if he *is* a Brain in a Vat. So if we *are* Brains in a Vat, we cannot *think* that we are, except in the bracketed sense [we are Brains in a Vat]; and this bracketed thought does not have reference conditions that would make it *true*. So it is not possible after all that we are Brains in a Vat.'

In other words, Putnam assumes the externalist perspective and shows that, given the theory of reference that follows from that perspective, the Brains in a Vat hypothesis is self-refuting. In this sense, his argument is primarily meant to be a tool at the disposal of the externalist philosopher to rebut the sceptic. Note that from the internalist perspective, this ingenious argument need not even turn on the conditions of the possibility of reference. If we assume Putnam's internal realism (or Kant's transcendental idealism), then the Brains in a Vat hypothesis becomes 'just a story' – a mere *logical* possibility, to use Kant's language. In fact, the sceptical story, as we have shown, implicitly assumes a God's eye point of view; it is told from the perspective of an 'eye' that does not belong to the world it sees. But to repeat, Putnam believes that his argument is capable of refuting the sceptic *even if one assumes the externalist perspective*; in this way he leaves aside any considerations regarding the opportunity to avoid a God's eye point of view.

Now, if this is true, the *need* to assume transcendental idealism in order to avoid the sceptical threat – a need on which we have so much insisted – would be readily falsified. In other words, if Putnam has correctly assessed the logic of his own argument, then transcendental idealism is *not*, as Kant argues, 'the only refuge.' On closer analysis, however, this reconstruction proves to be mistaken. Let us return to Putnam's argument. Its main thrust is that if we are brains in a vat, we cannot *think* (or *say*) that we are. More precisely, if we are brains in a vat and (therefore) we have to speak vat-English, we fall into self-contradiction as soon as we try to express our 'true' condition (*being* brains in a vat). It is rather evident, though, that this leaves intact the possibility that we *are* indeed brains in a vat *from the perspective of a putative external observer* (be it God or any other entity that falls outside the world we inhabit). The argument only shows that from within our world, we cannot even *express* our wretched condition. *From our perspective*, the Brains in a Vat hypothesis is a mere logical possibility, because it violates the conditions of possibility of reference. But the sceptic can very well reply that this is perfectly compatible with the possibility that the whole of our knowledge, if seen from the perspective of God, amounts to a systematic error, with the further complication that we would not even be able to formulate – without falling in contradiction or paradox – why this is so (that is, why we are brains in a vat). In sum, it is still possible that we are brains in a vat, that the externalist view of truth is right, and that truth (so defined) can never be achieved – not even in the case of the description of why this state of affairs holds.

Now, saying that this possibility does not concern us because it presupposes a point of view external to the world we inhabit amounts to assuming already some forms of internalism (or transcendental idealism).[33] Certainly, Putnam might reply that our objection presupposes, not just an 'external viewpoint,' but a viewpoint that transcends even the conditions of possibility of reference of our language. This reply, however, does not change much. Why, in fact, should this external viewer be bound to such conditions? Couldn't he be bound to reference conditions (if any) completely different from ours? And if so, wouldn't he be completely safe from the paradox that Putnam has shown to be an inevitable destiny that *we* face in describing our condition? Thus, in order to be satisfied with the fact that, if we are brains in a vat, then we cannot express this condition, we need to have already sided with a philosophical perspective that wants to remain within the sphere of successful (that is, non-paradoxical) use of our language, something very close to some form of internalism.[34]

From this, four main consequences follow. First, despite appearances, transcendental idealism (or internalism – the difference here does not matter) *is* a necessary premise of Putnam's antisceptical argument. Second, Putnam, unlike Kant, fails to make this logical dependence clear. Third, insofar as Putnam interprets his argument as a foundation of internalism, he seems to be arguing in a circular fashion.[35] And fourth, and most importantly for our purposes, Kant's argument, as we have reconstructed it, remains on a firmer footing than Putnam's, simply because its main premise (the truth of transcendental idealism) is not only clearly acknowledged, but *grounded* through the arguments we analysed in the third chapter, while I fail to see where Putnam's internalism finds a comparable foundation.

4 The Problem of Idealism between 1781 and 1787

In the preceding chapters we committed ourselves to an interpretation turning on two main theses. On the one hand, we have already seen that in 1781 Kant embraced a form of idealism that is sharply distinguished from phenomenalism, and that even the Fourth Paralogism, despite some tricky passages, vouches for a kind of (transcendental) idealism opposed to any negation of the external world's independent existence. On the other hand, we have been contending that the Fourth Paralogism, properly interpreted, contains the material for a powerful argument against the sceptic, provided that the truth of transcendental idealism is conceded. The development of Kant's thought from 1781 to 1787 can be seen as a test of the correctness of this interpretation. In fact, if the first point holds, we should not find after 1781 any attempt to refute the sceptic that turns on the identification of phenomena with mental entities that would be caused by a 'real' thing in itself. This was the hallmark of the 1770 antisceptical argument, which, as we have seen, Kant abandoned once and for all during his critical period. Moreover, if the Fourth Paralogism amounts to a successful refutation of the sceptic (the second point of our interpretation), one would expect Kant to be satisfied enough with it to keep it in the Second Edition. At most, one would expect minor stylistic changes.

Turning to the period between the two editions of the *Critique*, however, both these expectations appear to be frustrated. On the one hand, in two passages – one from the Metaphysics Mrongovius (dated shortly after 1781), the other from the *Prolegomena* (1783), Kant seems to retreat to the dogmatic argument of his 1770 *Dissertation*. At the same time, it is difficult to explain why, in the Second Edition, he has rewritten the Fourth Paralogism to the extent that the new one bears little resemblance to the original. The task of refuting the sceptic is now assigned to a completely new proof, the famous Refutation of Idealism. Does this radical change not suggest that Kant found some flaws in his original argument? Can we still point to the 1781 argument as Kant's best antisceptical proof if Kant himself seems to drop it in the Second Edition? Moreover, since the Refutation of Idealism seems to be independent of transcendental idealism, does this not contradict our thesis (and Kant's own) that transcendental idealism is 'the only refuge' against scepticism?

The present chapter serves as a bridge to the discussion of the 1787 argument per se. Its main purpose is to reply to those objections which will likely be raised against our interpretation. To this end, we need to consider the debate that the appearance of the *Critique of Pure Reason* provoked in the German intellectual world. In particular, we need to consider how Garve and Feder identified transcendental idealism with phenomenalism in their review and how Kant himself reacted to this gross misunderstanding of his thought. Once I have provided this historical background, it will be less difficult to reply to the above-mentioned objections.

The Garve–Feder Review and Kant's Reaction

In January 1782 the Zugabe zu den Göttingischen Anzeigen von gelehrten Sachen (Supplement to the Gottingen Bulletin of Scholarly Matters) hosted one of the first public responses to *Critique of Pure Reason* in the German intellectual world. Two anonymous authors, who would later be identified as Garve and Feder, published a review that turned on three main points. First, Kant's position was an 'idealism that treats equally spirit and matter, that transforms the world and ourselves into representations.'[1] Second, Kant's ideality of space and time was indistinguishable from the core of Berkeley's idealism. And third, the antisceptical argument contained in the Fourth Paralogism rested on the reduction of both external objects and thinking subjects to mere representations. As the reviewers put it: 'Vulgar, or as the author calls it, empirical idealism is thus refuted, not through a proof of the existence of bodies, but through the elimination of the privilege that the conviction of our own existence thought to possess compared to that of the existence of bodies.'

The first two points were inspired by the conflation between Kant and Berkeley that we analysed in chapter 2; the third point amounted to a new front in an assault on Kant's thought – one that merits particular attention. As we have seen, Kant's antisceptical strategy in the Fourth Paralogism *does* rest on the removal of a certain privilege that is usually accorded to inner knowledge. This was in fact the first step in the argument we analysed in the preceding chapter. Recall that on our interpretation, Kant removed a special kind of privilege of inner knowledge by locating the critique of the Cartesian sceptic in the Fourth Paralogism. Does this mean that the reviewers were correct in at least this respect?

Notwithstanding superficial analogies, it is easy to see that Kant's point in the Fourth Paralogism is very different from what the reviewers had in mind. They meant that the privilege is removed once both inner and outer knowledge are reduced to mere mental entities. In contrast, on our interpretation, by placing the antisceptical argument in the fourth part of the critique of rational psychology, Kant was clearing the way preliminarily from the belief that the existence of the subject can be inferred *analytically* from the 'I think' of apperception. This 'privilege' of inner knowledge was certainly denied by Kant in the Fourth Paralogism. But this had nothing to do with the 'transformation of ourselves into representations' claimed by the reviewers.

This specific interpretative mistake, however, is clearly the least serious of the reviewers' misunderstandings. Most important is that they identified Kant's idealism with Berkeley's – the core of the first two points. We sketched out in chapter 2 Kant's response to this interpretation. What is important to add here is that the reviewers' misreading became one of Kant's main preoccupations after 1781. Just to confine ourselves to the *Prolegomena*, Kant devotes to this point two long and dense 'observations' in paragraph 13, the entirety of paragraph 49, and a good part of the appendix. In these passages he applies a number of interesting strategies for making the distinction between his idealism and Berkeley's as clear as possible for readers. Of particular interest, besides the already noted introduction of the expression 'formal or critical idealism,' is Kant's emphasis on the fact that the affirmation of the epistemological dependence of all empirical objects on the senses does not entail their ontological dependence. Thus, for example:

> As little as the man who admits colors not to be properties of the object in itself but only to be modifications of the sense of sight should on that account be called an idealist, so little can my doctrine be named idealistic merely because I find that more, nay, *all the properties which constitute the intuition of a body belong merely to its appearance*. The existence of the thing

that appears is thereby not destroyed, as in genuine idealism, but it is only shown that we cannot possibly know it by the senses as it is in itself.[2]

Similarly, to underscore this same point, Kant notes that if we abstract from the conditions that make external objects epistemologically mind-dependent, we cannot even say that such objects *exist*. It is necessary to remain within the field of possible experience (the epistemological mind-dependence) even to make sense of the question regarding the existence of external objects (their ontological mind-independence):

> That there is something real outside us which not only corresponds but must correspond to our external perceptions can likewise be proved to be, not a connection of things in themselves, but for the sake of experience. This means that there is something empirical, i.e. some appearance in space outside us, that admits of a satisfactory proof; for we have nothing to do with other objects than those which belong to possible experience, because objects which cannot be given us in any experience are nothing for us.[3]

Moreover, the very first point Kant makes against the Garve–Feder review in the appendix centres on the distinction, missed by the reviewers, between his idealism and the Berkeleyian variety. Kant rather explicitly tells us that the main reason why he is bothering to reply to such a wrong-headed review is that he is eager to correct this mistake.[4] In a desperate effort to make this distinction clear, he notes that the essence of any true idealism is the following principle: 'All cognition through the senses and experience is nothing but sheer illusion, and only in the ideas of the pure understanding and reason is there truth.'[5] By contrast, his idealism teaches that 'all cognition merely from the pure understanding or pure reason is nothing but sheer illusion, and only in experience is there truth.'[6]

One could object that the principle of 'true idealism' does not capture very well Berkeley's position. In fact, in a certain sense, for Berkeley as well 'only in experience is there truth,' because being coincides with being experienced (or perceived). This inaccuracy, however, does not touch the crucial point. What Berkeley means by experience (ideas) is very different from what Kant means (genuine objects). The only reason why both positions can be called idealism, notes Kant, is that they share the thesis that space is not a property of the things considered in themselves. In the two systems, however, this thesis is interpreted in completely different ways: Berkeley holds that space (with all things in it) is nothing but an idea in our mind, whereas Kant believes that those mind-independent things which we encounter in our experience receive this formal property through their relation with our sensibility. This points to a profound difference regarding the ability to account for the a priori status of geometry; it also marks an equally profound difference relating to the ontological commitments of the two positions. In Kant's system, outer objects are epistemologically mind-dependent but epistemologically mind-independent; this distinction is completely lost to Berkeley.[7]

As we have said, responding to the reviewers' main misunderstanding became a key preoccupation for Kant in the years we are considering. Bearing this in mind will help us deal with the controversial passages that threaten our interpretation. To the analysis of these we now turn.

Two Puzzling Antisceptical Arguments

In Metaphysics Mrongovius, having exposed Berkeley's 'dogmatic or crude idealism, that no bodies exist outside us, but rather that appearances are nothing and lie merely in our senses and our power of imagination,' Kant says: 'But there is also a critical or transcendental idealism, when one assumes that appearances are indeed nothing in themselves, but that actually something unknown still underlies them. That is correct.'[8]

The impression here is that Kant is sinking again into the dogmatic antisceptical argument of the *Dissertation*. In particular, he seems to be relying on things in themselves as the sole ground for realism ('something unknown still underlies them'), while construing phenomena as the effects produced in us by the affections of things in themselves – that is, mental entities – and seemingly even identifying them with the 'appearances' the empirical idealist is committed to. Any attempt to reinterpret this passage so as to avoid attributing to Kant some form of phenomenalism (as we did with the Fourth Paralogism) appears hopeless. There is, however, a simple reason why this passage should not be taken as decisive evidence of Kant's return to phenomenalism or, even worse, as a rule that Kant gives us a posteriori when it comes to interpreting the Fourth Paralogism.

Kant's oral lectures, from which this passage is taken, are by their very nature and goal a simplified version of his doctrine. In fact, if we compare *any* argument discussed in the Lectures with the same argument as it is treated in the *Critique*, the difference in rigour is quite evident. This suggests that in case of a contradiction between the Lectures and a published work, we should as a general hermeneutical rule assign greater authority to the latter. Now, since the passage at hand is in direct contradiction with the Fourth Paralogism's denial that one can rely on things in themselves (the 'something unknown' that underlies appearances) to ground realism, it follows that instead of taking the passage as an indication of the opportunity to reconsider our entire assessment of the Fourth Paralogism, we should simply regard it as Kant's simplified albeit highly inaccurate way of letting his audience see immediately the difference between Berkeley's idealism and his own.

We saw in the preceding section that this was Kant's chief preoccupation in the years we are examining. To achieve this minimal result – so Kant probably thought – it is sufficient to emphasize the existence of things in themselves, which is precisely what the passage does. To be sure, one can wonder whether Kant in this way is actually distinguishing himself from Berkeley. In a sense, even for Berkeley there is a cause of the ideas we entertain – that is, ultimately, God. It follows that according to this passage the only difference between Kant and Berkeley seems to be that the former leaves undetermined this 'something' that affects our senses, deeming it systematically beyond our cognitive grasp, whereas the latter identifies it with the supreme entity. Obviously, if this is the entire difference between the two systems, then one should not be too harsh with Garve and Feder for their assessment of the *Critique*. The specific weaknesses of this line of thought, however, are rather secondary for our purposes. The crucial point is simply that, in a context far less formal than a published work, Kant probably felt justified to give this inaccurate and even misleading version of the difference between his philosophy and Berkeley's.

A rather different analysis is required for the passage from the *Prolegomena*. In response to sceptical idealism, which argues that things are nothing but representations to which no objects correspond, Kant argues: 'I say: there are things given to our sense as objects that are found outside us, but we know nothing of what they could be in themselves; we only know their phenomena, that is, the representations that they produce in us by affecting our senses.'[9]

Again, Kant here seems to be arguing against the sceptic that there are things outside us, although we know nothing about them, and that our knowledge is confined to phenomena, understood as the representations that things in themselves produce in our mind by affecting our senses. At first sight, this is nothing but a repetition of the 1770 argument: The sceptic is correct to reduce our knowledge to mental entities, but he forgets the things that produce them. Although we know nothing about them, they must exist as causes of our representations. The sceptic is in this way refuted. On closer examination, however, Kant is saying something very different.

The objects whose existence Kant is defending are not things in themselves, but 'things that are found outside us' that *considered as they are in themselves* are completely unknown to us, but that we know as phenomena – that is, *considered as they appear 'after' the organization of our senses*. The key here is to heed that Kant is affirming the existence of things 'given to our sense' without specifying whether these are things in themselves or phenomena. They are external things *in general*, better construed as transcendental objects that – depending on whether they are considered 'before' or 'after' their affection on our senses, are to be considered respectively as things in themselves or as phenomena. In fact, in the second part of the sentence Kant adds that, if regarded as they are in themselves, they remain completely unknown to us, while if considered 'after' their affection on our senses, they (the same things!) are to be viewed as phenomena. Unlike the passage in the Metaphysics Mrongovius, the present passage *does* makes room for an interpretation that removes the appearance of a controversial retreat to a precritical stance. In a sense, what seems to be a problematic passage turns out to be nothing but an expression of Kant's mature and critical stance.

To be sure, the present solution is not unanimously accepted by Kant interpreters. The problematic nature of these passages was first noted by Rousset, who pointed to a tension between the way in which Kant replies to the sceptic in the Fourth Paralogism and the way in which he replies to the accusation of idealism in the Lectures.[10] He also thought that Kant was relying explicitly on the thing in itself in the *Prolegomena*, after denying the validity of such a strategy in the Fourth Paralogism.[11] Ironically, though, from the awareness of this tension, Rousset drew an inference opposed to the one we are suggesting here. Instead of dismissing Kant's strategy in the Lectures as a vulgarized and rather inaccurate expression of his position and reinterpreting the passage in the *Prolegomena* in such a way as to make it compatible with the fundamental tenets of Kant's epistemology, he thought that the reference to the thing in itself was precisely what Kant meant and what his system required.

Actually, Rousset goes even further. Notwithstanding Kant's explicit denial, he thinks that the thing in itself plays a crucial role even in the

Fourth Paralogism. Thus, in his view, the passages we have analysed express a line of thought that was already present in the Fourth Paralogism but that Kant had not yet fully clarified to himself. In other words, we should view the strategy turning on the reference to things in themselves as the culmination of a line of thought already present in the 1781 argument, albeit in embryonic form. In general, Rousset seems to be inviting us to apply Kant's strategy in the Lectures and (supposedly) in the *Prolegomena* as a rule for interpreting the Fourth Paralogism over and above Kant's explicit denial that we can refer to things in themselves to refute the sceptic.

But where is the evidence to support this view? Rousset offers us a threefold argument. He tells us that we can find the implicit reference to the thing in itself in the Fourth Paralogism if we pay attention to its content, goal, and context. To begin with, in the Fourth Paralogism there is the admission that something unknown affects us. Moreover, its goal of grounding realism presupposes the reference to things 'really' other than ourselves – something that, for Rousset, cannot be accomplished by a phenomenon, which is 'in us.' Finally, the criticism of rational psychology – the context of the Fourth Paralogism – centres on the emptiness of the pure 'I think'; this would require that the content of our knowledge originate in something other than this empty 'I think,' which for Rousset means a thing in itself.

Given the results of our general analysis of the Fourth Paralogism in chapter 2, we should not find it difficult to reply to this interpretation. We have seen how Kant's admission that something unknown affects us does not commit him to the postulation that a genuine causal relation exists between a thing in itself and our intuitions and is in fact irrelevant to his proof. We have also seen how we can avoid the phenomenalistic reading on which rests Rousset's idea that a phenomenon cannot play the role of what is 'outside us.' Finally, though Kant certainly intends the Paralogism chapter to show the emptiness of the pure 'I think,' this does not in the least ground the necessity of referring to a thing in itself. The idea that the material of our knowledge comes from something other than the pure 'I think' does not necessarily mean that it comes from a thing in itself, which is what Rousset assumes. From an empirical point of view, the material of my knowledge simply comes from outer appearances, which clearly are other than the pure 'I think.'

This suggests a threefold conclusion. To begin with, the attempt to weaken Kant's explicit denial in the Fourth Paralogism that a thing in itself can play a role in the refutation of idealism stands on very shaky ground. Second, once the phenomenalistic reading is abandoned, there is no need to look for a supersensible object in order to refute idealism. The Fourth Paralogism does not refer to the thing in itself nor does it need to. Finally, since relying on things in themselves to refute the sceptic returns us back to a dogmatic version of transcendental idealism, we should consider the Fourth Paralogism (properly understood) as the expression of Kant's considered opinion and should regard the passage from Metaphysics Mrongovius as the outcome of some unfortunate simplification of his thought. Analogously, we should interpret the passage from the *Prolegomena* in such a way as to avoid a sheer contradiction with the main tenets of Kant's thought and with the direction of his development.

Is the Fourth Paralogism Really Repudiated in the Second Edition?

It is certainly true that the Fourth Paralogism in the Second Edition is very different from the Fourth Paralogism of 1781. Instead of a detailed treatment of Descartes's sceptical stance, we now find only the idea that from the undeniable fact that I think of myself as distinct from other things, 'I do not thereby learn whether this consciousness of myself would be even possible apart from things outside me, and whether, therefore, I could exist merely as a thinking being (*i.e.* without existing in a human form)' (B409). One might think that Kant here is referring to the central idea of the 1787 Refutation – namely, that a permanent external thing is necessary for the consciousness of my existence as determined in time. However, the fact that this consciousness is a consciousness of myself as a thinking being rules out this possibility. Indeed, if I regard myself as a thinking being I do not regard myself as a temporally determined succession of mental events. This passage is better understood as the familiar warning not to commit the mistake of drawing inferences about myself (and about the world around me) from the way in which I conceive of me (or am constrained to conceive of me). In any case, there is little doubt that this is very different from the detailed treatment of scepticism we encountered in the 1781 Fourth Paralogism.

But the mere fact that Kant changed his Fourth Paralogism radically is an insufficient basis to conclude that he was no longer satisfied with the main thrust of his original argument. There is no evidence to support this conclusion, and in fact there is evidence pointing to precisely the opposite. In the section of the Antinomy containing one of the few definitions of transcendental idealism in the first *Critique*, Kant emphasizes the difference between his idealism and empirical idealism and attempts to refute the latter through considerations very similar to those he uses in the Fourth Paralogism.

To begin with, Kant emphasizes the idea that the object of inner sense is as much an appearance as the object of outer sense. This echoes his critique of the idea of a special, intellectual access to the existence of the subject as a determinate entity – the hidden premise of scepticism that Kant had removed in 1781 by placing his critique in the Paralogism chapter. Second, he argues that empirical idealism is refuted because 'without objects in space there would be no empirical representation whatsoever,' which is identical with the second step in the standard strategy of the Fourth Paralogism. He also relies on the criterion for distinguishing dreams from experience that we saw at work in our argument.[12] Most importantly, he even provides roughly the same intuition that we used to reduce the sceptical hypothesis to an idle conjecture on the nature of the thing in itself. In fact, first Kant emphasizes that the very notion of reality is dependent on my actual or possible perception: 'Everything is real [*wirklich*] which stands in connection with a perception in accordance with the laws of empirical advance.'[13] This echoes both Kant's criterion for distinguishing experience from hallucination and the idea that reality is not to be found 'behind' our perceptions, but rather is immediately perceived (the immediacy thesis). Then, a few lines later, he suggests that 'the non-sensible cause of these representations [appearances] is completely unknown to us, and cannot therefore be intuited by us as an object' (A494/B522). This claim parallels the idea – which is crucial to the economy of our argument – that the hypothesis of an unknown 'X,' be it an Evil Genius or some other entity, can be incorporated and rendered harmless by transcendental idealism. Within this framework, the hypothesis that the non-sensible cause of our representations is the Evil Genius can be conceived and conceded without detriment to empirical realism.

Obviously, this still leaves us with the problem of determining why Kant removed the actual Fourth Paralogism while keeping its main thrust. A plausible explanation is that he realized that many passages in the old Fourth Paralogism had inspired the mistaken phenomenalistic readings of his position – misreadings that began right after the *Critique*'s appearance.[14] Nothing was further from Kant's intentions in the Fourth Paralogism (and anywhere in the *Critique*) than to support a phenomenalistic position; yet it is undeniable that the text was very much open to this kind of interpretative mistake. Kant must have been thinking that for the sake of clarity the original Fourth Paralogism – or more precisely the way in which he had presented its main thrust – needed to be sacrificed. But the fact that he kept the main thrust of its original argument in the Second Edition is strong evidence that he did not see any flaw in his original antisceptical strategy.[15] Whatever his reasons for writing a new Fourth Paralogism and a new and very different antisceptical argument, it would not be accurate to say that he found the main thrust of his antisceptical argument no longer convincing. All of this suggests that, contrary to what is usually assumed in the literature, we should begin to approach the 1787 Refutation of Idealism as an *additional* argument that Kant discovered in the Second Edition, rather than one that he intended to replace a previous unsuccessful attempt.[16]

This suggestion, obviously, conflicts with Kant's own characterization of the Refutation of Idealism as *the only possible* refutation of the sceptic. This characterization is to be found both in the introduction to the 1787 argument and in a footnote in the preface to the Second Edition.[17] Along these lines, one could also argue that Kant left the main intuition of the Fourth Paralogism in the Second Edition of the *Critique* simply because he had no time to change the entire book. This would be supported by Kant's own admission that time was too short to allow changes beyond the Paralogism chapter.[18]

In response to this last point, note that besides lack of time, Kant identifies an additional reason for not changing the rest of the *Critique*: he found 'among competent and impartial critics no misapprehension of the remaining sections.'[19] Thus he was satisfied with the understanding of the part of the *Critique* that follows after the Paralogism chapter, which suggests that he was also satisfied with what he wrote there. And obviously, the compressed version of the Fourth Paralogism that we discovered in Section 6 of the Antinomy falls precisely after the Paralogism chapter.

Moving to the more serious problem that Kant himself explicitly characterizes the 1787 refutation as the only one possible, if we pay attention to his language, it becomes clear that he considered the 1787 Refutation of Idealism the only possible *strict* refutation of the sceptic. This is evident in the passage from his footnote to the Second Edition's preface. By a strict proof, Kant probably means a reductio ad absurdum of scepticism, which is exactly what the Refutation of Idealism is. As we shall see, in this proof 'the game of idealism has been turned against itself,' because outer experience – which the Cartesian sceptic doubts – is shown to be a necessary condition of that inner experience to whose infallibility the sceptic is committed. A reductio of this sort obviously counts as a strict proof. Indeed, nothing can be as strict as a refutation that shows how our opponent does not realize that he doubts something that is a condition of the possibility of what he considers beyond doubt. But to introduce and even prefer a 'strict' proof of this sort is clearly compatible with the possibility of still believing in an alternative, non-strict – in the specified sense – proof.

I believe this captures Kant's assessment of his new and old proofs. The difference in his mind is not, respectively, between a successful and an unsuccessful argument, but between a straightforward proof that supposedly manages to turn the play of idealism against itself and an argument that, as we saw, instead of refuting scepticism directly, highlights the illegitimate, metaphysical nature of its questioning. Moreover, since there is no doubt that the Refutation of Idealism is more elegant, concise, and straightforward (although, as we shall see, ultimately unsuccessful) than the argument of the Fourth Paralogism, it comes as no surprise that Kant ultimately decided to keep only the former and sacrifice the latter, at least in its expanded version. But while this explains Kant's preference for the Refutation in the Second Edition, it certainly does not mean that he removed the Fourth Paralogism because he found some flaws in it. Finally, the same considerations can be used to explain why, in the Reflexionen that Kant devoted to the problem of scepticism after 1787, he clearly focused more on strengthening the Refutation (specifically, to rebutting possible objections to it) than to expanding the antisceptical lines of thought we encountered in the Fourth Paralogism.

5 The Refutation of Idealism

In the Second Edition of the *Critique*, Kant inserts a completely new section entitled 'Refutation of Idealism.' In it we find an antisceptical proof that turns on an alleged dependence of the empirical consciousness of our own existence (to whose certainty the Cartesian sceptic is thought to be committed) on the reality of outer experience. The core of the proof is that only outer knowledge contains the permanence necessary for the temporal determination of the succession of mental states, which Kant identifies with the empirical consciousness of our existence. As I have already indicated, Kant thought that with this proof 'the game of idealism had been turned against itself' (B276). This is so because, if outer knowledge is a condition of the possibility of inner knowledge, then one part of the 'game' of idealism – the certainty of inner knowledge – contradicts the other part, namely, the doubt about the existence of external objects.

Kant scholars have long found this argument intriguing, quite independently of its inherent merits. This interest comes as no surprise. To begin with, the very insertion of a new section in the Second Edition of the *Critique* raises a number of interpretative questions. Why did Kant find it necessary to add a new proof? And how does this proof differ from the 1781 argument? What general systematic repercussions does the new proof have for Kant's entire system? Also, the proof attacks an entire school – extremely influential in Kant's time and even later – based on the fundamental tenet of the 'way of ideas,' that is, the assumption that our knowledge is primarily about mental entities and only derivatively about genuine things. Such an important school is discredited (at least in its sceptical outcomes) through five very short steps and through an argumentative logic both clear and lethal: a reductio ad absurdum. Furthermore, since Strawson's *The Bounds of Sense*, many have seen in the 1787 Refutation the culmination of a Kantian strategy to ground the 'objectivity' of our knowledge, and consider this strategy particularly promising because it is apparently free from any commitment to transcendental idealism. Finally, quite independently of its significance for antiscepticism, the Refutation completes the theory of time determination introduced in the Analogies – a theory that many still view as Kant's most important contribution to epistemology.

In the context of this chapter, we shall focus on two main questions. The first concerns the placement of the Refutation both in the general context of the 1787 edition and in the specific context of the Postulates of Empirical Thought. The second concerns the very soundness of the proof. The latter is clearly the crucial question for any account of the Refutation; unfortunately, it is also the most difficult to answer. Commentators widely disagree about it, and furthermore, it is tied to a series of sub-questions relating to the single steps of the proof – questions that require careful attention. Thus, after an overview of the proof, I will analyse what I take as its most important (and controversial) points. My analysis will consider the following four issues: (a) the exact determination of the kind of self-knowledge that Kant is assuming in the Refutation; (b) whether he is entitled to attribute to Descartes this kind of self-knowledge; (c) exactly *what* the permanent is that is supposed to determine the temporal structure of my inner experience; and (d) why that permanent cannot be an inner object. My conclusion will be that even if we remove pseudo-difficulties that could undermine the success of the Refutation, the proof is still vulnerable to a crucial sceptical reply – one that Kant foresees and attempts to silence, albeit without convincing us much. In the third section I will concentrate on the sceptical objection and show that Kant's explicit self-defence is ultimately unsatisfactory. This chapter will end with an attempt to 'salvage' the Refutation by applying the antisceptical resources of the Fourth Paralogism.

The Placement of the Refutation

The placement of the Refutation poses a twofold problem. On the one hand, since it is an addition to the Second Edition, we might well wonder whether the modifications that Kant's general philosophy underwent between 1781 and 1787 are relevant to it. For example, is it accidental that Kant discovered this proof after 1781? Is it the case that he simply 'did not think of it,' or was the proof perhaps made possible by certain assumptions that Kant introduced only after 1781? At the same time, we have to consider the significance (if any) of the placement of the Refutation in the context of the Postulates of Empirical Thought. Why does Kant insert his new proof in a context entirely different from that of his old proof? We have already seen that the placement of the 1781 proof among the Paralogisms was extremely significant, in that it enabled us to reject the idea of a special, *intellectual* access to our existence. Does the new placement play a similarly significant role? Also, what is the significance of the 'migration' of the critique of scepticism from the Dialectic to the Analytic?

Starting with the first question, one crucial assumption on which the Refutation rests – as we shall see shortly – is that the permanent needed in order to determine my existence in time cannot be found in inner sense. But how can Kant assume that the permanent is not the self or the mind? After all, his standard theory of inner sense depicts precisely such entities as objects of inner sense. For example, he claims that '"I," as thinking, am an object of the inner sense, and am called "soul"' (A342/B400). Since built into the notion of 'self' or 'soul' is the idea of permanence or reidentifiability, it seems to be a perfect candidate for the permanence required. In the Second Edition, however, he introduces some substantial modifications to this theory. This modified theory, which I will spell out in some detail later in this chapter, turns on a strong asymmetry between inner and outer sense. While the latter generally yields the intuition of reidentifiable objects that function as property holders (ordinary objects with their properties), the former contains only a succession of representations with no intuition of a reidentifiable X to which these representations can be attributed as properties of a substance. Obviously, this asymmetry is crucial to the Refutation. If inner sense yielded the intuition of a reidentifiable object (if I had an impression of the Self), then there would be no need to 'look outside' to find the permanent required for the experience of the succession of my representations in time. All of this suggests that the qualifications of the theory of inner sense that Kant introduced in the Second Edition are essential to the Refutation. Kant's discovery of this argument after 1781 does not seem to be an accident, insofar as the modification of some central tenets of his theory of inner experience made such a discovery possible. The placement of the Refutation in the context of the Second Edition thus has precisely this significance.

Concerning the second question, Kant places the Refutation immediately after the Second Postulate of Empirical Thought. This postulate asserts: 'That which is bound up with the material conditions of experience, that is, with sensation, is *actual*' (A218/B266). In his discussion of the postulate, Kant points out that in order to assert the actuality (or existence) of an object, I do not always need a perception – that is, an intuition with a sensation – of the object itself. I can also assert its existence indirectly through the perceptions of some other objects combined with 'the principles of their empirical connection (the analogies)' (A225/B273). Kant gives the example of the perception of the motion of iron filings that informs us about the existence of some magnet. The existence of the magnet is thus determined mediately.

The reason given by Kant for placing the Refutation after the Second Postulate is that Cartesian idealism poses 'a serious objection to these rules for proving existence mediately' (B274). Note, however, that this justification is inaccurate and perhaps even misleading. To begin with, in the example quoted above, idealism does not question the plausibility of the inferences involved. For the idealist, even when I *directly* perceive an object, its existence is inferred mediately. In other words, the inference questioned by idealism is not that from a perceived object to an unperceived one (whose existence is affirmed through reference to the analogies). The inference is from a mental state to the object that supposedly caused it. The challenge is directed primarily against the perception of an object; a fortiori, it is about an object that is not directly perceived. Note also that by presenting the idealist challenge as a challenge against his own rules for proving the existence of objects *mediately*, Kant even invites us to think that the disagreement between him and the sceptic is about *specific* rules for inferring the existence of external objects, while they agree that existence must be proven mediately. But this is the opposite of the immediacy thesis, a position to which Kant, presumably, was still adhering in 1787.[1] It follows that Kant's stated justification for placing the Refutation where he does can hardly be accepted. It is plausible only because there is a vague resemblance between the inference Kant defends (from perceived to unperceived) and the inference the sceptic attacks (from a representation to its object). In general, however, his justification risks fostering serious misunderstandings.

This does not mean that the placement of the Refutation after the Second Postulate is completely self-defeating or even simply arbitrary. As in the First Edition, the discussion of scepticism is placed in correspondence to modality. The categories of modality – so Kant claims at the very beginning of his discussion of the Postulates of Empirical Thought – have the 'peculiarity' that 'in determining an object they do not in the least enlarge the concept to which they are attached as predicates. They only express the relation of the concept to the faculty of knowledge'(A219/B266). Thus the Second Postulate, to which the Refutation is attached, does not spell out any feature of possible experience, but merely the manner in which a certain object must relate to our faculty of knowledge if we are to consider it actual. This object, as the Postulate reads, 'must be bound up with the material conditions of experience, that is with sensation.'[2] Now, what the sceptic calls into question is precisely whether this condition (being bound up with sensation) is a reliable mark of actuality. It is thus only natural that Kant places what can serve as a defence of his Postulate – the Refutation – immediately after the exposition of the Postulate itself. Note also that to doubt that a sensation can be a reliable mark of existence (presumably because we need to infer from the sensation as effect to its cause) means to assume that our outer perception is mediate.

Why, then, does Kant fail to tell us explicitly that idealism questions the reliability of a sensation for determining an existence – that is, the immediacy of outer perception – like he did in the Fourth Paralogism? The reason might be that Kant, unlike in the First Edition, is trying to avoid a direct confrontation with the sceptic on the issue of the immediacy/mediacy of outer perception. Indeed, it seems that the Refutation does not rely at all on the immediacy thesis. Quite the contrary – Kant is very careful *not* to let his proof depend on this thesis. He states that 'the immediate consciousness of the existence of outer things is, in the preceding thesis, not presupposed, but proved'[3] because it is shown to be a condition of possibility of inner experience. By avoiding pointing to the immediacy thesis as the sceptic's target, Kant is also avoiding the necessity to centre his proof on a defence of it. More precisely, he avoids the necessity of starting his Refutation with the main point of disagreement with the sceptic, and enables himself to begin with a thesis – the temporal structure of inner experience – that he presumably shares with the sceptic. On this interpretation, it is therefore the reductio structure of the proof that dictates the hiding of the very point of disagreement and the rather misleading presentation of another one – the disagreement about 'these rules for proving existence mediately.'

As we have already noted, both the Fourth Paralogism and the Refutation are placed in correspondence to modality. But the similarity goes even deeper. Another interesting feature of the location of the Refutation is that, as in the First Edition, the category of existence is at stake. But there is a difference. While in the Fourth Paralogism the connection between existence and scepticism was that an existential claim (the hypostatization of the existence of the merely logical subject of thought into a substance or thing) was illegitimately affirmed by the sceptic, in the present case the point is rather that an existential claim (the existence of external objects through a sensation) is rightly affirmed, but illegitimately questioned or doubted by the sceptic.

It is intriguing that Kant perhaps moved his critique of scepticism from the Dialectic to the Analytic in part because of the different focus of the old and new arguments. Since his 1781 strategy focused on the need to deny the hypostatization of the subject in order to establish for outer knowledge the same immediacy that inner knowledge possesses, he was led to place his argument in the Paralogism. Although the denial of the hypostatization of the subject is hardly irrelevant for the new proof – it is necessary in order to block the sceptic's reply that we can ascertain our existence in an atemporal fashion – the focus is now on the fact that the determination of time is possible only through an external permanent. Since it is the First Analogy that establishes the necessity of a permanent for the experience of an alteration, the natural context of the new proof is no longer the Dialectic, but the Analytic – specifically, the Analytic of Principles, where this result is established.

The Proof: An Overview

The Refutation of Idealism consists of a Thesis, a Proof, and three explanatory Notes. The thesis states: 'The mere, but empirically determined, consciousness of my own existence proves the existence of objects in space outside me' (B275). The Proof reads:

> [1] I am conscious of my own existence as determined in time. [2] All determination of time presupposes something *permanent* in perception. [3] This permanent, however, cannot be something in me since it is only through this permanent that my existence in time can itself be determined. [4] Thus perception of this permanent is possible only through a thing outside me and not through the mere representation of a thing outside me; and consequently the determination of my existence in time is possible only through the existence of actual things which I perceive outside me. [5] Now consciousness [of my existence] in time is necessarily bound up with consciousness of the [condition of the] possibility of this time-determination; and it is therefore necessarily bound up with the existence of things outside me, as the condition of the time-determination. In other

words, the consciousness of my existence is at the same time an immediate consciousness of the existence of other things outside me. (B275–6)

The argument is rather straightforward. Kant defines self-knowledge as the consciousness of the succession of inner states of which I become aware when I reflect on myself. Given this temporal structure, he uses the results of the First Analogy to point out that in order to become aware of a temporal succession, I need a permanent that remains identical while the succession of different states continues to flow. Quite obscurely – especially if one is unaware of the modifications of Kant's view on inner sense in the Second Edition – he adds that this permanent cannot be found in me. It follows that this permanent must be found in external objects. Their existence therefore turns out to be a condition of the possibility of the experience of my own existence. The conclusion is that the Cartesian sceptic cannot consistently affirm the reality of the latter and doubt the reality of the former.

The idea that the sceptic is committed to the reality of the temporal structure of inner experience did not originate with Kant. In the 1770 letter to Kant, which we analysed in chapter 1, Lambert made precisely the same point: 'Even an idealist must grant at least that changes really exist and occur in his representations'[4] Perhaps this remark was Kant's inspiration for the Refutation. Whatever its historical origin, the proof presents a set of problematic points, some of them already noted in the literature, which can be grasped if we take a closer look at each step of the proof.

The Notion of Self-Consciousness at Work in the Refutation (Step 1)

In the first step of the argument ('I am conscious of my own existence as determined in time'), Kant defines the kind of self-knowledge that the Cartesian is supposed to accept as absolutely certain. The first problem concerns the ambiguity in the notion of being 'conscious of my own existence in time.' As we saw in the preceding chapter, Kant accounts in the *Critique* for two different kinds of self-consciousness, which correspond to two different ways in which the subject can become aware of its existence: (1) through apperception, which gives mere awareness of the existence of an indeterminate subject,[5] and (2) through inner sense, which provides empirical knowledge of the inner states of the mind – states that are ordered according to the form of inner sense, that is, time.[6] The references in the Thesis and in this first step to a consciousness that is 'empirically determined' and 'determined in time' suggest that Kant is concerned here with the latter notion of self-consciousness rather than with the former. Indeed, the mere awareness of existence given through apperception is not empirically determined in time; rather, it is purely intellectual because it is analytically deduced from the spontaneity of thought in general. Besides these textual indications, for the proof to even get off the ground, the access to my existence must be understood as empirical self-knowledge. Otherwise there would be no need for a permanent to determine the temporal structure that pertains to inner experience.[7]

For the sake of the rest of the argument, it is important that I highlight some features of this notion of empirical self-knowledge. To begin with, what exactly is the object of self-knowledge? In a crucial passage that he added to the Second Edition, Kant points out that 'the representations of the *outer senses* constitute the proper material with which we occupy our mind' (B67). This suggests that inner sense does not have material of its own, but instead is parasitic on the material provided by outer sense. In a footnote in Section 25 of the B Deduction, Kant holds that in any act of attention, the understanding determines inner sense. If we keep in mind that inner sense has no manifold of its own, this seems to mean that through the act of attention, the mind takes the representations provided by outer sense no longer as such, but as its own modifications. In other words, once the act of attention is accomplished, the representations are no longer representations of an external object, but reconceptualized by the mind as its states. Since time is the form of inner sense, the states of the mind are posited in a temporal succession. Thus to say that 'I am conscious of my existence as determined in time' is to say that I am conscious of the succession of representations reconceptualized as 'subjective objects' by a reflective act of attention.[8]

Note that this account seems to leave us with an object of inner sense and of inner experience quite different from the one indicated at times by Kant, especially in the First Edition. In fact, his theory would have it that the object of inner sense is the soul (or the mind).[9] This suggests that we are supposed to encounter in inner sense an abiding and reidentifiable object, whereas the present account allows for much less. To begin with, the object of inner sense seems to be a stream of representations. Moreover, the content of these representations comes from outer sense. Finally, and most importantly, these representations cannot be taken as properties of an object in the same way that, for example, colour, shape, or the size of a table are properties of this object. In inner sense there is no reidentifiable object to which these properties can be attributed. This suggests that the symmetry between inner and outer sense, on which Kant often insists (and at times still insists in the Second Edition), is not grounded. Given Kant's own assumptions, the representations that flow in my consciousness can at most be said to *belong to* the mind, but not to be representations *of* the mind.[10] At least, they are not representations *of* the mind in the same manner that the representations of colour, shape, and the size of the table in front of me are representations *of* this table. In the latter case we have a reidentifiable object to which these representations pertain as its properties; in the former case we have no such thing.

To be sure, there is a rather simple way to reconcile Kant's emphasis on the symmetry between inner and outer sense with his more or less explicit denial that inner sense has something reidentifiable as its object. We could say that when he claims that the soul is the object of inner sense, he simply *means* that the soul or the mind or the empirical 'I,' à la Hume, is no abiding object but simply a stream of representations.[11] Hence, even in the First Edition, Kant would make no room for a reidentifiable object as the object of inner sense. On this interpretation, Kant consistently holds that inner sense has its own object (hence the possibility of claiming the existence of *some kind* of symmetry) without ever considering this object to be reidentifiable as outer objects (the limits of the same symmetry). Even if correct, however, this approach to re-establishing some consistency within Kant's account of inner experience does not undermine the main point. In inner sense – in both editions and in the supposedly modified account of the 1787 edition – we have no abiding, reidentifiable object comparable to the objects of outer sense. Clearly, this point is crucial to the rest of the argument. In fact, the absence of such a reidentifiable object is Kant's ultimate motive for ruling out the possibility that the required permanent be just the 'Self,' understood precisely as an abiding object.

Certainly, this clarification of the notion of self-knowledge at work in the first step merely serves to highlight the real difficulty. Recall that this step is supposed to be shared by the Cartesian sceptic. The problem is whether the Cartesian is truly committed to the temporal structure of inner experience on which the first step insists and on which the entire Refutation rests. In fact, Kant assumes that we are conscious of our existence through awareness of the succession of our representations *over* time, regardless of how small the temporal span is. When we look at the very first expression of the cogito in the Second Meditation, however,

Descartes claims that 'I am, I exist, is necessarily true *each time* I pronounce it, or that I mentally conceive it.'[12] The reference to its being true 'each time' seems to indicate that the validity of the cogito does not go beyond each *instant* in which the cogito is performed. More importantly, regardless of whether Descartes interpreted the cogito in this way, arguably he should have. For the extension beyond the instant of the validity of the cogito seems to imply reliance on memory. Since this faculty could very easily be deceptively triggered by the Evil Genius, it seems that Descartes should not have extended the validity claim of the cogito beyond the instant.[13] If this is so, couldn't the sceptic simply ignore the Refutation by denying that I am conscious of my own existence through the experience of a succession of representations *over time*?[14]

This line of reasoning takes for granted that the recognition of the temporal succession of my mental states rests on memory. To be sure, at times Kant himself seems to characterize the empirical self-consciousness at stake precisely in this manner. In two pages of recently discovered notes, Kant construes empirical self-consciousness as involving the identification – presumably through memory – of the present 'I' with the 'I' of the past: 'The pure (transc.) apperception must be distinguished from the empirical *apperceptio percipientis* of the apperceptive perceived. The first says merely "I am." The second I was, I am, and I will be, i.e. I am a thing of the past, present and future time.'[15] But even if Kant at times construes empirical self-consciousness as resting on memory, it is far from obvious that it actually does.

Let us examine more closely what is involved in empirical self-consciousness. A condition of the representation of a succession, like that of one's own mental states, is that one is able to represent within a single act of consciousness the different items of the succession and the succession itself. When I entertain the succession in my consciousness of a representation A (say, the representation of this computer) and then of the representation B (say, the representation of the window on my left), I am not performing two distinct acts of consciousness in such a way that, when I am conscious of B, I must remember that I *was* conscious of A. Rather, in order to be able to experience the succession of these two items in my mind, I have to encompass their succession in a *single* act of consciousness. In other words, I must be able to encompass in a single act of consciousness not only the individual representations, but also their happening one after the other. This means that my consciousness extends beyond the instant and encompasses in a single act the temporal span in which the succession takes place.

The singleness of this act of consciousness is crucial, because it guarantees that I do not rely on memory. Since from a Cartesian (and Kantian) perspective whatever is present to consciousness is indubitable, it follows that the act of consciousness that encompasses this temporal span is as indubitable as one that has the instantaneous occurrence of a single representation as its object. In fact, these two kinds of consciousness can be at the root of two different but apparently equally legitimate instances of the cogito. One would be 'I think *this X*, therefore I am,' the other 'I think the succession of various *X*s in my consciousness, therefore I am.' Thus, although we can become aware of our existence through the consciousness of a single, instantaneous representation – something that admittedly does not entail any temporal structure – we can also use as a premise of the cogito a single complex act of consciousness. In the latter, we have a temporal dimension that does not rely on memory. It follows that the sceptic is committed to the certainty of this kind of consciousness, which extends beyond the instant. In turn, it follows that he cannot dismiss the Refutation by considering that it assumes a notion of self-consciousness the Cartesian would reject.[16]

To be sure, the Cartesian can still resort to the cogito interpreted as a single, non-temporal act of consciousness, and insist that at least in this case we have an bit of self-knowledge that is completely independent of any permanent external object. This might suffice to establish his cherished asymmetry between outer and inner knowledge and to escape the 'trap' of the Refutation. Despite an apparent plausibility that we have granted up till now for the sake of the argument, however, the very notion of an instantaneous, temporally unextended instance of the cogito is highly problematic. Even if we grant the possibility of such a thing as an instantaneous cognito, the entity that this instantaneous activity yields would be much less than what Descartes requires. The 'I's' whose existence would be proved through a certain number of occurrences of this activity would be completely unrelated. In other words, they could not be reidentified as moments of the same subjectivity. If the cognito has to prove the existence of a 'thing' (*res cognitans*), however, an array of fleeting, unrelated entities will not be sufficient. In fact, we usually say that a *thing* exists only if we can reidentify it *over time*. And if we cannot (say, if it ceases to exist because of sudden decomposition or similar), we still say that we could have done so if what caused its ceasing to exist had not occurred. In the case of the products of the instantaneous cognito, however, we cannot even say that, because *by definition* the unrelated 'I's' have no connection with one another. If they had one, then it would mean that we have reidentified them as instances of the same 'I.' This presupposes, though, a reidentification *in time* that would lead us back to the notion of self-knowledge that was avoided to escape the trap of the Refutation.

The clear identification of what Descartes requires from his cognito is crucial if we are to address another difficulty related to the first step of the Refutation. The problem now centres on Kant's admission that a consciousness of one's existence can be found in the pure 'I think' of apperception. This admission is repeated in the first of the three Notes that follow the Refutation: 'in the above proof we have shown that outer experience is really immediate, and that only by means of it is inner experience – *not indeed the consciousness of my own existence*, but the determination of it in time – possible.'[17] This consciousness of my own existence that is not dependent on outer knowledge is to be understood as the non-sensible self-consciousness through apperception that we have already discussed in chapter 3. Since through apperception the consciousness of my existence is a thought and not an intuition, it would seem that in it there is nothing even remotely resembling a temporal structure, and the obvious consequence would be that this self-consciousness does not require a permanent (external or internal) object. Thus, once again, it would seem that the Cartesian could dismiss the Refutation by pointing out that his notion of self-consciousness is not (or need not be) the empirical self-consciousness that presupposes an (external) permanent. It could rather be the non-sensible (and therefore non-temporal) self-consciousness that Kant himself concedes.

Certainly, Kant takes great care to point out that this consciousness only brings about the existence of an indeterminate 'I,' not the empirical 'I' with its mental history and all the particular determinations that make it an object distinct from others. For example, he writes:

> The 'I think' expresses the act of determining my existence. Existence is already given thereby, but the mode in which I am to determine this existence, that is, the manifold belonging to it, is not thereby given.[18]

And in the first of the Notes that he added to the proof, he is careful to add:

> Certainly, the representation 'I am,' which expresses the consciousness that can accompany all thought, immediately includes in itself the exist-

ence of a subject; but it does not so include in itself any *knowledge* of that subject, and therefore also no empirical knowledge, that is, no experience of it.[19]

But why should this indeterminate subject be different from the Cartesian thinking being? Couldn't the 'I' that figures in the Cartesian 'I think' be as indeterminate as the 'I' of apperception? Fortunately, in the preceding chapter we saw that it is illegitimate to identify the 'thing' that Descartes thought he could ascertain through the cogito with the 'I' whose existence is ascertainable through apperception.[20] Here we simply need to repeat the main point. The Cartesian cogito is supposed to yield the consciousness of a determinate object, the first entity (*res cogitans*) that is re-established after the radical doubt. This entity is determined at least to the extent that it contains the thoughts it entertains. For example, when I say 'I think X, therefore I am,' I need to include in my act of thought precisely the determination 'I am thinking X.' But this determination is precisely what the 'I' of apperception lacks. In fact, all that apperception yields is the author's completely empty thought of the activity of thinking. Through apperception, as we have seen, the number of things the world consists of is not increased. Only inner *experience*, with its temporal structure, can generate knowledge of the entity that Descartes hoped to establish through the cogito.

If the sceptic is committed to the temporal structure of inner experience, the next step in the proof is to spell out what this presupposes.

The Necessity of a (Spatial) Permanent (Step 2)

In the second step, Kant claims that 'all determination of time presupposes something *permanent* in perception.' This contention is borrowed from the First Analogy, in which he establishes this through a rather short and simple argument. All appearances are in time (as was established in the Transcendental Aesthetic).[21] The temporal relations among appearances (succession, coexistence, and duration[22]) can be represented only with reference to time, understood not as a fleeting succession of items but rather as an abiding substratum, 'as permanent form of inner intuition' (B224). Since time cannot be perceived, the substratum that represents time in general 'must be found in the objects of perception, that is, in the appearances.'[23] When Kant contends in the Refutation that 'all determination of time presupposes something *permanent* in perception,' he is simply appealing to the conclusion of this argument.

The necessity of permanence for the determination of any mode of time (succession, simultaneity, duration) is a minimal requirement and can be grasped intuitively. The basic point is that, given the successive nature of our apprehension, if we did not identify something as permanent, we would not have a comparison term against which we could contrast the succession itself and become aware of it. Also, without a permanent substratum we could not realize that an appearance A exists at the same time as an appearance B. We can say the latter only if, notwithstanding the successive nature of our apprehension, we consider each as simultaneous to something permanent. The simultaneity of the different states of the permanent functions as the model of the simultaneity of the appearances. Finally, the permanent also makes possible the measurement of time and thus the experience of duration.[24] Kant does not explain this point, but we can easily imagine how permanence makes the measurement of time possible. We measure time with reference to motion – for example, the motion of the planets. The experience of this motion presupposes the experience of a succession – the succession of the different places occupied by the planets – and of the coexistence of the series of these states with something permanent. But since, as we saw, the experience of succession and coexistence presupposes a permanent, it follows that the experience of duration, which in turn depends on that of succession and coexistence, presupposes the permanent as well.[25]

This minimal thesis is quite clearly distinguished from the thesis that all change must be taken as an alteration of a substance. These claims must indeed be distinguished: the latter does not claim only that a permanent is necessary for the determination of succession and coexistence; it also says that succession or coexistence can be represented only as succession or coexistence of states *of* the permanent – that is, as accidents of a substance.[26] Using Allison's helpful terminology, we shall refer to these claims respectively as the Backdrop thesis and the 'All Change Is Alteration' thesis.

The identification of these two different theses in the First Analogy is important because we have to decide which of them is used in the Refutation. If we decide that the Refutation uses the Backdrop thesis – and the phrasing of the second step strongly suggests it – then the permanent necessary for the determination of the temporal structure of my consciousness is going to be merely a reference point and not a kind of surrogate for the permanence of the self. On this reading, in the consciousness of one's existence in time there would be nothing more than consciousness of a temporally determined succession of mental states (and perhaps also the consciousness that they 'belong to me'), with no commitment to the idea that these mental states pertain to an abiding, identical 'I.' But if we decide that what is borrowed from the First Analogy is the 'All Change Is Alteration' thesis, then the permanent will be precisely a kind of external surrogate of the abiding self. The succession of representations in consciousness will be considered an alteration of something that retains its identity throughout the change of some of its features. In the present case, this would be nothing but the enduring self. On this reading, it will appear that the Refutation is meant to re-establish the identity of the self – an identity that was threatened by the modifications to the theory of inner sense that Kant introduced in the Second Edition.[27]

It is important to realize that this interpretation 'thickens' the notion of 'consciousness of my own existence as determined in time' in a completely arbitrary way. There is no evidence that the role of the permanent is to provide an awareness of the identity of the subject. The role Kant explicitly gives it is merely to make possible the temporal determination of the succession of my mental states. And this task can be accomplished even if I am *not* an identical subject – that is, even if all that my consciousness provides about me is a series of fleeting representations. Of course, this consciousness must contain also the thought that such representations *belong to me*. But this is still much less than the thought of an identical 'I' that underpins their succession. The role of the permanent is not to attribute such representations to some abiding substance, but simply to make possible their organization in a *temporal* series.

An additional problematic point connected with the First Analogy has to do with the very nature of the permanent. We do not want to deal here with the question of why the permanent cannot be found in inner sense. This is indeed the focus of the next step in the argument. The point that must be preliminarily examined is the following: even if we assume, as we do, that the Refutation borrows from the First Analogy only the minimal and apparently undeniable claim that we require a permanent substratum in order to become aware of the succession (and coexistence) of appearances, we still have to determine what this permanent is. This question is more difficult than it might first appear. A reasonable hypothesis is that Kant has in mind empirical ordinary objects, such as tables or chairs. Tables and chairs, however, themselves undergo changes. Hence the question: Do we have to understand that external objects can play the role of the permanent simply because they change *less* than the object of inner sense? After all, it is a plain and undeniable fact that external objects such as tables and chairs are more 'stable' and abiding than the object of inner sense, which, as we have seen, is constituted by a series of fleeting representations. In inner sense I have a continuous succession of thoughts, outer sense gives me a number of reidentifiable empirical objects; each of which could play the role of the substratum necessary for time determination. If the world were different, always changing in such a way that it was impossible to identify something that does not change, perhaps we would not have the necessary substratum. But what Kant wants to prove is the existence of *this* world, and this world certainly presents reidentifiable, relatively permanent things.[28]

But perhaps we can move beyond this minimal result. Is it really true that if the world were in constant flux, there would be nothing that could serve as permanent? Let us consider the following thought experiment. Let us imagine that all I see are objects moving at high speed and changing in their internal properties in such a way that no identification (let alone reidentification) is possible. Let us call them USOs (unidentified spinning objects, an extreme version of the familiar UFOs). Obviously, it is also assumed that I cannot see my body, which otherwise could very well serve as the permanent. In this situation, the question is whether we would lack what we need to determine inner experience temporally – that is, whether we would lack a permanent.

It is important to realize that even in this situation, the USOs, despite their motions and their internal changes, would still be taking place in an abiding framework – that is, in a space in which they find a determinate position with reference to me. When I experience a USO, I also intuit the framework in which this object moves. In fact, I experience its motion as a successive occupation of different parts of an already given framework. This framework is 'already given' in the sense that it is the horizon wherein this motion occurs. Moreover, this intuited framework is obviously permanent. We indeed conceive of the motion of the object as successively occupying parts of something that remains at rest while the motion takes place. Thus the perception of some objects in space, regardless of how rapidly they change and move, gives rise to the intuition of space as an abiding framework or system of reference. And this intuited framework serves as the required permanent.

Note that I am not assuming that you could see the object 'space,' which would be quite problematic from a Kantian perspective. Very clearly, Kant states that 'the mere form of intuition, without substance, is in itself no object, but the merely formal condition of an object (as appearance), as pure space and pure time (*ens imaginarium*). These are indeed something, as forms of intuition, but are not themselves objects that are intuited' (A291/B347). On the contrary, I am assuming that our USOs are necessary for the intuition of this system of reference. Once the USOs are perceived, the content of the pure intuition of space displays itself around these objects. But without it, with the mere pure intuition of space, my intuition would be completely empty.

It is crucial that external objects (no matter how changing) are necessary for the intuition of this framework. In fact, if a pure intuition of space – which clearly does not presuppose the existence of any object (or, as Kant says, is a mere '*ens imaginarium*') – were sufficient to provide the permanent, the Refutation would be immediately contradicted. We would have a time-determined inner experience without any external object, and Kant's antisceptical strategy to link inner and outer experience would prove completely ineffective.

This is, in fact, Robert Hanna's final assessment of the Refutation. In a suggestive article that has recently appeared, he argues that given Kant's account of space as something we can intuit even without objects in space, the pure intuition of space would be all Kant needs for the required permanence: 'The unique, non-empirical referent of pure spatial representations – that is space itself – has not been ruled out as the permanent Kant needs in order to meet the requirement of step 2.'[29] Hence, on Kant's own theory of space, the Refutation would *not* prove the necessity of external *things*. At best, it would show the need for some reference to the 'external.' But for the sake of time determination, an external spatial framework completely empty of material objects would be as good as a genuine external object.

As we saw, however, Kant quite explicitly denies that space (and time) are *objects* that can be intuited. He merely says that they are 'something, as forms of intuition, but are not themselves objects to be intuited' (A291/B347). Hence he is better interpreted (along the lines of Warren's thesis) as arguing that, *once objects are given in space*, something more coming from the forms of our mind is added to the mere intuition of these objects. This something more is simply the framework we suggested. The crucial point remains, however, that an empirical object, no matter how rapidly changing, is required to enable the intuition of the ever permanent framework 'space.' It is only through the former that the latter displays itself in front of the subject, making the determination of that subject's inner experience possible.

This notion of a system of reference or abiding framework is also crucial if we are to interpret correctly the important but deeply obscure Note 2, which follows the Refutation and in which Kant gives us a hint as to the nature of the permanent. Its central part runs as follows:

> Not only are we unable to perceive any determination of time save through change in outer relations (motion) relatively to the permanent in space (for instance, the motion of the sun relatively to objects on earth), we have nothing permanent on which, as intuition, we can base the concept of substance, save only *matter*; and even this permanence is not obtained from outer experience, but is presupposed *a priori* as a necessary condition of determination of time, and therefore also as a determination of inner sense in respect of [the determination of] our own existence through the existence of outer things. (B277–8)

In the first part of this passage, Kant seems to be taking the permanent as an empirical object. Time can be determined only through reference to motion relative to something permanent, such as the motion of the sun relative to objects at rest on earth.[30] In the second part, however, having emphasized that this permanent must be an intuition, Kant contends that the only thing that can serve as permanent, and that can thus make room for the application of the concept of substance, is matter. Moreover, this permanent 'is not obtained from outer experience.' This contention should strike us as puzzling. Weren't we supposed to find the permanent precisely in outer experience? If matter is really the only object of permanence and if this permanence is not to be found in outer experience, how can the Refutation contend that outer experience is necessary for inner experience?

The first step towards a solution to this difficulty is to clarify the notion of matter at stake in our quote. To do so, we must go back to the First Analogy. One important claim there is that there must be something absolutely permanent that could serve as the abiding substratum of *all* change ('the substrate of all change remains ever the same'[31]). Change might affect what usually serves as the substratum of change – namely, ordinary empirical objects such as chairs and tables, which obviously are only relatively permanent (they also pass out of existence). In order to experience the change even of these entities, we must presuppose some eternal matter that undergoes all possible alteration but that itself never ceases (or begins) to exist. In this way, when the ordinary objects that usually function as property holders or substances themselves pass out of existence, we can still refer to this matter as what underlies the process (and retain its identity). This matter functions as a condition of the possibility of representing changes of this sort.

When Kant says that 'we have nothing permanent on which, as intuition, we can base the concept of substance, save only *matter*,' he means that *ultimately* only matter can be said to be truly permanent because what usually serves as permanent can itself be subject to change. But how can Kant say that this matter can be given through an intuition and at the same time deny that the permanence that matter provides can be found in outer experience? The answer is that I do not perceive 'matter,' regardless of whether permanent or not; I perceive objects that I assume are ultimately made of matter. At the same time, however, there must be a feature of matter that can be intuited, thus making the application of the concept of substance possible. Now, what is this feature?

In the Architectonic of Pure Reason, Kant characterizes matter as 'impenetrable, lifeless extension.'[32] The reference to extension is crucial. It seems that this extension must be interpreted precisely as that external abiding framework we referred to. As we saw, when we experience external objects, regardless of how changing, we also intuit the spatial locations they occupy and the abiding framework that encompasses them (recall Warren's thesis). And it is this second-order intuition, made possible by the first order intuition of the object, that serves as the permanent. Note that Kant himself suggests this interpretation in the Reflexionen, in which he often identifies the permanent with 'space' (as opposed to a determinate spatial object).[33]

Thus Kant is correct to emphasize that the permanence of matter is not given in outer experience. To be sure, he confuses us by omitting that there *is* an intuitive datum of matter that is given to outer sense. This datum is precisely the intuition of the spatial framework in which the different parts of matter find themselves. This is also the datum we tried to highlight in our preceding thought experiment. The final result of our analysis is thus that the intuition of this abiding framework – itself made possible by the presence of (changing) objects – serves as the abiding permanent even in cases in which ordinary objects do not display a permanence sufficient for discharging that task. This shows that, after all, the Refutation does not *need* to rest on the contingent fact that external objects are more permanent than the inner object. Kant's reference to matter in the above quote, properly understood, suggests that there is a permanent intuitive datum that can function as the required permanent backdrop even if all ordinary empirical objects are in constant flux. We can now move to the next step, whose main function is to show that neither of these two kinds of permanent can be found 'in me.'

The Necessity to Look without for the Permanent (Step 3)

In a footnote to the Preface to the Second Edition, Kant asks us to replace the original claim that, 'all determination of time presupposes something *permanent* in perception' with the following: 'But this permanent cannot be an intuition in me. For all grounds of determination of my existence which are to be met with in me are representations; and as representations themselves require a permanent distinct from them, in relation to which their change, and so my existence in the time wherein they change, may be determined' (Bxl n.).

The first issue here is the reason for this replacement. Interpreters have already noted that the original version does not make clear why the required permanent cannot be either what Descartes means by a *res cogitans* or Kant's 'I' of apperception.[34] To be sure, the reference in the preceding step to the fact that the permanent must be found in 'perception,' and the clarification added in Note 1 that an intuition is required for knowledge of the subject, served to rule out this possibility. Immediately before publishing the Second Edition of the *Critique*, however, Kant must have thought that these claims were insufficient to preclude this possibility, and therefore made explicit in this step that the permanent must be given through an outer intuition ('this permanent cannot be an intuition in me').[35] More importantly, the new step, unlike the old one, spells out what we can find in inner sense – that is, representations (or better, a succession thereof), which as such cannot function as the required permanent.

Moving to the analysis of this new third step, we must bear in mind the modifications that Kant introduced in the Second Edition as to the nature of the object of inner sense. As we saw, inner sense has no material of its own. The representations we find in it are all products of acts of attention, through which we reconceptualize the representations of outer sense in order to take them as modifications of the mind. These acts of attention are successive; it follows that inner sense contains a succession of reinterpreted representations but no abiding, reidentifiable object that could function as a predicate holder. In this step of the Refutation, we can see Kant drawing the logical conclusion from these modifications about inner sense and inner experience scattered throughout the Second Edition. Now, if inner experience contains only this temporal series, we cannot find in it the permanent required for the very recognition of this succession. All the third step does is spell out that inner experience is unable to provide the permanent.

The idea that inner sense, unlike outer sense, contains a succession of representations is more problematic than it might appear. Kant often identifies the objects of all our experience, inner and outer, with representations. This suggests that we must distinguish between two senses of 'representations,' which we shall call R1 and R2. R1 are simply genuine objects of experience; R2 are mental items. In the Fourth Paralogism, as we saw, the term representation is used in the sense R1; in this step, however, it is clearly used in the sense R2. The R1/R2 distinction is also crucial if we are to understand the rather puzzling remark that Kant adds at the end of the footnote to the B Preface.[36] There Kant distinguishes between the representation of something permanent and a permanent representation, and contends that although all of our representations, 'not excluding that of matter,' are 'very transitory and variable,' the referent of some of them can still be something permanent. Using our distinction, this means that if I focus on the modification of my mind engaged in the cognition of an object, then I have nothing but a series of mental states (R2); however, if I focus on the referent (R1) of these representations, then I am referring to something permanent. The fleeting nature of R2 does not rule out the permanence of R1.[37]

Thus, by exploiting his modification of the theory of inner experience, Kant reaches his goal. Since the permanent cannot be found in inner experience, it must be found in outer experience, and furthermore, it must be a thing, not a mere representation (in the sense of R2). This is in fact the conclusion that Kant presents in the next step of the proof. As he puts it: 'Thus perception of this permanent is possible only through a *thing* outside me and not through the mere *representation* of a thing outside me; and consequently the determination [of my existence] in time is necessarily bound up with the existence of actual things which I perceived outside me' (B275–6).

If we were dealing merely with a representation of a thing (R2), then the permanent, quite simply, would not be permanent. Thus, Kant thinks, the necessity of a *thing* (as opposed to a mere representation thereof) for the temporal determination of inner experience is at last grounded. The final step (step 5) merely reiterates the thesis by arguing that 'consciousness [of my existence] in time is necessarily bound up with consciousness of the [condition of the] possibility of this time-determination; and it is therefore necessarily bound up with the existence of things outside me, as the condition of the time-determination.' Note that only at this stage does Kant insert a reference to the immediacy thesis: 'The consciousness of my existence is at the same time an immediate consciousness of the existence of other things outside me.'[38]

As we have already noted, Kant in the Refutation proves the immediacy thesis, instead of presupposing it as he did in the Fourth Paralogism, and he is deeply concerned about making this feature of the new proof clear to the reader, as the footnote to Note 1 indicates.

The 'Fatal Objection' and Kant's Two Strategies to Reply

In the footnote to the Preface to the Second Edition, and more explicitly in the Reflexionen, Kant begins to deal with an objection to his argument that will ultimately prove fatal to the Refutation. The objection is very simple: Even if it is true that the consciousness of our experience requires a permanent external object, cannot this object be itself a product of the imagination? Kant is well aware of this problem. In the footnote he identifies roughly the same point as *the* objection that would likely be raised against the Refutation:'To this proof it will probably be objected that I am immediately conscious only of what is in me, that is, of my *representation* of outer things; and consequently that it must still remain uncertain whether outside me there is anything corresponding to it, or not' (Bxln).

This contention may seem to be a mere repetition of the well-known sceptical challenge – that is, you cannot know that your experience is not constituted of mere representations. However, it acquires originality here because it is now referred not generically to the reality of any external object, but specifically to that of the permanent. In fact, only if the sceptical objection challenges the reality of the permanent does it make sense to say that the objection is directed against '*this* proof' rather than against any generic defence of the immediacy of outer experience. Moreover, that this is what Kant himself identifies as the crucial problem for the Refutation is clearly reflected in the frequency with which he deals with it in the Reflexionen.[39]

As Allison has pointed out, it is possible to identify two strategies that Kant uses to rebut the objection. The first is the same unsatisfactory strategy that we criticized in our discussion of the Fourth Paralogism: although the permanent on some occasions may be a product of the imagination, it cannot *always* be so, because the very functioning of the faculty of imagination rests on the existence of outer objects, the latter being those objects which furnish the material for the former. Having acknowledged the possibility that the permanent may be a mere representation (as in dreams and delusions), Kant adds that this does not really touch the main point of the refutation: 'Such representation is merely the reproduction of previous outer perceptions, which, as has been shown, are possible only through the reality of outer objects. All that we have here sought to prove is that inner experience in general is possible only though outer experience in general' (B278–9).

He repeats the same point in the footnote to Note 1, where he explains that 'should we merely imagine an outer sense, the faculty of intuition, which is to be determined by the faculty of imagination, would be annulled' (B277n). Note that besides all of the defects we listed in the previous chapter, the appeal to this strategy creates in the present context a further problem: it makes the entire refutation superfluous. If the permanent cannot be a product of the imagination on the grounds that all products of the imagination are ultimately mere reproductions of past (real) experiences, then we could refute idealism simply by blocking the sceptic's appeal to the imagination through these kinds of considerations. The whole story of a permanent necessary for time determination would simply be otiose.

The second strategy is more interesting. It turns on the idea that if the permanent is a product of the imagination or a hallucination, its illusory character will affect the reality of inner experience to which the Cartesian sceptic is committed. Although not very clearly, Kant suggests this line of thought in the footnote to the B Preface:

> But through inner *experience* I am conscious of *my existence* in time (consequently also of its determinability in time), and this is more than to be conscious merely of my representation. It is identical with the *empirical consciousness of my existence*, which is determinable only through relation to something which, while bound up with my existence, is outside me. This consciousness of my existence in time is bound up with in the way of identity with the consciousness of a relation to something outside me, and it is therefore experience not invention, sense not imagination, which inseparably connects this outside something with my inner sense. [Bxli]

Kant's strategy here is to exploit the sceptical commitment to the reality of the experience of my existence. This strategy – in conformity with the intuition that governs the entire Refutation – amounts to showing that the sceptical commitment to the reality of inner experience implies the reality of what makes this experience possible – that is, the reality of the permanent. In other words, if inner experience is to be real, which is what the sceptic assumes, then the rules of 'experience in general' must be respected – that is, the permanent cannot simply be imagined as external, but must actually exist outside of us. Conversely, if the permanent is merely imagined, then the sceptic should accept that we merely imagine having inner experience.[40]

Whatever the logical appeal of this strategy, Kant seems to miss the force of the sceptical objection. It is in fact true that the sceptic is committed to the reality of inner experience, but the point at issue now is whether this reality can be guaranteed by something other than an external object. The sceptic holds precisely that the illusory character of the permanent does *not* entail the illusory character of inner experience. That the sceptic is correct to hold this can be shown through an example as close as possible to ordinary experience. Let us go back to the example we applied in the preceding chapter to explain Kant's criterion for distinguishing hallucination from genuine experience. The scenario, it will be recalled, is that I find myself in a dark room. Since I am terrified of the dark and thus my nervous system fails to function properly, I 'perceive' a threatening individual. Suppose that, for any possible reason, I am in the mood to wonder whether I really exist *while I am having this* 'perception.' According to the Refutation, I will experience my existence as a temporal succession of inner states determined in time through reference to an 'external' permanent. Insofar as I 'use' this 'object' as the permanent, I have what is required in order to experience the temporal succession of my inner states as determined in time – that is, inner experience. The fact that this is a genuine bit of self-experience and not an illusion will be conceded if we consider that there is no feature that distinguishes it from another bit of inner experience made possible by a genuine external object. Or at least, I fail to see why it would be defective.

Another way to make the same point is as following: Even if we accept the transcendental apparatus on which the Refutation turns, all we can assume without begging the question is that the subject 'take' this permanent as a real object – namely, as something that endures while the succession of his inner states flows. But this task can be accomplished by a mere illusion. In this scenario, we might say, the permanent would be *empirically illusory* but *transcendentally real*, in the sense that it would do its transcendental job of making inner experience possible, although at the empirical level it would be just a hallucination. More importantly, insofar as the empirically illusory permanent serves its transcendental function for temporal determination, we cannot say that I am merely imagining inner experience or that the reality of inner experience is undermined. On the contrary – I am having a genuine inner experience.

Note also that the fact that the threatening individual could be detected post facto as a hallucination according to Kant's criterion because it would sooner or later violate some empirical laws (it would, for example disappear when I turn the light on), does not change anything. In fact, the recognition that what I was 'perceiving' was a hallucination does not retrospectively render illusory the inner experience that I temporally determined by relying on it. Once again, for the entire time that I was taking that object as a spatial, abiding object, I could determine the temporal structure of inner experience. Similarly, the consideration that hallucinations usually do not last long is of no avail. To begin with, this is empirically questionable. More importantly, this consideration is completely irrelevant. In fact, the point at issue now is whether the illusory nature of hallucinations translates itself into the illusory character of inner experience and not whether hallucinations last long enough to make the temporal determination of my inner states possible. Even if we deny that this is the case, clearly we have not shown that hallucinations make our inner experience in principle something less than what the sceptic is committed to.

So is it impossible to reply to the sceptic on this crucial point? Is there not a way to salvage the proof?

Salvaging the Refutation through the Fourth Paralogism

Note that although there is no way to say that normal cases of hallucination would render illusory the bits of inner experience that I temporally determine through them, it could be argued that the sceptical counter-reply rests on much more than an appeal to normal hallucinations. The point of the sceptical objection is that inner experience could *always* be determined through an illusory permanent. Indeed, to concede that this happens only on particular occasions would be to concede that on *other* occasions the temporal determination is made through a non-illusory permanent object – that is, through a real one – which would amount to self-defeat for the sceptic. But once we realize that the sceptic must construe his objection in these universal terms, we begin to see that we are in a situation similar to the one discussed in the Fourth Paralogism. In fact, what the sceptic is really contemplating is the possibility that our *entire* experience of permanent objects is illusory.

We saw, however, that permanence is a necessary feature of any possible world that we might intuit. This is because even in a world in constant flux, we could intuit space as an abiding external framework. Since space so understood is a necessary feature of *any* external experience, at least for cognitive beings like us – the sceptic is again asking to leave the particular and finite standpoint of our experience, and is wondering whether this world that appears and will always appear with this abiding framework could be different if viewed from a standpoint that is for us systematically negated.

This result is hardly surprising, given that the claim analysed in the preceding chapter that the world could be illusory is not very different from the present claim that the permanence of the world could be so. However, the present claim has the merit of underscoring the crucial fact that the sceptic cannot doubt the reality of the permanence in the world, without also doubting the empirical reality of something (space) that – from the standpoint of transcendental idealism – functions as a necessary and therefore indubitable datum of our experience. Consequently, although the hypothesis of a permanent provided by the imagination is sufficient to show the inadequacy of the Refutation as it stands, we cannot generalize from this to the postulation of a systematic deception as to the nature of the permanent without falling back into the difficulties we have already noted in our discussion of the Fourth Paralogism.

Thus the conclusion to which we are led is that by itself, the Refutation of Idealism only shows the conditions for the temporal determination of our experience – a result, to be sure, far from trivial. In order to bear the antisceptical weight that Kant assigns to it, however, it needs to appeal to the antisceptical material contained in the First Edition's argument. Obviously, this rescue operation comes at a cost. This cost is, primarily, the acceptance of transcendental idealism. Although I am sure this will dissatisfy those who praise the Refutation precisely for its independence from transcendental idealist premises, this cost seems nonetheless inevitable.

6 The Refutation of Idealism in the Reflexionen

Kant's confrontation with the problem of idealism does not end with the Second Edition of the *Critique*. In a series of Reflexionen that Adickes titled 'Reflexionen zum Idealismus' and that date from the late 1780s to the early 1790s, Kant came back to the problem that had captured his attention since 1755. The first question posed by these Reflexionen concerns Kant's reasons for returning to a problem he considered definitively solved in the *Critique*. As we have seen, Kant thinks that the Refutation of Idealism is capable of turning the game of idealism against itself, which amounts to silencing the sceptic once and for all.[1] Moreover, he tells us that his argument is the *only* possible strict proof that the external world exists.[2] Thus one would not expect to see Kant struggling, from 1788 on, to find new antisceptical arguments, to refine and strengthen his old ones, and to reply to possible objections to the 1787 Refutation (mainly what we indicated as the 'fatal objection'). Even less would one expect Kant, in a desperate attempt to find a solution, to appeal to an argument reminiscent of the old, dogmatic refutation of the 1770 *Dissertation*. But this is precisely what Kant does in the 'Reflexionen.' Why, then, does Kant return to a problem apparently solved? And why does he do it with arguments that at times even seem to push him back towards a precritical stance? The first part of this chapter is devoted to this question.

In addition, we need to verify whether these new arguments, and refinements of the preceding ones, really manage to improve Kant's overall criticism of scepticism. This task is rendered difficult by Kant's sketchy presentation, which at times is even abruptly interrupted; but also because Kant offers arguments that are merely apparently different, even though they depend on the same basic idea. In an attempt to introduce some order to the riddle of Kant's arguments, in the second part of the chapter we shall distinguish ten different arguments and show that they can be reduced to three main lines of thought: (a) arguments meant to refine the two defensive strategies he had already used in 1787 to rebut the 'fatal objection'; (b) seemingly metaphysical arguments presented in conjunction with the idea of an 'original passivity' of the subject; and (c) arguments turning on the relation between simultaneity and succession (the former considered as a condition of possibility of recognizing the latter). In the next three parts of the chapter we shall analyse and assess of these three lines of thought. We shall see that even if apparent difficulties are removed, these arguments do not constitute any significant improvement of Kant's overall critique. This negative assessment conflicts with Guyer's interpretation, which presents the Reflexionen, specifically (c), not only as Kant's sole successful refutation of the sceptic, but also as the foundation of Kant's entire epistemology. The final section of the chapter contains my reply to this interpretation.

Kant's Reasons for a New Confrontation with the Problem of Scepticism

It is fair to assume that Kant's reasons for returning to the problem of idealism after the 1787 Refutation could have been of two different sorts: first, they may have been external, by which I mean he was replying to objections that contemporary opponents were raising against the *Critique*; and second, they may have been internal, by which I mean he was attempting to remove weaknesses inherent in the 1787 Refutation. Heidemann argues that Kant was led to the 'Reflexionen zum Idealismus' mainly for external reasons and supports this hypothesis by reconstructing the criticisms aimed at the Second Edition in general and the Refutation of Idealism in particular.

Kant's main critics in this regard included Eberhard, who since 1788 had been editing *Philosophisches Magazin* and focusing his criticism specifically on transcendental philosophy, and Schulze, who in 1972 published anonymously *Aenesidemus oder über die Fundamente der von Herrn Professor Reinhold in Jena geliefertnen Elementar-Philosophie. Nebst einer Vertheitigung des Skepticismus gegen die Anmaassungen der Vernunftkritik*. As its title indicates, this book was not directed specifically against Kant, but rather against Reinhold, who during that era was the most prominent defender of Kant's philosophy.[3]

In the very first issue of *Philosophischen Magazin*, Eberhard gives his critique of the Refutation of Idealism. He assumes that transcendental idealism is no different from the Berkeleyan variety,[4] and he accuses Kant of reducing 'reason's consciousness of the permanent in us and our individual existence to illusion.'[5] Starting from these assumptions, he concludes that Kant shows that our consciousness of the existence of external things is immediate, but that this hardly counts as a foundation of the existence of the external world because it comes from the same author who reduces even our own existence to illusion.

Clearly, Eberhard's critique is based on serious misunderstandings of Kant's philosophy in general and of the Refutation in particular. We have already discussed the differences between Kant's idealism and Berkeley's. The idea that Kant reduces our own existence (or the 'permanent in us') to illusion is probably based on the Refutation's fundamental assumption that inner sense contains only a series of representations, but 'no impression of the Self,' understood as an abiding substance. As we saw, even the intervention of an external permanent is not meant to establish the 'permanence' or 'identity of the self.' It is only meant to make possible the temporal determination of the series of representations in our consciousness. Yet it would be misleading to infer from this that Kant reduces our existence to mere illusion. Although I do not experience myself as an entity identical throughout time, I do experience the temporally determined succession of my representations. The experience of this succession involves the experience of my existence. The latter, like the former, is for Kant no illusion. Kant ridicules any form of scepticism about ourselves,[6] and furthermore, the Refutation never suggests that the identification of the consciousness of our existence with the consciousness of the succession of mental items makes that very existence dubious, let alone illusory.

Serious misunderstandings characterize Schulze's critique as well. In *Aenesidemus* he argues that the Refutation of Idealism is meant to prove the existence of things in themselves. Kant's argument would boil down to the idea that something must cause our intuitions. Given this, Schulze can easily dismiss the Refutation on the grounds that it dogmatically takes for granted what the sceptic doubts – namely, that the cause of our intuitions is a mind-independent object. Moreover, Schulze thinks that this (bad) argument is directed against Berkeley and accuses Kant of ignoring that the English bishop would agree with his point.

Clearly, Schulze's criticisms, like Eberhard's, miss their target. To begin with, Schulze accuses Kant of embracing an argument that he explicitly rejects in 1781 and that he by no means rehabilitates in 1787. In fact, while the Fourth Paralogism explicitly rejects any attempt to ground the existence of the external world through a causal argument (it sees this line of reasoning as actually opening the way for the sceptic), the Refutation does not rest in the least on an inference from our intuitions to their alleged causes. Moreover, Kant explicitly states that the Refutation is not directed against Berkeley, whose philosophy he never considers as a form of 'scepticism,' contrary to what Schulze believes. Unlike Descartes, Berkeley is always viewed by Kant as a dogmatist, not a sceptic.

Kant was certainly aware of Eberhard's and Schulze's criticisms. In a letter to Beck dated to 10 November 1792, he mentions and dismisses them as based on a misunderstanding of his theory of the ideality of space and time. Relying on this fact, Heidemann argues that Kant was pushed to go back to the problem of idealism after 1787 mainly in an effort to provide a full reply to this new generation of critics, who by and large were repeating the same interpretative mistakes as the reviewers of the First Edition.[7] If so, the 'Reflexionen zum Idealismus' are mainly a reply to these opponents.

Despite its attractiveness, Heidemann's suggestion is difficult to accept. To begin with, as he recognizes, Kant never mentions these critics by name in the 'Reflexionen.' If Kant's main concern were with them, given his tendency to attack quite violently and explicitly those who misunderstood the nature of his idealism, we would expect to find at least an oblique reference to them or an invitation to the author of *Aenesidemus* – similar to that sent to the reviewer of the First Edition – to 'step out of his incognito.'[8] More importantly, the Reflexionen deal neither with the refutation of Berkeley's idealism nor with the distinction between phenomenalism and transcendental idealism. Kant mentions Berkeley once in the Reflexionen, and this is only to clarify that he is *not* going to deal with his dogmatic idealism.[9] Yet as Heidemann well knows, the conflation of Berkeley's and Kant's idealism is the main point of Eberhard's and Schulze's critique. If they were Kant's main targets, why would he ignore Berkeley's idealism and the mistaken identification of the latter with his standpoint?

If external factors do not seem to be a strong motivation behind the Reflexionen, what did motivate this return to the problem of scepticism? A plausible hypothesis is that Kant was not confident that he had silenced the sceptic with the 1787 Refutation. Indirect evidence in favour of this hypothesis comes from his last-minute emendation to the argument contained in the footnote to the Preface to the Second Edition. The very existence of this emendation suggests that Kant was not completely satisfied with his original argument. But, more importantly, in the footnote Kant specifically attempts to improve his reply to the 'fatal objection.' Since the Reflexionen are mainly characterized by the same attempt, they can plausibly be seen as a continuation of the refinements inaugurated in the footnote. Thus internal factors, rather than external ones, seem to have been the basis of Kant's return to the problem of scepticism.

The Antisceptical Arguments in the Reflexionen: An Overview

It is possible to identify a considerable number of arguments that Kant sketches in the 'Reflexionen zum Idealismus.' Sometimes they differ among themselves only in some detail. Other times they arise from a completely different intuition. A tentative list follows:

I   All objects of our experience are representations, but those of outer sense (permanent objects) are necessary for the temporal determination of those of inner sense. (Ak. 18: 614–15, 31–2/1–9)

II External objects cannot be systematically products of the imagination because the material that the imagination uses for its play ultimately comes from the perception of external objects. (Ak. 18: 309, 31–4; 310, 24–8; 332, 10–22; 613, 26–31; 619, 1–5)

III If the permanent, necessary for the temporal determination of self-knowledge, is a product of the imagination, and thus an illusion, then self-knowledge itself becomes illusory. But the sceptic is committed to the reality of self-knowledge. Therefore, the sceptic must concede the existence of non-illusory permanent external objects. (Ak. 18: 308, 25–9)

IV The intuition of things other than me presupposes the consciousness of the determinability of me by things other than me (original passivity). It is impossible to be conscious of things other than me without being truly passive (as opposed to merely imagining to be so). (Ak. 18: 307, 13–24; 312, 9–18)

V   The empirical consciousness of our existence must be given at the same time as (or presupposes) the intellectual consciousness (or intellectual intuition) of things outside me.[10] (Ak. 18: 306, 11–25)

VI The permanent cannot be systematically a product of the imagination. If this were so, the permanent would be a representation – that is, a mental entity – which, as such, would be one of the succeeding items in my consciousness and therefore could not play the role of the permanent. (Ak. 18: 308, 5–11; 313, 18–21; 612, 6–13; 615, 10–14)

VII There is a distinction between pure (or transcendental) and empirical self-consciousness; the former is a consciousness that is independent of knowledge of external things, whereas the latter requires an external permanent that is to be found in external knowledge.[11] (Ak. 18: 306, 11–17; 615, 15–24)

VIII Radical heterogeneity of inner sense and outer sense: I can neither represent time outside me nor space inside me; therefore, if I had no outer sense, I could not represent space and therefore permanence, which is, however, necessary for determining the temporal dimension of inner experience. (Ak. 18: 310, 1–6; 313, 11–17; 612–3, 23–9/1–2, 613, 9–16; 618, 14–21; 620–1, 21–31/1–4)

IX The condition of the possibility of experiencing simultaneity is the ability to go forwards and backwards in the apprehension of the manifold. This is possible only with an external abiding object, not with a mere representation. But the experience of simultaneity is necessary for the experience of succession (specifically, for the experience of the succession of our representations). Therefore, there must be external abiding objects. (Ak. 18: 614, 12–30; 615, 24–31; 616, 4–12)

X It is possible to transform a product of the imagination (such as a hallucination) into an object of inner sense (that is, it is possible to realize that it is a mere product of the imagination and not a genuine object), while it is not possible to make a spatial object into an object of inner sense, because this would mean to represent space as time – that is, in one dimension – which is contradictory. Therefore, real objects and mere products of the imagination are distinguishable. (Ak. 18: 611–12, 20–9/1–4)

As noted earlier, we can organize these various arguments into three main groups: (a) those which resolve around the main idea of the 1787 Refutation and attempt to deal with some of its weaknesses – specifically, the possibility that the permanent can be a product of the imagination (I, II, III, VI, VII, VIII, X); (b) the idea of the original passivity of the subject (IV), presented in conjunction with the problematic assumption of an intellectual intuition of things other than ourselves (V); and

(c) an argument that turns on the condition of possibility of recognizing simultaneity (IX). Let us analyse each of these.

Defending the Refutation from the 'Fatal Objection'

Given that we have already discussed the two defensive strategies that Kant adopts against the 'fatal objection,' our analysis of the first group can be rather short. Arguments I and II are merely repetitions of these two strategies. Note, however, that, compared to the formulations in the *Critique*, they are expressed more clearly as well as distinguished more clearly from each other. In R5709, Kant writes: 'Without an outer sense, whose representations we repeat only and combine in other manners (as it happens also with inner sense when we fantasize), there would be no dreams at all.'[12]

The significance of this passage lies in the fact that Kant clarifies that he is not denying the imagination's ability to *combine* representations in such a way as to produce images of things never before seen. His argument is not that for any representation, there must be a corresponding object that we have experienced (though in fact he does at times contend this).[13] If this were his argument, the example of the representation of a golden mountain that arises from the combination of previously experienced mountains and golden things would be sufficient to refute him. The point is, rather, that the imagination cannot produce something whose constituting elements had not previously been intuited by one of the senses. Since inner sense has no intuition of anything permanent, the imagination must ultimately borrow it from outer sense.

To be sure, despite these important qualifications, the first defensive strategy is still unsatisfactory. As we noted in the preceding chapter, the possibility remains that the representation of the permanent may be the product of some unknown faculty. In that case, the fact that we have no intuition of something permanent in our inner sense and therefore that we could not have produced permanence through the imagination would obviously be insufficient to conclude that we must have experienced genuine permanent objects through outer sense. The representation of permanent objects could simply be the product of this unknown faculty.

As we have seen, already in 1787 Kant has an alternative strategy against the 'fatal objection.' This strategy is also to be found in the Reflexionen, and is perhaps more clearly expressed there than in the

Critique. In Reflexion 5653 he writes: 'The fact is: the empirical consciousness of my existence in time is necessarily bound up with the empirical consciousness of a relation to something outside us and *the former is so little an illusion ... as the latter.*'[14]

While the formulation of the same strategy in the *Critique* insisted that the reality of my inner experience requires the reality of the permanent ('but through inner *experience* I am conscious of *my existence* in time (consequently also of its determinability in time), and this is more than to be conscious merely of my representation'[15]), this formulation has the virtue of letting the true core of the argument emerge – namely, that the *cost* of reducing the permanent to a mere representation (that is, to an illusion) is that of reducing inner experience to something equally illusory ('the former is so little an illusion ... as the latter'). Obviously, at bottom this is precisely the same idea as in the *Critique*. If anything, it is more clearly formulated. Despite its merits, however, this formulation does not remove the difficulties we have already encountered. It is still unclear *why* the fact that the permanent is an illusion makes inner experience an illusion as well.

Another attempt to reply to the 'fatal objection' is argument X. In a very obscure passage Kant denies with the following reasoning that the permanent can be (systematically) a product of the imagination:

> If one wanted to say that also the representation of the permanent given through outer sense is merely a perception given through inner sense that is represented as given through outer sense only through the imagination, it should be possible in general (although not for us) to be conscious of it as belonging to inner sense. But then the representation of space would be transformed into one of time, that is, it would be possible to represent space as time (in one dimension), which is self-contradictory.[16]

It is difficult to understand what Kant means by 'it should be possible in general (although not for us) to be conscious of it as belonging to inner sense.' Perhaps he has in mind the following: if I entertain in my mind a representation produced by the imagination, then I can always become (at least in principle, or 'in general,' as Kant puts it) conscious of this representation as belonging to inner sense. For example, when I imagine my parents' house, I certainly imagine a spatial content, and I can even almost see it as in front of me (depending on the vividness of my memory). But I can always realize that this is merely a mental item with a spatial content, as opposed to an object that occupies a place outside me. The possibility of placing this imagined external object back in my mind introduces an irreducible phenomenological difference between the perception of a real object outside me and the mere imagination of it. A genuine external object 'resists' this placing of itself in the mind. To contend that one can place an external object in the mind means to assume that we can represent space as time – that is, something three-dimensional as one-dimensional – which Kant takes as patently absurd.

As the last sentence of the passage makes clear, the core of the argument, on this interpretation, is Kant's familiar claim that space and time have heterogeneous and irreducible contents. As such it stands in an interesting connection to argument VI, which centres on the idea that if the permanent were a mere mental item, it would be one of the succeeding items in my consciousness and therefore could not play the role of the permanent. The arguments are similar in that both rest on a denial of the possibility that a representation ultimately belonging to inner sense could play the role of the permanent. They are different because while VI simply affirms (or assumes) that images of external objects cannot play the role of the permanent because they are ultimately mental entities, the present argument, on my interpretation, at least gives us a hint as to why this is so. The reference to the possibility of becoming aware of products of the imagination as mere mental entities and therefore to the irreducible phenomenological difference between products of the imagination and genuine external objects is precisely such a hint.[17]

Obviously, this does not mean that the argument is satisfactory. It is questionable whether products of the imagination such as hallucinations are truly phenomenologically different from genuine objects, or that we can always 'uncover' them as mere objects of inner sense; more importantly, Kant is again simply ignoring the possibility that 'genuine' external objects phenomenologically different from the products of the imagination may be given by some unknown faculty or an Evil Genius. In that case, the phenomenological difference to which Kant is appealing would still be respected, but would be insufficient to yield the desired result.

Let us move to the two remaining groups of arguments.

The Original Passivity: A Metaphysical Argument?

Scattered throughout the Reflexionen is a line of argument that seems to be both clearly incompatible with the limitations that transcendental idealism places on our knowledge as well as reminiscent of the metaphysical argument of the 1770 *Dissertation*. In Reflexion 5653, Kant replies as follows to the claim made by 'material idealism' that only the consciousness of our existence is immediate:

> Against this argument it is sufficient to notice that the transcendental consciousness of ourselves, which accompanies the spontaneity of all our intellectual acts, but consists of the mere 'I' without the determination of my existence in time, is certainly immediate, but the empirical consciousness of myself, which amounts to [*ausmacht*] inner sense (as the former [amounts] to the form of the intellectual character of my subjectivity), by no means takes place immediately; and that the consciousness of things other than myself (which must be also presupposed as intellectual and, insofar as it is not a representation of them in space, can be called intellectual intuition, through which we have no knowledge of things) and the determination of their existence in space must be [given] at the same time with the determination of my existence in time; thus, I [am conscious of] my own empirically determined existence no more than that of the things (which I do not know how they are in themselves).[18]

In another passage he wonders how the consciousness of a representation, which is a passive determination (a mental entity) and therefore presents no permanence, can be a representation of something permanent. The answer he gives is as astonishing as the preceding passage:

> Here it must be noted only that the object, which, however, is only in the understanding, means something distinct from the representation; therefore, inner sense itself, which makes ourselves objects of our representations, relates to something distinct from ourselves (as transcendental object of apperception). Thus, if we did not refer the representations to something distinct from us, they would never deliver knowledge; for, as far as inner sense is concerned, it consists only of the relation of the representations to the subject, whether or not they mean anything.[19]

In both passages Kant seems to be appealing problematically to what is beyond appearances in order to refute the sceptic. In the first passage, the consciousness of things other than me is characterized as an 'intellectual consciousness' and even as an 'intellectual intuition.'[20] Clearly, the object of an intellectual intuition is not an appearance. Also, in the second passage we find that the object to which our representations necessarily refer is the equivalent in outer knowledge to the 'transcendental object of apperception.' Moreover, it is 'only in the understanding.' Thus the permanent that is supposed to make the temporal determination of our inner knowledge possible is not an empirical object but the 'transcendental object.' Kant seems to be claiming roughly the same thing when he affirms in Reflexion 6312 that '[the permanent] must lie either in what is simultaneous, or in the intelligible, which contains the ground of appearances.'[21]

Taken in isolation, these passages are clearly incompatible with the limitations that transcendental idealism imposes on our knowledge. To begin with, Kant repeatedly denies that we have an intellectual intuition. The essence of his position, as we saw in chapter 2, is that our intuition is necessarily bound to sensible forms (space and time). On this idea rests the entire distinction between appearances and things in themselves. To be sure, Kant also says in this passage that an intellectual intuition yields no knowledge of the intuited things. Nonetheless, this intellectual intuition is the vehicle through which we are supposed to acquire the consciousness of things other than ourselves, which in turn is what supposedly refutes the sceptic. Moreover, in the second passage Kant relies on the idea of the necessary reference of our representations (which he clearly identifies with mental entities) to an object that remains beyond them. In fact, the core of his argument is that both inner sense and outer sense entertain only representations, but both refer to an 'object' (transcendental subject or transcendental object) distinct from them. Although he does not formulate this argument in causal terms, the fact that he relies on the transcendental object in order to refute scepticism makes this argument strikingly similar to the dogmatic argument of the *Dissertation*, which, we shall recall, turned on the idea that our representations (mental entities) are caused by extra-sensible objects.

However, both the impression that Kant has violated his own most fundamental epistemological tenets and the impression of a straightforward return to a dogmatic refutation of scepticism can be, if not removed, at least strongly mitigated if we heed the context in which these puzzling passages appear. This context is the idea of the 'original passivity' of the subject, which Kant presents as follows:

> The intuition of a thing other than me presupposes the consciousness of a determinability of my subject through a factor other than myself, and that,

therefore, does not belong to spontaneity, because the determining factor is not in me. And in fact I cannot think any space in me. Thus, the possibility of representing things in space through an intuition rests on the consciousness of a determination, of which I am not responsible at all, through other things, which means nothing but my original passivity [...] To receive a representation of something other than myself originally, without being really [*in der That*] passive, is impossible.²²

In other words, without the consciousness of being a passive entity, determinable through something other than my spontaneous thinking, I would not be able to represent something other than myself. Kant is appealing to the consciousness that each of us has of our determinability by things other than ourselves. To this he rather dogmatically adds that if we were not 'really' passive – as opposed to imagined to be so – we would never be able to represent something outer.

The crucial feature in this line of argument, independently of its strength, is the conceptual framework within which Kant is operating. He is assuming determinable subjects and determining objects other than the subjects *before the determination or affection takes place*. Given this framework, the object (other than ourselves) that does the determining cannot be described as an empirical object. In fact, the thought of an object *before* it affects our sensibility is the thought of it as transcendental object. It cannot be an empirical object because the very idea of the subject's determinability imposes the thought of a determining object *before* the determination. Thus it is quite natural that such an object 'is only in the understanding,' and even that the intuition thereof is not a sensible one. It follows that when Kant characterizes this intuition as intellectual, he is not violating one of the most fundamental tenets of his epistemology. Rather, he is respecting the conceptual setting that the idea of an 'original passivity' or 'determinability' imposes. In fact, the introduction of the problematic notion of intellectual intuition is immediately counterbalanced by the reminder that through it we have no knowledge of things.

This may remove the impression of a straightforward violation of Kant's own epistemological rules; yet it also seems to point to the weakness of the argument. In his attempt to refute the sceptic, Kant seems be to appealing to the existence of an object about which, by his own admission, we know nothing. The present argument would thus face the same problems as the 1770 argument. But even this reading would not do justice to Kant's intentions. Unlike the argument of the *Dissertation*, the present antisceptical strategy does not point to a non-sensible object as the object whose existence is supposed to refute the sceptic. Kant, rather, is focusing on the phenomenological fact that we are not completely active or spontaneous beings. His point is that we immediately take ourselves as passive – that is, as determinable by things other than ourselves. We confront the brute datum of an exteriority that affects us, and there is no way that we can reinterpret this exteriority as something that 'belongs to us.' This is why he inserts the reference to the impossibility of representing any space in us as a confirmation of the main idea of our original passivity ('And in fact I cannot think any space in me.').

To be sure, Kant realizes that in the case of dreams (and hallucinations) we merely seem to be determined by other things; but the representations with which we occupy our minds are actually products of self-affection. His reply to this obvious retort turns on the familiar idea that all of these illusions presuppose genuine outer representations. Thus the 'original passivity' argument ultimately implodes into argument I and suffers the same difficulties. Yet, Kant's argument, although invalid, is at least not as dogmatic or as metaphysical as it appears.

Moreover, and this is crucial for the validity of the historical reconstruction I have suggested, he is not contradicting the direction – from dogmatism to criticism – that we have indicated is key to the development of his antisceptical strategy from the 1770 *Dissertation* to the critical period. That Kant did not abandon this crucial insight is also confirmed by a passage in which he reaffirms the Fourth Paralogism's warning against the temptation to let the refutation of the sceptic rest on a reference to things in themselves. In this passage he contends: 'If we take our knowledge as knowledge of things in themselves, we will never be able to ground the existence of the external world, because we will always be bound to an invalid inference from the effect (our representations) to their cause (things in themselves).'[23]

Finally, note that our interpretation helps remove the mystery of the very coexistence of the passage just quoted and of argument IV within the 'Reflexionen.' In fact, without the mitigation of the dogmatic import of IV it would be impossible not to charge Kant with sheer inconsistency for claiming that we must rely on the object of an intellectual intuition in order to refute the sceptic and that we would never be able to prove the reality of outer things 'if our knowledge of outer objects is supposed to be a knowledge of them (and of space) as things in themselves.'[24]

Simultaneity and Succession

In Reflexionen 6313 to 6315, Kant introduces the familiar idea of the 1787 Refutation that a permanent is required for the temporal determination of inner experience, but with an interesting variation. He now interprets the permanent as what allows the experience of simultaneity, which in turn he considers necessary for the experience of the succession of our mental items. In the passage that perhaps most clearly expresses this line of thought, he writes: 'The simultaneity of A and B cannot be represented without a permanent. For all apprehension is actually successive. For the succession to go not only forward from A to B, but also backward from B to A, it is necessary that A endure. The sensible representations A and B must have a ground other than inner sense, but still in some sense, and therefore in outer sense. Therefore, there must be objects of outer sense.'[25]

Kant's point here is rather simple. Since a condition of possibility of the representation of simultaneity is that I can go backwards and forwards in the apprehension of the simultaneous items, they all must pertain to an *abiding* object or state of affairs. Therefore, simultaneity cannot be represented without a permanent. The interpretation of the permanent in terms of 'what is simultaneous' allows Kant to confront what we have called the 'fatal objection' in a new manner – namely, by focusing on the conditions of the possibility of experiencing simultaneity. In order to experience simultaneity, it must be possible to go forwards and backwards in the apprehension of the manifold. Now, this is possible only with a genuine abiding object, not with a representation of inner sense. In fact, in inner sense I have only the one directional succession of mental items, none of which endures. Given that inner sense is unable to represent simultaneity, we must 'look without' for some external abiding object that makes possible the experience of simultaneity and thus the temporal determination of my inner experience.

Although the idea that it must be necessary to go backwards and forwards for the experience of simultaneity clarifies as much as we could hope why the succession of the items in inner sense cannot contain the permanent object necessary for the temporal determination of the same succession, it is doubtful whether it really helps us see why a product of the imagination could not allow this 'going forward and backward.' Unless Kant explains that there is some phenomenological difference between a product of the imagination and a genuine external object, it is difficult to see why I could not go backwards and forwards in the apprehension of the various parts of a merely imagined external object, say a table. Thus it seems that all this argument does is spell out the necessary condition for the experience of simultaneity, which makes it very clear that we require the experience of something different from the items of inner sense. A different question, however, is whether it succeeds in showing that a product of the imagination could not meet such condition as well as a genuine object.

To be sure, Kant is well aware of this problem, and in an important passage he attempts to rule out just this possibility:

> Since the imagination (and its product) is itself only an object of inner sense, the empirical consciousness (*apprehentio*) of this condition can contain only succession. But this itself cannot be represented except by means of something that endures, with which that which is successive is simultaneous. This enduring thing, with which that which is successive is simultaneous, that is, space, cannot in turn be a representation of the mere imagination but must be a representation of sense, for otherwise that which lasts would not be in the sensibility at all.[26]

Kant points out that a product of the imagination is nothing but an object of inner sense. As such, it will be apprehended in our consciousness as a series of temporally successive items. But in order to represent these items, we need 'something that endures' that will be experienced simultaneously with the succession of the states of this product of the imagination ('with which that which is successive is simultaneous'). In turn, this 'something that endures' cannot be itself a product of the imagination. If this were so, it would be apprehended as a series of successive items and it could not play its role. And for Kant this is what rebuts the 'fatal objection.'

Clearly, the crucial step of the entire argument is the first, in which Kant reduces a product of the imagination to a fleeting series of mental items (an object of inner sense). This permits the denial that such a product could present itself as a permanent object. But this crucial step amounts to a sheer assertion that begs the whole question. In fact, that a product of the imagination (or a hallucination) appears to us as distinguishable from a genuine external object is just the point at stake. On what grounds does Kant affirm that the various features of the hallucinated or imagined object endure less (or do not endure at all) than the features of a genuine object? As far I can see, Kant offers no help in answering this question.

Guyer's 'Central Argument'

This negative assessment of the strength of the present argument conflicts with Guyer's interpretation, which finds in the above-quoted passage not only Kant's sole successful attempt to deal with the weaknesses of the published version of the Refutation, but also the true foundation of Kant's entire epistemology. In order to appreciate this point, it is necessary to sketch the basic features of Guyer's interpretation and then verify whether the passage in question is able to bear the philosophical significance that Guyer places on it.

Following Strawson's tradition, although starting from rather different assumptions, Guyer contends that the Refutation of Idealism, far from being merely an ad hominem criticism of Cartesian scepticism, is the real solution to the central problem of the *Critique*. This is so because, if we show that external objects are necessary for the time-determination of inner states – which the sceptic assumes we know with absolute certainty – then *at once* we prove the existence of the external world and show that the rules and principles necessary for the time-determination (categories and analogies) of any kind of succession, even the merely subjective succession of inner states, are likewise indubitable. In fact, Guyer believes that among the various tactics Kant uses in the Transcendental Deduction of the categories, the only successful one is the one that refers to the crucial role of the categories for time-determination. The Refutation of Idealism is thus the completion of Kant's transcendental theory of experience, which for Guyer is nothing but the identification and justification of the conditions on which it is possible to determine the temporal structure of our cognition. The fact that Kant never said that the Refutation plays this crucial role, even for the destiny of the Transcendental Deduction, is explained by Kant's 'natural attachment to the architectonic he had finally created, particularly to the idea of a direct inference from *a priori* certainty of apperception to its transcendental ground.'[27] Moreover, Guyer thinks that the published version of the Refutation fails to fulfil this crucial mission and that it is only in these Reflexionen – particularly in the passage we are considering – that the final solution is to be found.

Leaving aside any comment on Guyer's reconstruction of the Transcendental Deduction and on the alleged necessity for it to refer to time-determination, let us consider again the passage in question and see how Guyer argues for the existence in it of such an essential line of thought. According to Guyer, Kant assumes that the mere happening of a succession of representations in our consciousness is insufficient for the recognition of such a succession. There is no problem here. In fact, we would think this is why a permanent is needed. But this is not what Guyer has in mind. He states: 'Kant's further claim that such recognition can be grounded "only on something which endures, with which that which is successive is simultaneous" can then mean only that successive representations in one's own experience can be judged to be successive only if they are judged to be severally simultaneous with the severally successive states of some enduring object.'[28]

In other words Kant, according to Guyer, is not rephrasing the familiar claim that what endures (the permanent) must be given simultaneously with what is successive (the mental items in my consciousness), if the temporal determination of this succession is to be possible. Rather, Kant would have in mind something much more sophisticated. In order to judge two items in my consciousness to be successive (as opposed to simultaneous) I must relate them to the two successive objective facts that cause them. For example, I can tell the difference between scenario 1, in which representation A occurs before representation B in my consciousness (I now perceive B and remember having perceived A), and scenario 2, in which representation A and representation B occur simultaneously in my consciousness (I now perceive A and B as simultaneous parts of a complex representation AB), only if I correlate A and B to respectively successive or simultaneous objective states. Thus, by knowing that the object causing B entered my perceptual field only after the object that caused A, I know that scenario 1 is the correct description of what happens in my consciousness, whereas by knowing that the two objects are objectively simultaneous, I know that scenario 2 is the correct one.[29] Without this reference to the objective state of affairs, I could not decide between 1 and 2 because the order of the succession of my mental items is not something that is immediately grasped by the mind.

This is, for Guyer, the deep meaning of the crucial passage at A99 where Kant affirms that intuition certainly gives us a manifold, but such a manifold can be represented 'only insofar as the mind distinguishes the time in the sequence of one impression upon another.' The order of the representations in my consciousness (the order of the apprehension of the manifold) is thus not immediately given, but rather must be determined. For Guyer, it can be determined only by referring to the objective state of affairs that caused it. Inner experience, understood as a time-determined succession of subjective representations, is possible only under the condition of the existence of a simultaneous succession of objective states that caused the representations. This would be the 'central argument' of the Refutation and – insofar as it completes Kant's account of the conditions for time-determination in general – it is also the central argument of the critical epistemology.

Leaving aside whether Guyer is correct in his interpretation of A99 – where Kant clearly indicates that what is needed for the apprehension of the manifold is a synthesis of apprehension and not the relating of the items of the manifold to the objective states that caused them – it is not clear why the words 'the enduring object, with which all that is successive is simultaneous' can be interpreted 'only' in Guyer's manner. Actually, there is no indication that the relation between 'the enduring object and 'what is successive' must be understood in the manner suggested – that is, as a correlation between objective and subjective states where the former cause the latter. In fact, there are at least three good reasons to believe that this is *not* the way in which the relation should be taken.

To begin with, on Guyer's interpretation the permanent becomes something that constantly changes; it follows that the role Kant assigns to it is completely lost. Kant repeatedly instructs us that the permanent stands as something which does not change throughout the succession of subjective representations, and which, precisely because it does not, makes the experience of the succession possible. But on Guyer's reading, the permanent is as fleeting as the succession of our representations.

Moreover, it seems that the constraints the objective order is supposed to place on the order of our mental items could be placed by some sort of Evil Genius equally well, especially if the relation between the constraining object and the order of our representations is interpreted causally. It seems that I could distinguish between scenarios 1 and 2 even if the objective states causing my mental states were merely imagined.

Finally, from a linguistic standpoint, the phrase that in German reads 'das Beharrliche, womit jenes successive [das empirische Bewusstsein] zugleich ist' does not support Guyer's interpretation. If we keep the adverbial sense of 'zugleich' (which is indeed an adverb and not an adjective), the sentence seems to contain nothing more than Kant's usual and familiar claim that in order to represent succession, I must represent the permanent at the same time as the succession itself. As such, the Reflexion seems incapable of supporting the philosophical weight that Guyer places on it. Kant's present argument, which turns on the relation between succession and simultaneity does not constitute a substantial divergence from the main idea of the Refutation, and as such it shares the Refutation's inability to be a convincing reply to the sceptic.

The Reflexion 'Vom inneren Sinne'

The final text relevant for our purposes, and probably the last text that Kant devoted to the problem of idealism (if one abstracts from very brief and oblique passages in the *Opus Postumum*), is a recently discovered Reflexion entitled 'Vom inneren Sinne.'[30] The argumentative strategies that we have already noted in the 'Reflexionene zum Idealismus' are here represented, and this text appears as a sort of summary of the various antisceptical arguments of Kant's late thought. As Heidemann has rightly pointed out, this Reflexion must have been composed later than the 'Reflexionen zum Idealismus' precisely because it contains all the arguments that we can find in them and serves as a sort of summary of Kant's attempts to silence the sceptic. And since the 'Reflexionen zum Idealismus' are dated roughly from 1787 to 1793, this text can reasonably be dated around the middle or end of the 1790s.[31]

Besides representing well-known antisceptical arguments – the 1787 Refutation of Idealism (I), the original passivity of the subject (IV), the condition of possibility of the experience of simultaneity (IX), and, especially, the radical heterogeneity of the contents of inner and outer sense (VIII) – Kant seems to be insisting on a theme that was only sketched in the 'Reflexionen zum Idealismus.' This theme goes back to the modified theory of inner sense as presented in the Second Edition of the *Critique*. Recall that according to this modified theory, inner sense has no manifold of its own, as Kant held in 1781; rather, it owes its material to outer sense. In other words, the contents of inner sense are nothing but the representations of outer sense reinterpreted by the mind no longer as representations of external objects, but as modifications of the mind itself. The novelty now is that Kant uses this modified theory as an independent antisceptical argument. Thus, in the context of the usual distinction between intellectual self-consciousness and empirical self-experience, Kant is contending that 'in inner experience [...], which I posit, I affect myself by bringing the representations of outer sense in an empirical consciousness of my state.'[32] Then a few lines later he adds:

> Only the (synthetic) apprehension of these representations [of outer sense] is bound up with the consciousness of the state of my representations in

time whose representation is merely the subjective form of my sensibility, the way I appear to myself in inner sense.

And even more explicitly, towards the end of the Reflexion, he notes:

> That we can affect ourselves (something that certainly must be assumed if at least one sense in general is to exist) is only possible insofar as we apprehend the representations of things that affect us, that is, of outer things, for in such a way we affect ourselves and the time is actually the form of the apprehension of the representation that concerns something outside us.

Note the importance of the parenthetic sentence. In it one finds what the sceptic must concede – namely, the existence and certainty of at least one sense, in this case, inner sense. In other words, the sceptic must concede that we are affected at least by ourselves in inner sense, and thus the question is, 'What are the causal factors of this affection?' Given Kant's modified theory, these are simply the representations of outer objects whose existence is thus necessary (so thinks Kant) for the very possibility of self-affection, which in turn is necessary for inner experience.

This line of thought has found some support in Heidemann's *Kant und das Problem des metaphysischen Idealismus*, which constitutes the most recent and perhaps most complete account of our subject in the literature. Heidemann points out that all Kantian arguments seem to presuppose the genuine existence of something given to outer sense; for this reason they seem viciously circular. For example, the 1787 Refutation of Idealism ultimately presupposes the reality of the permanent object necessary for the temporal determination of inner experience. As we have seen, similar considerations could be applied to the other arguments we have so far listed. However, continues Heidemann, against this charge of circularity Kant can and does argue as follows: 'On the basis of the critical determination of the relation between inner and outer sense he simply notices that the contents of our representations cannot be produced either from the thinking "I" or from inner sense, but – as the Postulate of Actuality posits – they must arise from outer sense.'[33]

Heidemann seems to treat this as an indisputable fact on which Kant can easily rely for his refutation. According to him, it is impossible to wonder within a Kantian framework about the 'true' origin of the contents of our representations 'because the objects of our knowledge are given to us through sensibility.' This rules out any 'a priori deduction' – by which Heidemann seems to mean a reduction to something else – of these sensible contents. In other words, one cannot doubt about the true origin of these contents, which we experience as coming from outer sense and which are then reconceptualized by the mind into the contents of self-knowledge. Even the transcendental realist must concede this point in that he is equally committed to the 'givenness' of the objects of our experience. And his sceptical ally, the empirical idealist, can refuse it only through his 'ungrounded metaphysical conception.'[34]

Unfortunately, it is far from obvious that Kant can appeal to this fundamental tenet of this epistemology to refute the sceptic. Although Heidemann is certainly correct that Kant places much emphasis on the radical heterogeneity of the contents of inner and outer sense and that, starting with the Second Edition he more or less explicitly views outer sense as the source of *all* the material of our knowledge, one might raise a number of objections regarding Kant's ability to mount a convincing refutation of the Cartesian sceptic on this basis. To begin with, while the new view of the relation between inner and outer sense is in itself a legitimate epistemological opinion, it becomes a mere *petitio principii* if it is used to remove doubts about the existence of the external world. After all, these doubts turn on the possibility that inner sense, or the imagination, is capable of providing all the material of our knowledge in such a way that what we think comes from external objects is actually a product of the imagination or the trick of some Evil Genius. If this is the challenge, it is question-begging to state merely that all the material of our knowledge comes from outer sense. Moreover, even if we leave aside this consideration, it is undeniable – as the literature on the Refutation has largely recognized and as we have already repeatedly noted – that on this reconstruction, Kant's refutation of the sceptic would rest on bold assumptions about the limits of our imaginative power or, even worse, on a failure to take seriously Descartes's idea that we could have an unknown faculty that could be the true origin of those contents which we usually assign to outer sense. Thus, even this last antisceptical strategy shares the failure of those already considered in the 'Reflexionen zum Idealismus,' and despite its historical interest, the Reflexion 'Vom inneren Sinne' fails to constitute a significant theoretical improvement on Kant's tactic against the sceptic.

Conclusion

In the preceding pages I have offered a reconstruction of the development of Kant's antisceptical arguments that challenges the mainstream reading on this topic in Kant's philosophy. I find this reading both incomplete and inaccurate. It is incomplete because scant attention has been paid to Kant's precritical confrontation with scepticism, even though it is so crucial not only for the completeness of any account of his confrontation with scepticism, but also and more importantly for the avoidance of profound and still widespread mistakes in the interpretation of the *Critique of Pure Reason* as a whole. And it is *inaccurate* because the same mistakes, which turn on the persistent conflation between Kant's idealism and phenomenalism, make it impossible to appreciate the antisceptical potential of the Fourth Paralogism in the A Edition. This text has long been dismissed as a dubious attempt to refute Descartes's scepticism as to the existence of external objects by reducing the latter to mental entities. Properly interpreted, however, the Fourth Paralogism is both a powerful antisceptical argument and, quite surprisingly, the ultimate expression of the empirical realism that constitutes the foundation of Kant's mature philosophy.

This book should at least have made it clear that once the phenomenalistic reading is abandoned, it is possible to find in the Fourth Paralogism the material for an antisceptical argument that deserves our attention. Since this argument depends on transcendental idealism, I could not have rehabilitated the Fourth Paralogism without defending this philosophical standpoint, at least as far as its *nature* is concerned. Although my defence certainly does not count as an exhaustive treatment of this enormous issue – the foundation of transcendental idealism has been arbitrarily limited to the Aesthetic, and even on that more should be said – I believe that I have made the case for an assessment of Kant's idealism more favourable than the one usually offered. We have seen that once transcendental idealism is brought into the picture, scepticism loses the ground on which it stands. Its cherished thesis that outer perception is mediated is readily contradicted. Since space is a form of outer sense – not a feature that must be 'picked up' from experience – any object other than me affecting my sensibility is immediately placed in space. At the same time, the question as to the 'real' ingredients of the world *beyond the way in which this world appears to us* (whether ordinary things or the ideas instilled in our mind by an Evil Genius) becomes absurd because it violates the limits that transcendental idealism places on the questions we can legitimately raise.

A final word on the nature of the antisceptical argument I have advocated in this study: This argument rests on the combination of two points – the immediacy thesis and the identification of Descartes's hypothesis that the world is the product of an Evil Genius with a vain enquiry into the nature of the thing in itself. While the first thesis removes an obstacle that would make any refutation impossible – if our experience is primarily about mental entities, the sceptic can always raise doubts about the correspondence of those to real objects; the second thesis builds on this result by ruling out the possibility that the world we immediately see is a hallucination. It does so by noting that even to entertain the thought of our experience as entirely hallucinatory, we would have to go behind the world of experience and think of some unknown X that is different from what appears to us, be it an Evil Genius or some other philosophical fantasy. This is the link between the sceptical hypothesis and an inquiry into the nature of the thing in itself.

This link provides the crux of the entire argument. Once this is recognized, the transcendental idealist can easily dismiss the sceptic's challenge. When this identification is not made explicit, however, the transcendental idealist seems as vulnerable to scepticism as anyone else, even if the immediacy thesis is conceded. In fact, Kant clearly recognizes the reality of hallucinations, and it is not clear in what sense hallucinations could be considered less 'immediate' than genuine perceptions, so it would seem that the possibility that the world is one 'big' hallucination still threatens the transcendental idealist. In order to rule out that possibility, the anti-metaphysical resources of transcendental idealism must be brought into play.

I am aware that precisely because of its reliance on transcendental idealism, this argument is open to criticism by those who view this doctrine unfavourably. Since presumably many of them are not sceptics, however, I think it is fair to place on them the burden of finding a successful refutation of scepticism that is independent of transcendental idealism. In this book, I have analysed some attempts of this sort, and they have all ended up being either ineffective (Guyer's, but also Kant's own 1787 argument), or rather obscure (Reid's), or dependent on hidden assumptions (Putnam's), or they have strengthened the impression that empirical realism and scepticism are on the same footing or even capable of furthering the sceptic's cause (Carnap's). As long as a refutation of this sort is not found, I am tempted to take seriously Kant's characterization of transcendental idealism as 'the only refuge.' I am also tempted to interpret the failure of those refutations of scepticism which operate, more or less consciously, within a transcendentally realistic perspective as indirect evidence *in favour of* transcendental idealism. As a matter of fact, the entire Fourth Paralogism, with its insistence that transcendental idealism is 'the only refuge,' can be viewed as an indirect foundation of that doctrine, to be added to the foundations of the Aesthetic and the Dialectic. I do not know whether this was Kant's intention, but I think that the possibility of appreciating the Fourth Paralogism in this way is both plausible and fascinating.

Notes

(Author's note: Kant's works are usually cited from the most appropriate English translation. If one is not available or if it is useful to give reference to the original German, I quote from Kant, *Gesammette Schriften*, cited as Ak. with volume and page number.)

Introduction

1 Hilary Putnam, *Reason, Truth, and History*, 1–22.
2 Barry Stroud, *The Significance of Philosophical Scepticism*.
3 The only exception is Hoyos Jaramillo (*Kant und die Idealismusfrage*, 94–110), who, however, pays scant attention to the Lectures on Metaphysics, which, as I will show, constitute a crucial part of this reconstruction.
4 This is the position of Kemp Smith (see *A Commentary to Kant's 'Critique of Pure Reason,'* pp. 301–7).
5 K. Ameriks, *Kant's Theory of the Mind*, pp. 64–72, 111–23; in this category one can also include all interpreters who think that Kant manages to refute the sceptic only when he appeals to the thing in itself. Indeed this would amount to requiring that Kant be satisfied with a pyrric victory. This line of interpretation is popular in the old literature, but can be detected also in important recent accounts such as Rousset's; see *La doctrine kantienne de l'objectivité*, 153.
6 B. Rousset, *La doctrine*, 145–7; Müller-Lauter, 'Kants Widerlegung des materialen Idealismus,' 67; L. Agosta, 'Kant's Problem of the Existence of the External World,' 391; P. Guyer, *Kant and the Claims of Knowledge*, 279–332 (for his particular rejection of the Fourth Paralogism on the grounds of Kant's alleged commitment to phenomenalism, see 280–2); Hoyos Jaramillo, *Kant und die Idealismusfrage*, 146–8; D.H. Heidemann, *Kant und das Problem des metaphysischen Idealismus*, 234; H. Allison, *Kant's Transcendental Idealism*, 1st ed., 294–304 (Allison, though, does not claim that the Fourth Paralogism fails).
7 To be sure, some interpreters believe that even the Refutation of Idealism presupposes transcendental idealism. See Allison, *Kant's Transcendental Idealism*, 2nd ed., 300.

8 Most notably ibid.

1. The Problem of Idealism in the Pre-critical Period

1 Although some commentators have analysed Kant's precritical stance towards idealism, their accounts are deficient in two main respects. To begin with, no one considers all the relevant material that one can obtain from close scrutiny of Kant's lectures, which are of crucial importance for the intelligibility of the whole development. Moreover, scant or no attention is paid to the question of how the treatment of idealism reflects Kant's general philosophical commitments. In other words, no *systematic* account of this aspect of Kant's precritical thought has ever been provided. The most comprehensive treatment in the literature is by Hoyos Jaramillo (*Kant und die Idealismusfrage*, 94–110). Hoyos Jaramillo, however, considers only marginally the Lectures on Metaphysics, which, as I will show, constitute a crucial part of this reconstruction. See also Kemp Smith, *A Commentary to Kant's Critique of Pure Reason*, 298–300.
2 Ak. 1: 410.
3 Ak. 1: 411. The first sentence is translated by me. For the second I follow Guyer's translation (Guyer, *Kant and the Claims of Knowledge*, 11–12). It is difficult to understand precisely which 'healthier philosophy' Kant has in mind. Perhaps this is a generic reference to philosophers, such as Locke, who maintain the existence of things corresponding to the 'ideas,' despite our knowledge being limited to the latter. Given this passage, I fail to understand what De Vleeschauwer means when he claims that 'there is no question here [in the *Nova Dilucidatio*] – and it is worth insisting on this point – of any problem of realism; Kant never gives it a thought.' See H.J. De Vleeschauwer, *The Development of Kantian Thought*, 23.
4 In the Fourth Paralogism, Kant says: 'The inference from a given effect to a determinate cause is always uncertain, since the effect may be due to more than one cause' (A368). All references to the *Critique of Pure Reason* are to the standard First and Second Edition pagination. I follow Kemp Smith's translation of the *Critique* (New York: St Martin's Press, 1965).
5 In this case, this would mean to overlook the possibility that the inner changes of the mind own be self-produced, as happens, for example, in cases of hallucination.
6 See Ak. 1: 228.
7 E. Cassirer, *Kant's Life and Thought*, 53.
8 Ak. 2: 33.
9 Kant contrasts the mathematical method, which starts from 'explanation' –

in the sense of definition – of an object (for example, a triangle), with the metaphysical method, which should never start from definitions because unlike mathematics, metaphysics does not 'construct' its object. He writes: 'In metaphysics I can never begin with the explanation; rather the definition is so far from being the first thing I know of an object, that it is almost always the last' (Ak. 2: 283). See also Ak. 2: 285–6.

10 See Ak. 2: 66. Even in the most metaphysical work of this pre-critical period, then, we find extreme caution. Metaphysics is a 'groundless abyss [*bodenloser Abgrund*].' One must enter this 'ocean' like one who, sailing on an unknown sea, must constantly check whether something has led him astray. It is no accident that Divine Providence made the conviction that God exists rest on commonsense rather than on a metaphysical proof. Beiser, in a crisp and informative essay on the development of Kant's thought (Paul Guyer, ed., *Cambridge Companion to Kant*, 26–61), has called the years 1760 to 1766 Kant's period of 'disillusionment' after his 'infatuation' with metaphysics of the years 1746 to 1759. See in particular page 26.

11 Ak. 28: 42–3.

12 Elsewhere in the *Metaphysica*, Baumgarten offers the definition of 'idealista' that Kant here borrows. Baumgarten's definitions of 'egoista' and 'idealista' are respectively in *Metaphysica*, §392, 438 and §402, 438. The part that corresponds to our paragraph is §392.

13 See Ak. 1: 314, 317, 321.

14 Although Kant still accepts the inference to a wise creator, he no longer believes that one can infer all the predicates that traditionally are thought in the concept of God. See Ak. 2: 124–5.

15 Cassirer, *Kant's Life and Thought*, 65.

16 Ibid., 76 has noted that this empirical orientation conflicts with the highly metaphysical *Beweisgrund*: 'It is especially discordant for Kant on the one hand to consign reason in its determination of actuality completely to the data of experience, and on the other to entrust to it the power of bringing us to unconditional certainty regarding an infinite being lying beyond all possibility of experience.' One should remember, though, that even in the *Beweisgrund* Kant warns us that metaphysics is a 'groundless abyss' and that the belief in the existence of God would inevitably be shaky if had to rest on a metaphysical proof.

17 John Locke, *Essay concerning Human Understanding*, 122–3.

18 Ibid.

19 David Hume, *A Treatise of Human Nature*, 191.

20 Ibid.

21 I. Kant, *Dreams of a Spirit-Seer*, 108.

22 See ibid., 108 ff.
23 Note how Kant seems to be under the direct influence of Hume. Indeed, it was in the 1760s that Hume entered the German philosophical world. In particular, his work touched a theme that was already much debated in Germany, namely, the possibility – defended by the Leibnizians and denied (among others) by Crusius – that the principle of sufficient reason could be reduced to that of non-contradiction (see on this point De Vleeschauwer, *Development*, 12). Kant sounds influenced by Hume even in his language when he says that 'questions like 'How something can be a cause, or possess a power,' can never be known through reason; but these relations must be taken from experience alone' (*Dreams*, 117). In a letter to Herz (1768), Kant explicitly praises Hume as one of the greatest philosophers: 'I confidently look forward to this epoch ... in which Montaigne occupies the lowest place and Hume so far as I know the highest' (Ak. 10: 70).
24 My analysis of how Kant narrows down possible causal relations to those effectively suggested by experience in *Dreams*, and of the relevance of this for the refutation of idealism, is indebted to L.E. Hoyos Jaramillo, *Kant und die Idealismusfrage* (100–1).
25 But the significance of *Dreams* for the question of idealism goes beyond this dismissive attitude. Almost in passing, Kant introduces at least two ideas that are worth noting. First, we find a defence of the reliability of outer sense that anticipates insights of the critical period. Kant claims: 'We find, however, in using our external senses, that besides the clearness with which the objects are seen, we perceive at the same time their location, perhaps not always with the same accuracy, *still as a necessary condition of sensation, without which it would be impossible to perceive things as being outside of ourselves*' (*Dreams*, 77; my italics). The importance of this passage is clear enough: it seems to anticipate the idea of the Transcendental Aesthetic that space is a condition of the possibility of our representation of objects as 'outside of ourselves'; this, in turn, is the basis for the idea of the immediacy of outer perception on which the Fourth Paralogism rests. It would be impossible to represent things 'as being outside of ourselves' if we could not grasp in the sensation also their location. The experience of an object distinct from myself is not composed of two successive moments – one in which sense data appear in my mind and another in which I attribute to them (or perhaps to their cause) a spatial location. This is the picture of external knowledge that, as we shall see in the Fourth Paralogism, necessarily leads to scepticism. The experience of something as distinct from ourselves presupposes that we put it in space. Second, the antimetaphysical attitude that dominates *Dreams* also leads Kant to give a quasi-neuro-

logical explanation of what happens in the brain of a visionary – Swedenborg, for example. Visions, assuming that those who experience them really see those spiritual substances which they claim to see, can be treated as cases of brain malfunctioning. A healthy brain places the point (*focus imaginarium*) at which the light rays or the sounds intersect outside the subject, if the source is an external object, and inside the subject, if the source is internal, such as in cases of fantasies or products of the imagination. To the contrary, a sick brain misplaces the *focus imaginarium* in such a way that what in normal conditions would be taken as a self-produced representation is mistaken for a representation originating from outside. This is precisely what happens in the brains of those who claim (sincerely) to see spirits. Applying this scientific result to the problem of idealism, one could say that in normal circumstances we do distinguish imagining from perceiving and that the situation in which the former is undeniably mistaken for the latter should not be generalized, as the sceptic does. These cases of malfunctioning are explainable in the scientific framework that obviously presupposes the reality of outer objects, including our body and our brain. Thus the sceptic's doubt is revealed as an illegitimate generalization of phenomena that can easily be handled in the context of our realistic scientific framework. Obviously, this line of thought cannot count as a strict refutation either of the visionary or of the idealist. Kant's argument does not rule out the possibility that people who claim to see spirits do see them and are not merely victims of misplacement of their own representations; in just the same way, the application of his argument to the problem of idealism does not rule out the possibility that the whole of our experience – including this explanation of cases of images-taken-for-reality – is nothing but a trick of some Evil Genius. The point, however, is not whether this argument is a strict refutation of the sceptic; it is rather that Kant's 'neurological' explanation is a clear sign of his present *attitude* concerning metaphysical problems. After all, Kant himself admits that any foolish hypothesis can be somehow consistently held. Therefore, he himself would not take these considerations as a strict refutation of the spirit-seer or the idealist. He is aware that it is vain to hope for a logical refutation of these metaphysical exercises. Nevertheless, they *can* be refuted, if they are not taken too seriously, and if we can show that the cases presented as support of such speculations can in fact easily be explained by science.
26 Kant, *Dreams*, 83.
27 In the first part of Section VII of Book I, we are presented with two dilemmas that force Hume to rethink his entire position. The first dilemma is the following: either we bow to our imagination in our scientific pursuits or we

reject all imagination and adhere to our concrete understanding. In the first case, we rely on a 'false reason' whereas in the second we embrace a faculty that was already shown to be faulty and unreliable by Hume in section 1 of Book I; ('no reason at all'). We can be rescued from the absolute scepticism that constitutes the second horn of the dilemma only thanks to the imagination's reluctance to enter into such subtle reasoning and be impressed by it. The question then becomes whether we should make it a general rule to abstain from *any* abstruse reasoning, in our cognitive pursuits. This gives rise to another dilemma. If we assume this general rule, we reject all science and philosophy and also fall into contradicting ourselves because the maxim that banishes all abstract reasoning is itself based on subtle or abstract reasoning. But if we do not accept it, and if we again open the gates to abstract reasoning, then we find ourselves pushed back to the self-subversion of reason (see Section 1). So we are at the point where reason cannot tell us what to do: 'I know not what ought to be done in the present case' (Hume, *Treatise*, 268). It seems that there is no rational solution to this dilemma. Insofar as we rely on reason alone, we will never emerge from this paralysis. Thus the lesson to draw is that we must avoid all kinds of abstract speculations in order also to avoid such self-defeating results. In Hume's own terms, one must reject 'total scepticism' and embrace 'true scepticism' (ibid., 273).
28 Perhaps the interpreter who argues most convincingly against the impression of a dramatic shift is Beiser: see 'Kant's Intellectual Development,' 48–52.
29 The former group is championed by Guyer (see *Kant and the Claim of Knowledge*, 21–2), the latter by Hoyos Jaramillo (*Kant und die Idealismusfrage*, 105–6).
30 See, Guyer, *Kant and the Claim of Knowledge*, 21–2.
31 Ibid., 335.
32 The other two are in the A27–B43/A28–B44 and A490–B518/A493–B522.
33 See Lambert's letter of 13 October 1770, in Kant, *Philosophical Correspondence*, 61.
34 Ibid., 75.
35 Ibid.
36 Ibid.; my emphasis.
37 Kant does not say this is why the question of whether things in themselves change rests on a sort of category mistake. I offer this explanation simply as a hypothesis of what Kant means.
38 The same unfortunate formula is to be found in Metaphysics Mrongovius (1782–3). See Ak. 29: 928–9: 'But there is also a critical or transcendental ide-

alism, when one assumes that appearances are indeed nothing in themselves, but that actually something unknown still underlies them. That is correct.' We shall deal with this passage in chapter 4.

39 The analysis of this text is indebted to Rousset (see *La doctrine kantienne de l'objectivité*, 140–1). Rousset, however, believes that the Fourth Paralogism removes the idea of a radical asymmetry between inner and outer sense, but with it also the distinction between representation and object. This is because for Rousset, the Fourth Paralogism is heavily committed to phenomenalism. Moreover, he believes that Kant's realism must ultimately be grounded in the thing in itself. My interpretation will challenge these two claims.

40 For further details on the dispute, see Ameriks and Narazon's introduction to *Lectures on Metaphysics* (xxviii–xl). For the dating of Metaphysics L_1 see xxx–xxxiii.

41 For a similar statement about the absolute certainty of inner sense, see Ak. 28: 224. One should note, however, that here Kant may simply be presenting Descartes's position.

42 See Baumgarten, *Metaphysica*, §394–5.

43 See Ak. 28: 207.

44 See ibid. There are two versions of this sentence: (1) 'bleibt der Egoismus und Idealismus in der Philosophie problematisch,' according to Lehman's reading, and (2) 'bleibt Egoismus und Idealismus als problematisch in Philosophie' according to Pölitz's reading, which is followed by Ameriks. The former suggests that idealism remains as a problem in philosophy, whereas the latter suggests that problematic (as opposed to dogmatic) idealism remains in philosophy. We will follow the latter, which is more coherent in relation to the beginning of the following paragraph. Note, however, that the discarded reading suggests even more strongly that Kant considers idealism as a problem yet to be solved.

45 R5400; my translation.

46 It will be crucial for our interpretation to spell out precisely *what sort* of epistemic parity Kant has in mind. Indeed, given that he recognizes the usual phenomena of hallucinations and the like – to which, admittedly, only outer sense is subject – this parity can be affirmed only with qualifications.

47 *Critique of Pure Reason*, A371.

2. The Nature of Transcendental Idealism and Its Foundation

1 See A378.
2 The only interpreter who thinks that (a) Kant does express a Berkeleyian

position in the Fourth Paralogism and (b) that this Berkeleyan position is a successful refutation of scepticism about the existence of the external world is Colin Turbayne (see his 'Kant's Refutation of Dogmatic Idealism'). Turbayne's interpretation rests on the assumption that Berkeley does have a proof of the external world – specifically, in the third dialogue between Hylas and Philonous. This assumption, however, is extremely difficult to accept. In that dialogue Philonous/Berkeley shows that there is no reason to be sceptical about the existence of matter, understood as what is immediately given to our senses. At the same time, however, he insists that one can be absolutely certain that matter, understood as a substance existing independently of a perceiving mind, does not exist. Since this matter is clearly mind-dependent in the sense that its existence depends on whether someone (ultimately God) perceives it, I do not see how this can count as a foundation of the existence of the external world, at least insofar as we understand by that the world that Descartes doubted and that Kant wanted to prove.

3 I will not espouse any *specific* non-phenomenalistic reading, although I find Allison's notion of epistemic condition as key to the proper understanding of the Kantian notion of appearances. For my purposes, it is enough to show that the attribution of phenomenalism regarding appearances to the mature Kant is both textually dubious and systematically disastrous; it is also contradicted by the direction of his intellectual evolution.

4 Guyer contends that Kant was free from any commitment to phenomenalism only in the years immediately surrounding the *Inaugural Dissertation* (1770), in the Refutation of Idealism of the second edition and in its later refinements in the Reflexionen (See Guyer, *Kant and the Claims of Knowledge*, 24). Van Cleve has recently proposed an interpretation of Kantian appearances as 'virtual objects' that reduces the ontological reality of an appearance to a state of the intuiting subject. According to Van Cleve's interpretation, the appearance 'red object' for an intuiting subject X amounts to nothing but X's sensing redly. Moreover, he claims that the Berkeleyan *esse est percipi* is the proper mode of being for appearances (see James Van Cleve, *Problems from Kant*, 3–14, esp. 8–12).

5 Kant, *Prolegomena*, 153. Collins focuses on this passage in his passionate defence of a non-phenomenalistic reading of Kant's idealism; see A. Collins, *Possible Experience*, 2.

6 Obviously, this is compatible with saying that there is in the objects something that causes the appearance of redness, warmth, and the like in our minds. This would be a moderate interpretation of the ideality of secondary qualities.

7 On the difference between Kant's and Berkeley's treatment of the primary–secondary qualities distinction see also Allison, 'Kant's Critique of Berkeley,' 52–7. For a more favourable assessment of the secondary qualities analogy, see Collins, *Possible Experience*, 60–73.
8 See B519n.
9 See Bxxvii; my emphasis.
10 Ibid.
11 B69. Kant attempts to do the same, although less clearly, in the *Prolegomena* (see 44–9).
12 See A42/B59; my emphasis.
13 A490/B518.
14 Kant constantly attempts to refute this rival form of idealism. This is obvious in the case of the Fourth Paralogism, but it is noteworthy that Kant also presents the same antisceptical argument of the Paralogism in the Antinomy (A492/B520–1; we will discuss this point in detail in the next chapter). This should not come as a surprise to readers. In the preceding chapter we saw that the reaching of Kant's mature philosophy and the refutation of scepticism were two inseparable intellectual achievements.
15 For a debate on this crucial passage, see Hoke Robinson, 'Two Perspectives on Kant's Appearances and Things in Themselves,' 411–41; and Allison, *Idealism and Freedom*, 12–17. For a criticism of the one-world-view interpretation, see James Van Cleve, *Problems from Kant*, 134–71. Van Cleve argues that the textual evidence in favour of the two-world view is at least as strong as that in favour of the alternative view. Moreover, using as examples passages from Locke and Berkeley, Van Cleve points out that sometimes authors inadvertently use 'double-aspect language to express what is plainly a double-object view' (ibid., 145). While part of the alleged evidence in favour of the two-world view is discussed later in this chapter, Van Cleve's second point is rather puzzling. Proving that some authors (Locke, Leibniz) use double-aspect language to mean something quite different does not prove that Kant makes the same mistake. If we are to interpret passages in which Kant talks about appearances and things in themselves as 'the same things' (Bxxvii–xxviii) to mean precisely the opposite, we need a reason to do so that is quite independent of other people's misleading style of writing. Van Cleve's point – that sometimes authors mean something different from what they have in mind – hardly counts as such a reason.
16 Ak. XX, 335.
17 A740/B768.
18 See L. Agosta, 'Kant's Problem of the Existence of the External World,' 391;

Guyer, *Kant and the Claims of Knowledge*, 280–1. The best refutation of the phenomenalistic reading of the Fourth Paralogism is found in G. Bird. *Kant's Theory of Knowledge*, 43–6.

19 See Kemp Smith, *A Commentary*, 304–5.
20 See C. Turbayne, 'Kant's Refutation of Dogmatic Idealism,' 225–44.
21 H. Robinson, 'Two Perspectives,' 419n. The passages Robinson cites are A104, A109, A113, B164, A190/236, A191/B236, A250, A369, A372, A372, A375, A377, A383, A386, A390, A391, A490/B518, A492/B520, A493/B521, A494/B523, A498/B527, A507/B535, A563/B591, and A793/B821; and *Prolegomena*, Ak. 4, 288, 289, 292, 305, 307, 319, 341, and 342.
22 These are A369 (in addition to the one Robinson has in mind), two passages at A370 (in addition to the one Jacobi has in mind), A371, and A376.
23 The very same point is made by H.E. Matthews in 'Strawson on Transcendental Idealism,' 132–49. See also G. Bird, *Kant's Theory of Knowledge*, ch. 3; and D.P. Dryer, *Kant's Solution for Verification in Metaphysics*, ch. 11, section vi.
24 See A373.
25 This analysis should also be applied to the murky passage in the Antinomy where Kant claims that 'the object is in our brain' (A484/B512).
26 The denial that the objects of our experience exist independently outside our thoughts is also expressed in the 'Consideration of Pure Psychology as a Whole, in View of these Paralogisms,' which immediately follows the Fourth Paralogism. There, Kant writes: 'If I remove the thinking subject the whole corporeal world must at once vanish' (A383).
27 In *Three Dialogues between Hylas and Philonous*, Hylas concedes to Philonous that the existence of matter is 'highly improbable.' To this, Philonous replies that he has proved much more – namely, that such existence is impossible: 'I deny it [matter] to be possible; and have, if I mistake not, evidently proved from your own concessions that it is not. In the common sense of the word *matter*, is there any more implied, than an extended, solid figured, moveable substance existing without the mind? And have you not acknowledged over and over, that you have seen evident reason for the denying the possibility of such a substance'; and similarly: 'I do not deny the existence of material substance merely because I have no notion of it, but because the notion of it is inconsistent.' See George Berkeley, *The Works*, 224–5.
28 See A376. Note that Kant normally uses the terms 'Wirklich' and 'Wirklichkeit' to indicate the existence of an object, not the empirical manifold given to us by the perception of an object (for which Kant uses 'Real' and 'Realität'). This suggests that in these passages Kant is not merely saying that the

empirical manifold pertaining to an object is simply the perception of it (something quite unproblematic). Rather, it seems that Kant is actually identifying perception (whether the act or the content) with the thing perceived. That is why these passages constitute a real challenge to our interpretation.

29 See Rousset, *La doctrine kantienne de l'objectivité*, 145. Rousset's work is intended as a response to Pierre Lachièze-Rey's strongly idealistic reading of Kant in *L'idéalism kantien*.

30 I borrow the characterization of the third and fourth arguments as metaphysical and theological respectively from Guyer. Note that if the absurdity on which the fourth argument rests is interpreted as based in the fact that placing God in space and time would involve assigning a temporal determination to creation and thus a temporal limit to the world, then this argument can be seen as anticipating the First Antinomy.

31 The argument from the status of Euclidean geometry is rejected because Euclidean geometry is no longer seen as a science whose truth is necessary and universal. The other arguments are rejected because they turn on dogmatic premises. Against the very possibility of considering the argument from geometry and the argument from the Metaphysical Exposition as independent, Brandt has contended recently that the former must be considered as something 'not superfluous [*unentbehrlicher*]' to the economy of the entire Transcendental Aesthetic ('Transzendentale Ästhetik, 1–3,' pp. 90–1). In fact, Brandt argues, the mere demonstration that space and time are forms of sensibility does not guarantee their 'actuality' – that is, their capacity to be properties of empirical objects. By showing that his theory can raise geometry to the status of an a priori science, Kant would provide such guarantee. Note, however, that this interpretation – which considers the argument from the standpoint of geometry as a sort of transcendental deduction of the forms of sensibility – ignores the fact that such guarantee for Kant *is* superfluous. As he puts it: 'That objects of sensible intuition must conform to the formal conditions of sensibility which lie *a priori* in the mind is evident, because otherwise they would not be objects for us' (A90/B122–3).

32 For the formulation of this principle, see Allison, *Kant's Transcendental Idealism*, 1st ed., 27. It is clearly at work in Allison's discussion of the argument (83–6).

33 Warren, 'Kant and the Apriority of Space,' 179–224, esp. 202. As Warren himself notes, Charles Parsons makes a similar response to the criticism that Kant's argument makes all concepts a priori. In fact, if Kant's claim is taken in the form 'in order to represent (or recognize) X, I already have to

have the representation X,' then even an empirical concept such as, 'table' turns out to be a priori. But if Kant's claim is taken in the sense that the representation of space must be presupposed in order to represent particular spatial regions, then the objection no longer applies. Note also that according to Allison's interpretation, the argument does not suffer this embarrassing consequence. If the representation of space is taken as a necessary condition in the proper sense, it makes possible the very individuation of objects (their being given in the first place as objects). As such, the representation of space cannot be associated with that of a concept the possession of which makes possible the recognition of particular instances falling under that concept. In fact, on this interpretation the representation of space would enable the very intuitions from which – through abstraction or any other concept formation device – that concept is formed.

34 Ibid., 202n31.
35 Ibid., 204.
36 Ibid., 187.
37 Note, however, that there are reasons to doubt that Kant ever meant to convey Warren's Thesis in the first apriority argument. Even if *ausser uns* and *ausser- und nebeneinander* must be taken in a spatial sense, as Warren contends, Kant's point is that we must presuppose the representation of space in order to represent spatially *sensations*, not objects ('in order that certain sensations be referred to something outside me'). If Kant's thesis in the first apriority argument were what Warren thinks – that is, that the representation of space is necessary for representing spatial relations among objects *already constituted as such* – Kant would probably say that this representation is necessary to represent objects, not sensations, as distinct from myself and from one another. The fact that he talks about sensations, however, indicates that what he has in mind is that one needs the representation of space in order to make certain sensations into objects of experience. And this is very close to the idea that space is a necessary condition of experience.
38 Terry Greenwood, 'Kant and the Modalities of Space,' 118.
39 The same kind of reply can be used against criticisms, such as those of Charles Parsons ('The Transcendental Aesthetic,' 72–3), that turn on the idea that one can explain the fact that our experience is necessarily spatial ('the inconceivability of the absence of space') as the mere result of the evolution of human beings in an environment that *is* spatio-temporal. Thus, as the evolutionary epistemology of Donald Campbell and Karl Popper holds, space and time would be a priori for the individual but a posteriori for the species. But again, this amounts to a complete failure to grasp the meaning

of necessary condition. If space and time are conditions of the representation of objects, then one cannot say that long-term exposure imprinted them in our mind. They make possible the experience even of our ancestors. A naturalistic account of this sort can never capture the idea that Kant is trying to establish in these arguments. If we keep in mind this strong notion of condition of the possibility of experience, we can also reply to Parsons's idea that Kant's claim, although phenomenologically sound, cannot rule out the possibility that 'in our objective description of the world, we would in the end be able to carry out a reduction of reference to space to reference to relations of underlying objects such as Leibniz's individual substances (monads)' (72). If the representation of space functions as a necessary condition in the proper sense, this ultimate reduction of it to the relations of objects in space is only *logically* conceivable; in actuality, it is impossible because, once again, it presupposes that we have access to the objects in space independently of the condition that, we agreed, was necessary for the representation of these very objects.

40 Greenwood, 'Kant,' 124.
41 Greenwood's critique depends entirely on the success of his refutation of the apriority thesis. This refutation is essential for rejecting both Kant's critique of relationalist accounts of space and what Greenwood calls the Principle of Transcendental Idealism (see 'Kant,' 124–5). By denying the latter, Greenwood is also denying Kant's rejection of the absolutistic theory of space (see 125). Thus, the rejection of the apriority thesis is the basis for Greenwood's proof that Kant's argument by elimination for the thesis of the ideality of space and time is a complete failure because it cannot eliminate either of its two rival theories.
42 Parson, 'Transcendental,' 69.
43 See A21/B35; and *Prolegomena*, 36.
44 Kant denies this in several places in the *Critique*. For example: 'The mere form of intuition, without substance, is in itself no object, but the merely formal condition of an object (as appearance), as pure space and pure time (*ens imaginarium*). These are indeed something, as forms of intuition, but are not themselves objects that are intuited' (A291/B347; see also A433/B461). This will be crucial to our discussion of the Refutation of Idealism – specifically, of the nature of the 'permanent' that is claimed to be necessary for the time determination of self-knowledge.
45 Parsons, 'Transcendental,' 69.
46 Greenwood, 'Kant,' 124.
47 See Warren, 'Kant,' 210.
48 Kemp Smith's translation rather obscures this last point. In the original it is

quite clear that 'und zwar a priori mit apodiktischer Gewissheit' is a mere addition to the main point – that is, that geometrical truths can be derived only 'aus der Anschaung.' But the English leaves it open the possibility of interpreting 'mit apodiktischer Gewissheit' as modifying 'aus der Anschaung,' thus giving the impression that the main point is that we can derive these geometrical truths 'from intuition ... *with apodictic certainty*' rather than '*from intuition*, and this indeed a priori, [that is,] with apodictic certainty.'

49 See Allison, *Kant's Transcendental Idealiism*, 1st ed., 92.
50 To be sure, there is also here a kind of phenomenological fact to which Kant appeals. This is that space is represented as 'containing an infinite number of representations *within* itself.' But whereas in the old argument the phenomenological fact coincides with the conclusion (space is given, as an intuition, and not represented, through a concept, as infinite), at least the new argument grounds the fact that space is given as an intuition through appeal to a distinct (and perhaps easier to accept) phenomenological fact.
51 Parson, 'Transcendental,' 71.
52 Kant has here Crusius in mind. In the letter to Marcus Herz, Kant claims that Crusius 'assumed certain implanted rules for judgments and assumed certain concepts that God had already planted – in human soul – such as they must be in order to harmonize with things.' And he suggestively calls this system 'that of preestablished intellectual harmony (*harmonia praestabilita intellectuale*).' See *Philosophical Correspondence*, xxx.
53 L. Falkenstein, 'Kant's Argument for the Non-Spatiality of Things in Themselves,' 267.
54 Ibid., 274–6.
55 In fact, Allison has recognized that Falkenstein's analysis, far from being incompatible with his reply, completes it (see Allison, *Idealism and Freedom*, 10–11).
56 Guyer, *Kant and the Claims*, 347.
57 Note that this criticism cannot easily be dismissed because it points to a real difficulty. Since Kant argues by elimination, he is vulnerable to the obvious response that something other than the ideality of space and time could account for the features of the representations of space and time established in the Metaphysical Exposition. Indeed, Guyer's criticism is simply a version of the neglected alternative objection that we have already discussed. Recall, the objection turns on the idea that Kant assumes that space and time either are forms of our sensibility or are objective features, but overlooks the possibility that they are both. The only novelty Guyer introduces to this old objection is that for him, Kant does not *overlook* or *neglect* this

possibility, but rather attempts (without success) to rule it out by arguing from the thesis that space and time are not properties of things in themselves (the first Conclusion) to the thesis that they are *only* forms of sensibility (the second Conclusion). See Guyer, *Kant and the Claims of Knowledge*, 363.
58 Ibid. 349.
59 Ibid., 364.
60 Perhaps this is why Kant himself in the *Prolegomena* (50–1) holds that without transcendental idealism even a posteriori knowledge becomes impossible.
61 In chapter 5 we shall see that Guyer's specific reading of Kant's refutation of the sceptic is also very dubious.

3. The Antisceptical Argument of the Fourth Paralogism

1 At A396, Kant writes: 'All *illusion* may be said to consist in treating the *subjective* condition of thinking as being knowledge of the *object*.'
2 The others are at A295–6/B352, B427, and A422/B449–50.
3 Existence is at stake in the Fourth Paralogism because from each group is selected only the category that expresses 'absolute unity' (A401), or, as Kant says elsewhere, 'form(s) the basis of the unity of the others in a possible perception, namely subsistence, reality, unity (not plurality), and existence' (A403). This is so because the selected categories are supposed to express features of the pure 'I think,' which is the paradigm of unity. In fact the 'I think' is what gives unity to the categories in the first place. Note that Kant does not explain why existence, and not possibility or necessity, expresses absolute unity. Perhaps the point is that if an object is merely possible, its unity is only thought, but not realized; whereas to say that an object is necessary means only that it must exist necessarily – that is, that the unity expressed by its existence must be necessary. But the thought of the unity is still provided by the category of existence.
4 On my interpretation, the Fourth Paralogism legitimately belongs to the critique of rational psychology. As we saw, the placement of the Fourth Paralogism within Kant's general discussion of the Cartesian project plays a crucial logical role in the overall antisceptical argument. Kalter and Bennett (see A. Kalter, *Kants vierter Paralogismus*, and J. Bennett, *Kant's Dialectic*), hold the opposite opinion, denying that the Fourth Paralogism belongs to the general discussion of rational psychology.
5 See also B158n ('The "I think" expresses the act of determining my existence. Existence is already given thereby'); and *Prolegomena*, 100n ('it [the

representation of the apperception (the Ego)] is nothing more than the feeling of an existence without the least definite conception').

6 The problem cannot be avoided by approaching the idea of an intellectual access to our existence as a novelty introduced in the Second Edition. It is also to be found – albeit less explicitly – in the First Edition. For example, in the 1781 version of the Transcendental Deduction, Kant distinguishes between empirical and transcendental apperception. Both are presented as forms of self-consciousness; but whereas the former does not yield knowledge of a 'fixed and abiding self,' the latter represents the numerically identical subject, and this 'cannot be thought as such through empirical data' (A107). If the idea of a non-sensible access to our existence is also in the First Edition, it is especially incumbent on us to show how the main point of the Fourth Paralogism – that we know our existence 'in the same manner' as we know the existence of external objects – is compatible with this very idea.

7 See A320/B377.

8 Note that Kant also distinguishes between *immediate* inferences of the understanding and *mediate* inferences of reason (see A303/B359–60). Since, as we saw, some intervention of cognitive faculties other than sensibility (judgment or understanding) is necessary in perception, one could be led to assume that an immediate perception is nothing but an immediate inference of the understanding. This impression, however, would be mistaken for two main reasons. To begin with, Kant in the Fourth Paralogism seems to define immediacy in opposition to any inference whatsoever. More importantly, the immediate inferences of the understanding are not judgments of the sort that are involved in perception. The former are logical inferences from a proposition such as 'all men are mortal' to another such as 'some men are mortal.' Such inferences do not require a middle term and are for this reason immediate. In contrast, the judgment involved in perception is presumably determinative judgment – that is, when we are faced with some object X, our judgment subsumes it under a universal (empirical concept). A determinative judgment obviously has nothing to do with logical inferences such as the one that leads us from 'all men are mortal' to 'some men are mortal.' Kant himself affirms the distinction in *Logic*, at 120n, where he explicitly distinguishes between mediate inference of reason and mediate inference of judgment.

9 On this point see G. Bird, *Kant's Theory of Knowledge*, 43–4.

10 See on this point Stroud's convincing argument against Quine's rejection of scepticism. Stroud argues that if nowadays science – the framework in

which Quine recommends we stay in order to solve epistemological problems – sees knowledge as a mere, to use Quine's own characterization, 'projection' of the torrential output of our experience from meager sense data in our mind, then scepticism is not only not refuted, it is actually strengthened. Indeed, nowadays science would be suggesting precisely the transcendental realist idea that the immediate objects of our experience are sense data. See B. Stroud, *The Significance of Philosophical Scepticism*, 209–253. That Quine accepts the transcendental realists' model of perception is also evident from his *The Roots of Reference*, in which he states (on the opening page) that bodies are not given in our sensations, but merely inferred from them. I thank Mario De Caro for suggesting this reference to me.

11 This metaphor obviously does not do justice to the fact that space and time are not spontaneously imposed as the intellectual forms are. Rather, they are merely the form of our receptivity. I do not think, however, that this inaccuracy undermines the metaphor's ability to capture the idea of immediacy.

12 Both points are established in the Transcendental Aesthetic. See A24–5/B39–40 and A26–7/B42–3.

13 That this horizon is given to us immediately arises from the fact that the representation of space is an intuition, as proved in the Transcendental Aesthetic. In the Transcendental Deduction, however, Kant makes it clear that the unity of this formal intuition – which he had treated in the Transcendental Aesthetic as belonging merely to sensibility – actually 'presupposes a synthesis' and thus the intervention of the understanding (see B160–1 and the related footnote). Since this synthesis, leading ultimately to the required unity, can only occur through the application of some concepts, we find again – this time no longer at the level of perception, but at that of pure intuition – the spectre of a weakening of the immediacy thesis owing to the necessary intervention of the understanding. This time, what is at risk is not the immediacy of an empirical intuition (or perception), but the immediacy of this *formal intuition*. And since immediacy is a necessary feature of intuition, this really amounts to questioning whether the representation of space can be an intuition in the first place. The same considerations that helped us show that the notion of immediacy of perception is not contradictory can be applied with little modification to the present problem as well. Whatever unity the understanding can give to the pure manifold, it will always be a unity that is added to something that is already given. The unity is an intellectual contribution, but the

immediate presence to the mind of the not yet unified pure spatial manifold is not. Indeed, the unity that is added will always be a determination of a pre-given spatial horizon. This given imposes *limits* on the unification of the understanding. The pure horizon can be intellectually determined either to form the representation of space as object (as in geometry) or, once it is filled with some empirical manifold, to form the representation of an empirical object. But it will always be a determination of something spatial. Moreover, this something spatial is given immediately.

14 We could thus say that the seeds of the presence of an external world lie in the constitution of the mind. Our acquaintance with this externality constituted by this formal intuition of space is even prior to the cognition of the particular spatial objects we encounter in it. This idea of the priority of space over the matter that occupies it is a topic of the *Critique* that is not confined to the Transcendental Aesthetic. In the Antinomy, specifically in opposition to the Leibnizians, Kant repeats the same point: 'The form of intuition (as a subjective property of sensibility) is prior to all matter (sensations); space and time come before all appearances and before all data of experience, and are indeed what make the latter at all possible' (A267/B323).

15 Compare this idea with what Lachièze-Rey says about the relationship between space and the objects in it that affect our sensibility. His point is that our passivity towards objects has to be considered in terms of a passivity towards something that consciousness has itself contributed, rather than simply in terms of passivity towards things completely extrinsic to sensibility itself (see *L'idéalism kantien*, p. 239).

16 Note the similarity to Kant's first argument for the apriority of the representation of space (see A23/B38).

17 For example, Reid contends: 'It is further to be observed, that hardness and softness, roughness and smoothness, figure and motion, do all suppose extension and cannot be conceived without it; yet I think it must, on the other hand, be allowed, that if we had never felt any thing hard or soft, rough or smooth, figured or moved, we should never have had the conception of extension: so that as there is a good ground to believe, that the notion of extension could not be prior to that of other primary qualities; so it is certain that it could not be posterior to the notion of any of them, *being necessarily implied in them all*.' (See Thomas Reid, *An Inquiry into the Human Mind*, 70; my emphasis). Note that Reid is treating sensations of touch merely as occasions for the arising of the representation of extension, which is the only one that has a real priority.

18 Ibid., 71.
19 See A376. Kant alludes to the same criterion also at Bxli, A492/B520, and in the *Prolegomena*, 46.
20 Indeed, up to this point in the text the two terms, taken without further qualification such as 'transcendental' or 'empirical,' were defined respectively as the position that holds an 'uncertainty' about the existence of the external object and the position that holds 'a possible certainty in regards to objects of outer sense' (A367).
21 Kemp Smith introduces an 'and' between the two theses, absent in the original, thus suggesting that Kant takes them as individually necessary but only jointly sufficient. However, when one looks at the original text, the impression is rather that Kant in listing two theses, each of which he considers sufficient. That this is his position is confirmed in the Reflexionen, where each of the two theses is often presented without the other and each is taken as sufficient grounds to refute the sceptic. See *A Commentary*.
22 See, for example, Allison, *Kant's Transcendental Idealism*, 1st ed., 301–2.
23 Ibid., 302.
24 Descartes, *Discourse on Method* and *Meditations*, 96.
25 Understanding the failure of this strategy, which Kant would also use in the Refutation of Idealism, is also crucial when it comes to assessing a series of strategies that are no more than variations of it. Here we note only that the most recent study of this topic (D.W. Heidemann, *Kant und das Problem des metaphysischen Idealismus*) indicates that Kant's sole successful strategy against the sceptic is his idea (from the Second Edition) that *all* the material of our knowledge comes from outer sense; this idea, however, is simply a variation of our strategy and thus shares the same destiny. It merely assumes what it should prove – namely, that there is no heightened power of the imagination that could reduce our experience to a mere interplay of mental forces.
26 This is 'hyper-imagination' because obviously, it cannot be identical to the imagination as we know it. The latter – as Kant often points out – borrows its material from genuine perception. Therefore, by itself it could not generate the representation of the world.
27 See A380. An alternative approach to understanding the metaphysical illegitimate nature of the sceptical question is to focus on the very *notion* of the world with which the sceptic operates. According to Kant, our experience is always an experience of particular events. We do not experience the world in its totality. The world, as the sum total of all appearances, is not the object of a possible intuition, but an idea of reason. The particular 'bits' of our experience can be genuine objects, or they can be hallucinations,

which we can detect through the criterion mentioned earlier. When the sceptic raises his question, he is really asking us to leave the standpoint of the particular event, because this certainly vouches for the existence of external objects (along with that of hallucinations), and to wonder about the nature of a whole that cannot be captured by particular experiences. In other words, the sceptic is asking us to wonder about the referent of a mere idea of reason. At the same time, however, the sceptic presupposes that at least in principle we can intuit such an object. Otherwise, the sceptic's hypothesis would lose all ability to describe 'how things really are' (or might be). A comparison of the sceptical question to the metaphysical reasoning of the Antinomy is also important if we hope to understand a subtler feature of sceptical reasoning. Recall that one of the features that distinguishes the Antinomy from both the Paralogism and the Ideal is that the idea of reason is not a noumenal object such as the Soul, or God; rather, it is the sum of all appearances, or as Kant puts it, 'the unconditioned unity of the objective conditions *in the field of appearances*' (A406/B433). This phenomenal dimension of the Antinomy, which obscures the metaphysical assumption that underlies each of the positions treated in the Thesis and in the Antithesis – namely, that the world is a whole existing in itself – parallels the apparent empirical ground of the sceptical position (it arises from particular, 'empirical' cases of delusion of the imagination), which obscures the metaphysical and absolute point of view that, as we saw, it presupposes. Thus, this comparison brings to light the misleading feature of scepticism: its seemingly empirical dimension masks its metaphysical nature. Precisely this feature is what makes scepticism both so convincing and so difficult to rebut.

28 Incidentally, note that this passage provides further-evidence for the non-phenomenalistic interpretation of transcendental idealism presented in chapter 2. The case of the 'spiritualist' entangled in the appearances/things in themselves conflation suggests that according to Kant, one can hold that everything is spiritual (perceiving subjects and perceived objects) and still be a transcendental realist. In other words, one does not abandon transcendental realism by reducing external objects to mental entities. It follows that transcendental idealism cannot be construed as a version of Berkeley's *esse est percipi*.
29 Rudolf Carnap, *The Logical Structure of the World*, 333–4.
30 Dummett himself uses this example; see *The Logical Basis of Metaphysics*, 334.
31 Not surprisingly, in his defence of scepticism against Carnap's charge of

meaninglessness, Stroud can easily show that if the truth of statements such as 'there is an object X out there' depends on the choice of a linguistic framework, the existence of such an object has been made dependent on a subjective decision, such as to adopt language that includes such things. And, as Stroud correctly points out, this results in an 'idealism of truly heroic proportions' (*The Significance*, 193). Note, however, that this result is merely a consequence of an assumption we have already criticized – that is, that sense data have a sort of priority and that the entire edifice of knowledge must be built upon them. Once we assume that much, it is inevitable that the existence of external objects becomes either doubtful, as the sceptic wants, or simply a matter of subjective choice of linguistic framework, as Carnap holds.

32 Hilary Putnam, *Reason, Truth and History*, 15.
33 There is no need to specify the difference between Putnam's internalism and Kant's transcendental idealism in this context. They have in common the intuition that the objects of our experience owe something to the 'way' in which we describe them. Kant believes that this 'way' is determined by the sensible forms to which our intuition is bound, whereas Putnam refers to the specific 'system of description' that we assume, or that we are bound to assume (ibid., 49). On this point, see Ameriks's distinction between specific and non-specific definitions of transcendental idealism in 'Kantian Idealism Today,' 329–42, 333–4. For a detailed comparison of Kant's transcendental idealism and Putnam's internal realism, see Van Cleve, *Problems from Kant*, ch. 13, esp. 212–19.
34 For a similar charge of circularity, see Dell'Utri, *Le vie del realismo*, 117. Other critical assessments of Putnam's argument can be found in D. Lewis, 'Putnam's Paradox,' 221–36; J.E. McCarthy, 'Putnam's Vat World,' 731–2; J. McIntyre, 'Putnam's Brains,' 59–61; J. Stephens and L.M. Russow, 'Brains in Vats,' 205–12; A.L. Brueckner, 'Brains in a Vat,'148–67; idem, 'If I Am a Brain in a Vat,' 123–8; F.B. Farrell, 'Putnam and the Vat People,' 147–60; M. Kinghan, 'The External World Sceptic,' 161–6; A. Malachowski, 'Metaphysical Review Semantic,' 167–74; P. Tichy, 'Putnam on Brains,' 137–46; P. Coppock, 'Putnam's Transcendental Arguments,' 14–28; J. Heil, 'Are We Brains in a Vat?' 427–36; and T. Tymoczko, 'In Defense of Putnam's Brains,' 281–97. See also M. Capozzi, 'Realism and Truth,' 157–64.
35 That Putnam interprets his argument in this way is suggested, among other things, by the fact that he points out that the internalist philosopher does not need to appeal to such a complicated argument to refute the sceptic. As we saw, *from within the internalist perspective*, the refutation of the sceptic,

according to Putnam, is straightforward: the Brains in a Vat hypothesis cannot even be raised within a perspective that denies the legitimacy of a God's eye point of view – that is, the point of view from which the 'story' is necessarily told.

4. The Problem of Idealism between 1781 and 1787

1 I. Kant, *Prolegomena* (1977), 100.
2 Ibid., 30.
3 Ibid., 72.
4 I. Kant, Ak. 4: 376.
5 I. Kant, *Prolegomena* (1977), 107.
6 Ibid.
7 The importance of the idealism issue in these years is also revealed in the exchange of letters between Kant and Garve following the 1782 review. For a complete analysis of this exchange see Heidemann, *Kant*, 87–94.
8 See Ak. 29: 928–9.
9 Kant, *Prolegomena*, 43.
10 See, *La doctrine*, 146–7.
11 Rousset refers to Kant, *Prolegomena*, 43.
12 Kant writes: 'The empirical truth of appearances in space and time is, however, sufficiently secured; it is adequately distinguished from dreams, if both dreams and genuine appearances cohere truly and completely in one experience, in accordance with empirical laws' (A492/B520).
13 See A493/B521. These laws of the empirical advance are simply the transcendental laws that make the perception of an event possible (for example, necessary presence of a cause for a given effect) and that are therefore supposed to be respected also in the perception of new events – namely, in the empirical advance.
14 Most importantly, the Garve-Feder review (see *Zugabe zu den Göttingischen Anzeigen von gelehrten Sachen*, Göttingen, 1770–82, III, 40–8). This review and the polemical discussion that followed between Kant and Feder after 1781 has been shown by Heidemann to have been extremely important for the Second Edition of the *Critique* – specifically, for the removal of the Fourth Paralogism and the elaboration of a new refutation of idealism (Heidemann, *Kant*, 87–94).
15 That Kant's intentions were not to move from phenomenalism to non-phenomenalism in the passage from the Fourth Paralogism to the Refutation of Idealism is clearly indicated by Kant himself when he notes that the new

proof differentiates itself from the original for 'the method of proof only'(Bxl n). For a completely different assessment of this remark, see Guyer, *Kant*, 281–2. Guyer, influenced by his phenomenalistic reading of the Fourth Paralogism, tends to interpret this remark as misleading because it would suggest that the 1787 proof itself is infected by phenomenalism, whereas for him, one of the great advantages of the Refutation is precisely that Kant there happily combines 'epistemological subjectivism' with 'ontological realism' – that is, the view that objects as we know them are different from the way they are in themselves, but that they are nonetheless numerically distinct from the subject.
16 The idea that Kant removed the Fourth Paralogism because he no longer viewed it as a viable refutation is often a consequence of the assumption that the Fourth Paralogism is committed to phenomenalism. The clearest expression of this view is perhaps to be found in Rousset (see *La doctrine*, 148).
17 See Bxl n and B275.
18 See Bxl.
19 Ibid.

5. The Refutation of Idealism

1 In the first Note that Kant inserts after the proof, he criticizes scepticism because it assumes that 'the only immediate experience is inner experience, and that from it we can only *infer* outer things.' This suggests that the 1781 immediacy thesis was still being endorsed by Kant in 1787. Note however that, as Kant says in the footnote attached to the Note, the immediacy of outer experience is not assumed (as in the Fourth Paralogism, where it was simply introduced as a consequence of transcendental idealism); rather, it is proved. Indeed, the proof allegedly shows that inner experience is possible only on the condition that we have experience of things, not of representations thereof, which means that we have immediate outer experience.
2 See A218/B266. This point was also made in the Fourth Paralogism: 'It is sensation, therefore, that indicates a reality in space and time' (A373).
3 B277n.
4 A. Zweig, (ed.), *Philosophical Correspondence*, 61 (Ak. X: 102).
5 See B157, B158n, B422n.
6 See A33/B49–50, A34/B50–1, and B67.
7 In 'Personal Identity and Kant's "Refutation of Idealism"' (259–78), Aquila

argues convincingly against Strawson's and Bennett's interpretation of the notion of self-consciousness in the Refutation. See esp. 260–5.
8 In a recently discovered Reflexion (see Brandt and Stark, *Neue Autographen*, 18), Kant expresses this point by saying that 'in inner experience ... I bring the representations of the outer senses in the empirical consciousness.' To bring the representations of outer sense into inner experience means to reconceptualize them along the lines we have described.
9 See A34/B50–1, A342/B400. Note that Kant leaves the passages that indicate the soul to be the proper object of inner sense in the Second Edition; furthermore, he reintroduces this idea in what he adds in the Second Edition; see B427.
10 Allison, *Kant's*, 261.
11 This would explain why, in the Second Edition, Kant allows to coexist the idea that the soul is the object of inner sense (see A22/B37, A342/B400) with the passage at B67 (quoted above) in which he introduces the idea – crucial for the Refutation itself – that inner sense contains only a temporal series of representations.
12 Descartes, *Philosophical Works*, 150; my emphasis. Roughly the same point is repeated later when Descartes states that 'I am, I exist, that is certain. But how long? Just when I think' (see ibid., 151). In the preceding quote, I emended the English translation by replacing 'how often' with 'how long.'
13 On this point, see Lachièze-Rey, *L'idéalisme kantien*, 18–19.
14 This point was first noted by Lachièze-Rey, who, starting from the assumption that Descartes restricted the validity of the cogito to the instant, concludes that the position Kant attacks in the Refutation, despite his explicit pronouncements, cannot be Descartes's. He then suggests that the real targets are Lambert, Mendelssohn, and Schultz, who, by defending the reality of time (as we saw during our discussion of the Kant–Lambert dispute), would have committed themselves to the temporal structure of inner experience and thus to the proof structure of the Refutation (see Lechièze-Rey, *L'idéalisme kantien*, 68n). This suggestion cannot be accepted, for two simple reasons: (a) Kant explicitly considers Descartes as his target (see B274); and (b) there is nothing in the defence of the reality of time by these thinkers that could entail some doubt about the reality of space and of the things in it. Kant, on this interpretation, would be refuting the scepticism of philosophers who are not sceptics.
15 Brandt and Stark, *Neue Autographen*, 19; my translation.
16 Obviously, the time that is contained in this single act of consciousness does not need to be identical with the putative objective time that applies outside of consciousness. Although this is clearly a very un-Kantian

assumption, there is no need to assume that the flow of representations in my consciousness and external phenomena belong to the same all-inclusive time. The Refutation's proof structure requires only that there be *a* temporal structure to inner experience, no matter how 'private,' and quite independently of the possibility of mapping this subjective time onto the objective one.

17 B276–7; my emphasis.
18 See B158n.
19 See B277.
20 Lachièze-Rey, whose entire interpretation of the *Critique* turns on the attempt to show that for Kant, regardless of his own hesitations, there would be an 'autoposition du *je*' (see *L'idéalisme kantien*, 61), obviously has a different opinion on this issue. For him, 'Kant, despite certain appearances, recognizes after all the autonomy and independence of the Cartesian principle [the *cogito ergo sum*]' (see ibid., 63). By that, Lachièze-Rey means precisely that Kant would acknowledge that a thinking substance can posit itself through apperception.
21 See A34/B50.
22 Kant's account of the different 'modes of time' is notoriously problematic. His so-called official theory is that 'the three modes of time are duration, succession, coexistence' (A173/B219). It has already been noted (see, for example, Allison, *Kant's*, 358) that there is a question concerning the very meaning of the notion of 'mode of time'; yet another question centres on the apparent tension between this 'official' definition and the denial contained in the First Analogy that succession (or change) and coexistence are modes of time. Note that the two questions are interdependent. The solution proposed by Kemp Smith to the second question – that coexistence and succession are modes of the things in time, not of time itself, which neither passes nor, properly, coexists, but only endures – also sheds light on the first. Indeed, at the very least it suggests that the expression 'modes of time' is short for 'modes of the determination of things in time.' This, however, does not exhaust the difficulties. Kant is often inconsistent even about the number of these modes. Sometimes he considers succession and coexistence as the sole relations possible in time ('Time can determine [appearances] in a twofold manner, either as in succession to one another or as coexisting'; A182, and see also A182/B226). But in the same paragraph he seems to consider duration, not only as an additional time relation determinable through reference to the permanent, but also as the *only* time relation or, alternatively, as capable of summarizing in itself all possible modes of time: 'Only through the permanent does existence in different parts of

the time-series acquire a magnitude which can be entitled duration ... Without the permanent there is therefore no time relation' (A183/B226).
23 See B225. Note the apparent paradox: what determines temporally the appearances must be found in the appearances themselves. This paradox is, however, highly instructive. It points to the need for us to 'decide' for ourselves what will count as a permanent among appearances. In other words, it already points to the necessity to apply an intellectual rule (permanence) to appearances in order to 'build' the required permanent. This is not immediately given, as an intuitive datum. Rather, it must be intellectually determined.
24 See A183/B226.
25 All Kant says is that 'only through the permanent does existence in different parts of the time-series acquire a magnitude, which can be entitled duration' (A183/B226). Note that the reference to time-series – previously associated with succession – suggests the connection between succession and duration that we applied in providing the argument for this claim. Also, note that if duration is a derivative of succession and coexistence, as our argument suggests, this could explain why sometimes Kant drops it from the list of the modes of time.
26 The two theses are not clearly distinguished in the First Edition, in which Kant does not bother to introduce first this minimal thesis and then the more substantial 'all change is an alteration' thesis. He immediately presents the permanent not as a mere reference point, but rather as a substance and change/succession as alterations of the substance. In fact, he claims that change and succession can be represented because they are 'only so many ways (modes of time) in which the permanent exists' (A182/B226).
27 In fact some interpreters think that the external permanent is what makes possible the recognition (or the very constitution) of the *identity* of the self. Aquila has suggested this interpretation; see 'Personal Identity,' 265.
28 Robert Hanna similarly believes that the Refutation does not need the controversial assumption of an absolutely permanent substrate but merely that of a relatively or temporally permanent one ('Kant's "Refutation" Reconsidered,' 153).
29 Ibid., 161.
30 The fact that the motion of the sun is apparent is obviously irrelevant. In this context, we are talking about the condition of the possibility of determining time through reference to any kind of motion, actual or apparent.
31 See B225.
32 See A848/B876. I take the suggestion about this passage, as well as the idea that Kant considers eternal matter necessary as a condition of the possibil-

ity of the experience of the passing in and out of existence of those objects that normally function as 'substances' or subjects of change, from Allison (*Kant's*, 207–10).

33 See R6313 (Ak. XVIII: 614). There Kant writes: 'This permanent ... *that is, space*, cannot be in turn representation of the mere imagination, but of the sense.' See also R5653 (Ak. XVIII: 308): 'The permanence depends essentially on the representation of space' and 'the representation of space lies at the basis of the temporal determination of permanence' (my translation).

34 Allison, *Kant's Transcendental Idealism*, 1st ed., 298–9. Also, Guyer recognizes that this step improves on the original, but for a different reason. For Guyer, more than signaling to the reader that we are not talking about the 'I' of apperception, the new version clarifies that 'the empirical self is presented only by means of such transitory representations' (*Kant and the Claims of Knowledge*, 285) – something that, as we shall see, Kant cannot take for self-explanatory and that is in fact the product of his general theory of the object of inner sense, as modified in the Second Edition.

35 The 'official' reason that Kant gives for replacing this step of the proof is that in the original step 'there is some obscurity' (Bxln). Perhaps the obscurity he had in mind was caused precisely by the failure to reiterate the necessarily sensible nature of the permanent.

36 See Bxli.

37 Note that when Kant points out that since inner sense provides only representations (R2), the perception of the required permanent is possible only through a *thing* outside me, this permanent 'thing' could very well be called a representation, but in the sense of R1, not of R2.

38 Hanna thinks that the 'at the same time' (*zugleich*) in this passage is to be taken in the temporal sense. On this reading, Kant would be introducing a simultaneity condition. Any bit of inner experience I am having now presupposes a simultaneous veridical bit of outer experience. Hanna criticizes this idea on the grounds that Kant himself, by recognizing the existence of hallucinatory events, makes room for the possibility of inner experience without a simultaneous bit of outer experience (Hanna, 'Kant's "Refutation,"' 162–3). I doubt, however, that we need to take the 'at the same time' in this temporal sense. Precisely for the reasons Hanna cites, it is more generous to interpret the 'at the same time' in a (perhaps looser) logical sense: inner experience *by itself* (or ipso facto) presupposes outer experience.

39 See R5653, Ak. XVIII: 308–9, 310; R5709, Ak. XVIII: 332; R6311, Ak. XVIII: 611; R6313, Ak. XVIII: 614.

40 Kant presents – perhaps more clearly expressed – the same strategy in a Reflexion, when he argues: 'The fact is: the empirical consciousness of my

existence in time is necessarily bound up with the empirical consciousness of a relation to something outside us and the former is so little an illusion ... as the latter' (Ak. 18: 308).

6. The Refutation of Idealism in the Reflexionen

1. See B276.
2. Bxln. As I showed at the end of the preceding chapter, this assessment of the 1787 Refutation does not entail that there may be other *non-strict*, albeit sound, refutations, such as the argument of the Fourth Paralogism. As we shall see, however, in the 'Reflexionen' Kant seems to be after other *strict* refutations. Thus the tension between Kant's assessment and the very existence of these supplementary proofs cannot easily be removed.
3. Reinhold defends Kant's philosophy by attempting to give a sort of foundation to it. See his *Versuch einer neuen Theorie, Briefe*, and *Beyträge zur Berichtigung*.
4. This identification is implicit in the first issue, but explicit in the third. See Eberhard, ed., *Philosophischen Magazin* 3: 243–62, esp. 260.
5. Ibid., 1 (1788): 9–29, esp. 27. It is not clear what Eberhard has in mind here. His accusation would at least be meaningful if he had in mind the Paralogisms in which Kant shows the impossibility of inferring substantiality, simplicity, and personality (understood as numerical identity of the self at different times and therefore as permanence) from the pure 'I think.' The fact that he uses the terminology of the Refutation, however, indicates that he is giving his (highly dubious) interpretation of the Refutation and not of the Paralogisms.
6. Kant considered as 'an absurdity of which no one has yet been guilty' (B71) the idea of doubting (let alone denying) the reality of self-knowledge.
7. For a brief account of the Garve–Feder review, see ch. 2.
8. See, *Kant Prolegomena*, 158.
9. See Ak. 18: 614.
10. Kant also presents two other apparently metaphysical arguments: (a) inner and outer representations necessarily refer to something other than themselves, which is only in the understanding (Ak. 18: 312, 23–31); and (b) the temporal determination of our representations presupposes a permanent that must lie either in what is simultaneous or in what contains the ground of appearances, that is, the intelligible (Ak. 18: 612, 15–18). See also R6317, where Kant characterizes the permanent objects necessary for the temporal determination of my self-consciousness as 'Sachen an sich' (Ak. 18: 627).

11 In Reflexion 6315 this distinction becomes threefold: (1) pure (or transcendental); (2) empirical self-consciousness; and (3) knowledge of myself as a being determined in time. Only the latter requires an external permanent. Lachièze-Rey considers Kant's acknowledgment that there could be an empirical consciousness of my existence *independent* of external objects evidence in support of his idea that Kant accepts Descartes's *cogito ergo sum* and never intends to make the determination of the existence of the subject – at least as a not yet objectified entity – dependent on the existence of outer things. In fact, according to Lachièze-Rey, the problematic idealism that Kant attacks is not Descartes's (see Lachièze-Rey, *L'idéalisme kantien*, 63–71).
12 Ak. 18: 310; all passages from the 'Reflexionen zum Idealismus' are translated by me unless otherwise indicated.
13 See for example Ak. 18: 332: 'This representation [of the permanent] cannot be grounded on the mere image of a permanent outside us, because an image to which no corresponding object can be given is impossible.'
14 Ak. 18: 308; my emphasis.
15 Bxln.
16 Ak. 18: 611–12.
17 Kant seems to rely on another phenomenological fact for rebutting the 'fatal objection' when he claims: 'If there were no outer objects of our sense, therefore no sense at all, but only imagination, then it would at least be possible to become aware of its [the imagination's] action as a spontaneity' (Ak. 18: 312).
18 Ak. 18: 306.
19 Ak. 18: 312.
20 Actually, there could be a way to remove any difficulty about this passage. We could take the phrase 'the consciousness of things other than myself (which must be also presupposed as intellectual)' to mean simply that the consciousness of things other than myself, like the consciousness of myself, is twofold: sensible, but also 'intellectual.' If this is what Kant means, despite its prima facie characterization of our *whole* consciousness of external things as intellectual, then the passage clearly makes a familiar and unproblematic point.
21 Ak. 18: 612.
22 Ak. 18: 307.
23 Ak. 18: 614–15, 31–2/1–9.
24 Ak. 18: 614. This denial of the possibility of relying on things in themselves must be used for the correct interpretation of Reflexion 6312, where Kant affirms that 'the permanent must lie either in what is simultaneous or in the intelligible, which contains the ground of appearances' (Ak. 18: 612). In

light of that denial, Kant should not be taken as contemplating two possible candidates (either what is simultaneous or the intelligible) for the role of the permanent; rather, he is actually affirming the first only and noting that without the first we would be left with the second possibility, *which however is not available for us*. Evidence in favour of this interpretation is that Kant elsewhere makes precisely this point: 'This enduring thing ... must be a representation of sense, for otherwise that which lasts would not be in the sensibility at all' (Ak. 18: 614).

25 Ak. 18: 614.
26 See Ak.18: 614. I follow here Guyer's translation (*Kant and the Claims of Knowledge*, 305).
27 Guyer, *Kant and the Claims of Knowledge*, 279.
28 Ibid., 306.
29 Guyer spells out this argument in some detail at ibid., 306–7.
30 For background on the discovery of this text, for a placement of it within Kant's general confrontation of the problem of idealism, and, in particular, for a comparison of the theses contained in the text and Kant's precritical thought, see Reinhard Brandt, 'Eine neu aufgefundene Reflexion,' in Brandt and Stark, eds., *Neue Autographen*, 1–17.
31 See Heidemann, *Kant*, 221.
32 Brandt and Stark, *Neue Autographen*, 18; my translation.
33 Heidemann, *Kant*, 238; my translation.
34 Ibid.

Bibliography

Works by Kant

Critique of Pure Reason. Trans. N. Kemp Smith. New York: St Martin's Press, 1965.
Dreams of a Spirit-Seer. Trans. E.F. Goerwitz, ed. F. Sewall. Bristol: Thoemmes Press, 1992.
Gesammelte Schriften. Ed. Königlich Preussischen Akademie der Wissenschaften. Berlin and Leipzig: De Gruyter, 1922.
Kant's Inaugural Dissertation of 1770. Trans. W.J. Eckoff. New York: Columbia College, 1894.
Kritik der reinen Vernunft. Ed. R. Schmidt. Hamburg: Felix Meiner, 1990.
Lectures on Metaphysics. Ed. and trans. K. Ameriks and S. Naragon. Cambridge: Cambridge University Press, 1997.
Logic. Trans. R. Hartman and W. Schwarz. New York: Dover, 1988.
'On a Discovery according to Which Any New Critique of Pure Reason Has Been Made Superfluous by an Earlier One.' In *The Kant-Eberhard Controversy*. Ed. and trans. H.E. Allison. Baltimore: Johns Hopkins University Press, 1973.
Philosophical Correspondence 1759–99. Ed. and trans. A. Zweig. Chicago: University of Chicago Press, 1970.
Prolegomena to Any Future Metaphysics That Can Qualify as a Science. Trans. P. Carus. Chicago and La Salle: Open Court Publishing, 1902; Indianapolis: Hackett, 1977.
Selected Pre-critical Writings and Correspondence with Beck. Trans. G.B. Kerferd and D.E. Walford. Manchester: Manchester University Press, 1968.
'Vom inneren Sinne' (Loses Blatt Leningrad 1). In *Neue Autographen und Dokumente zu Kants Leben, Schriften und Vorlesungen*. Ed. R. Brandt and W. Stark. Hamburg: Felix Meiner Verlag, 1987.

Vorkritische Schriften von Immanuel Kant. Ed. A. Buchenau. Berlin: Bruno Cassirer Verlag, 1922.

Other Works

Adams, R.M. 'Things in Themselves.' *Philosophy and Phenomenological Research* 57 (1997): 801–25.
Adickes, E. *Kants Lehre von der doppeltten Affektion anseres Ich als Schüssel zu seiner Erkenntnistheorie.* Tübingen: J.C. Mohr, 1929.
Agosta, L. 'Kant's Problem of the Existence of the External World.' In *Akten des fünften Internationalen Kant-Kongresses,* ed. G. Funke, 387–93. Bonn: Bouvier, 1981.
Allison, H.E. *Idealism and Freedom.* Cambridge: Cambridge University Press, 1996.
- 'Kant's Concept of the Transcendental Object.' *Kant-Studien* 59 (1968): 165–86.
- 'Kant's Critique of Berkeley.' *Journal of the History of Philosophy* 11 (1973): 43–63.
- 'Kant's Refutation of Realism.' *Dialectica* 30 (1976): 223–53.
- *Kant's Transcendental Idealism: An Interpretation and Defense.* New Haven and London: Yale University Press, 1983. Revised and enlarged edition, 2004.
- 'The Non-Spatiality of Things in Themselves for Kant.' *Journal of the History of Philosophy* 14 (1976): 313–21.
- 'Things in Themselves, Noumena, and the Transcendental Object.' *Dialectica* 32 (1978): 41–76.
- 'Transcendental Idealism and Descriptive Metaphysics.' *Kant-Studien* 60 (1969): 216–23.
Ameriks, K. 'Kantian Idealism Today.' *History of Philosophy Quarterly* 9 (1992): 329–42.
- *Kant's Theory of Mind: An Analysis of the Paralogisms of Pure Reason.* Oxford: Clarendon Press, 1982.
- 'Recent Work on Kant's Theoretical Philosophy.' *American Philosophical Quarterly* 19 (1982): 1–24.
Aquila, R. 'Personal Identity and Kant's "Refutation of Idealism."' *Kant-Studien* 70 (1979): 257–78.
Baum, M. 'Kant on Pure Intuition.' In *Minds, Ideas, and Object: Essays on the Theory of Representation in modern Philosophy,* ed. P.D. Cummins and G. Zoeller, 303–15. Atascadero, CA: Kidgeview, 1992.
Baumgarten, A.G. *Metaphysica.* Halle: Nackdruck Hildesheim 1963.
Bayle, P. *Dictionaire historique et critique,* 5th ed. Amsterdam: Compagnie des Librariwes, 1734.

Beck, L.W. *Essays on Kant and Hume.* New Haven: Yale University Press, 1978.
- ed. *Kant Studies Today.* La Salle, IL: Open Court, 1969.
Beiser, F.C. 'Kant's Intellectual Development: 1746–1781.' In *Cambridge Companion to Kant,* ed. P. Guyer, 26–61 Cambridge: Cambridge University Press, 1992.
Bennett, J. *Kant's Analytic.* Cambridge: Cambridge University Press, 1966.
- *Kant's Dialectic.* Cambridge: Cambridge University Press, 1974.
Berkeley, G. *The Works of George Berkeley, Bishop of Cloyne,* ed. A.A. Luce and T.E. Jessop. London: Thomas Nelson and Sons, 1948.
Bird, G. *Kant's Theory of Knowledge.* London: Routledge and Kegan Paul, 1962.
Brandt, R. 'Transzendentale Ästhetik, 1–3.' In *Kant's Kritik der reinen Vernunft,* 80–105. Berlin: Akademie Verlag, 1998.
Brandt, R., and W. Stark, eds. *Neue Autographen und Dokumente zu Kants Leben, Schriften und Vorlesungen.* Hamburg: Felix Meiner Verlag, 1987.
Britain, G.G., Jr. *Kant's Theory of Science.* Princeton: Princeton University Press, 1992.
Broad, C.D. *Kant: An Introduction.* Cambridge: Cambridge University Press, 1978.
Brueckner, A.L. 'Brains in a Vat.' *Journal of Philosophy* 83 (1986): 148–67.
- 'If I Am a Brain in a Vat, Then I Am Not a Brain in a Vat.' *Mind* 101 (1992): 123–8.
Caird, E. *The Critical Philosophy of Kant.* Glasgow: J. Meclehose, 1909.
Capozzi, M. 'Realism and Truth; Putnam and Kant.' In *Filosofia della scienza e fondamenti della probabilità e della statistica,* 157–64. Bologna: Corsi e Sambin, 1991.
Carnap, R. *The Logical Structure of the World and Pseudoproblems in Philosophy.* Berkeley: University of California Press, 1967.
Cassirer, E. *Kant's Life and Thought,* trans. J. Haden. New Haven: Yale University Press, 1981.
Collins, A. *Possible Experience.* Berkely: University of California Press, 1999.
Coppock, P. 'Putnam's Transcendental Arguments.' *Pacific Philosophical Quarterly* 68 (1987): 14–28.
Crusius, C.A. *Die Philosophische Hauptwerke,* ed. G. Tonelli. New York: Geerge Olms Verlag, 1999.
Cummins, P.D., adn G. Zoeller, eds. *Minds, Ideas, and Objects: Essays on the Theory of Representation in Modern Philosophy.* North American Kant Atascadero, CA: Ridgeview, 1992. Society Studies in Philosophy 2.
Dell'Utri, Massimo. *Le vie del realismo.* Milan: Franco Angeli, 1992.
Den Ouden, B., ed. *New Essays on Kant.* New York: Peter Lang, 1987.

Descartes, R. *Discourse on Method* and *Meditations*, trans. L.J. Lafleur. Indianapolis: Bobbs-Merril, 1996.
– *Philosophical Works of Descartes*, trans. E.S. Haldane and G.R.T. Ross. Cambridge: Cambridge University Press, 1968.
de Vleeschauwer, H.J. *The Development of Kantian Thought*. New York: Thomas Nelson and Sons 1962.
Doney, W., ed. *Descartes: A Collection of Critical Essays*. Notre Dame: University of Notre Dame Press, 1968.
Dryer, D.P. *Kant's Solution for Verification in Metaphysics*. London: Allen & Unwin, 1966.
Dummett, M. *The Logical Basis of Metaphysics*. Cambridge: Harvard University Press, 1991.
Eberhard, J.A., ed. *Philosophischen Magazin* (1788 and ff.).
Falkenstein, L.' Kant's Argument for the Non-Spatiality of Things in Themselves.' *Kant-Studien* 80 (1989): 265–83.
– *Kant's Intuitionism*. Toronto: University of Toronto Press, 1995.
Farrell, F.B. 'Putnam and the Vat People.' *Philosophia* 16 (1986): 147–60.
Feder, J.H., and C.F. Garve. '*Kritik der reinen Vernunft*. Von Imman. Kant. 1781.' In *Zugabe zu den Göttingischen Königl. Gesellschaft der Wissenschaften*, 1, 1782, 3, 40–8.
Föster, E. 'Kant's Refutation of Idealism.' In *Philosophy: Its History and Historiography*, ed. A.J. Holland. Dortrecht: D. Reidel, 1985.
Frangiotti, M.A. 'Refuting Kant's Refutation of Idealism.' *Idealistic Studies* 25(1995): 93–106.
Gäbe, L. 'Die Paralogismen der reinen Vernunft in der ersten und zweiten Auflage von Kants Kritik.' PhD dissertation, Marburg University, 1954.
Gochnauer, M. 'Kant's Refutation of Idealism.' *Journal of the History of Philosophy* 12 (1974): 195–206.
Greenwood, T. 'Kant and the Modalities of Space.' In Reading Kant, ed. E. Scharper and W. Vossenkuhl, 117–39. Stuttgart: Klett-Colta, 1984.
Grier, M. *Kant's Doctrine of Transcendental Illusion*. Cambridge: Cambridge University Press, 1992.
Guyer, P. 'Direckes Wissen und die Widerlegung des Idealismus.' In *Akten des fünften Internationalen Kant-Kongresses*, ed. G. Funke, 236–42. Bonn, 1982.
– *Kant and the Claims of Knowledge*. Cambridge: Cambridge University Press, 1987.
– 'Kant's Intentions in the Refutation of Idealism.' *Philosophical Review* 92 (1983): 329–83.
– ed. *The Cambridge Companion to Kant*. Cambridge: Cambridge University Press, 1992.

Hanna, R. *Kant and the Foundations of Analytic Philosophy.* Oxford: Clarendon/ Oxford University Press, 2001.
- 'Kant's "Refutation" Reconsidered.' *Ratio* 13 (2000): 146–74.
Heidemann, D.H. *Kant und das Problem des metaphysischen Idealismus.* Berlin: de Gruyter, 1998.
Heil, J. 'Are We Brains in a Vat? Top Philosophers Say "No".' *Canadian Journal of Philosophy* 17 (1987): 427–36.
Henrich, D. *Identität und Objectivität. Eine Untersuchung über Kants transzendentale Deduktion.* Heidelberg: Carl Winter Universität Verlag, 1976.
- 'The Proof-Structure of Kant's Transcendental Deduction.' *Review of Metaphysics* 22 (1969): 640–59.
Hintikka, J. 'On Kant's Notion of Intuition.' *Kant Studies Today*, ed. L.W. Beck. La Salle, IL: Open Court 1992.
Hoyos Jaramillo, L.E. *Kant und die Idealismusfrage: Eine Untersuchung über Kants Widerlegung des Idealismus.* Mainz: Gardez! Verlag, 1994.
Hume, D. *A Treatise of Human Nature*, ed. L.A. Selby-Bigge. Oxford: Clarendon Press, 1896.
Hymers, M. 'The Role of Kant's Refutation of Idealism.' *Southern Journal of Philosophy* (1991): 51–68.
Kalter, A. *Kants vierter Paralogismus. Eine entwicklungsgeschichtliche Untersuchung zum Paralogismenkapitel der ersten Ausgabe der Kritik der reinen Vernunft.* Meisenheim am Glan: Hain, 1975.
Kaulbach, F. 'Kant's Beweis des "Daseins der Gegenstände im Raum ausser mir."' *Kant-Studien* 50 (1958–9): 323–47.
Klotz, C. *Kants Widerlegung des problematischen Idealismus.* Göttingen: Vandenhoeck and Ruprecht, 1993.
Kemp Smith, N. *A Commentary to Kant's Critique of Pure Reason.* New York: Humanities Press, 1962.
Kenny, A. *Descartes: A Study of His Philosophy.* New York: Random House, 1968.
Kinghan, M. 'The External World Sceptic Escapes Again.' *Philosophical Review* 88 (1986): 161–6.
Körner, S. *Kant.* London: Penguin Books, 1995.
Lachièze-Rey, P. *L'idéalisme kantien.* Paris: Libraire Philosophique J. Vrin, 1950.
Langton, R., *Kantian Humility: Our Ignorance of Things in Themselves.* Oxford: Oxford University Press, 1998.
Lehmann, G. 'Kants Widerlegung des Idealismus.' *Kant-Studien* 50 (1958–9): 348–62.
Lewis, D. 'Putnam's Paradox.' *Australasian Journal of Philosophy* 62 (1984): 221–36.

Malachowski, A. 'Metaphysical Review Semantic: Some Moral Desiderata.' *Philosophia* 16 (1986): 167–74.
Matthews, H.E., 'Strawson on Transcendental Idealism.' In *Kant on Pure Reason*, ed. R.C.C. Walker. Oxford: Oxford University Press, 1982.
McCarthy, J.E. 'Putnam's Vat World and the Skeptical Method.' *Journal of Philosophy* 81 (1984): 731–2.
McIntyre, J. 'Putnam's Brains.' *Analysis* 44 (1984): 59–61.
Meerbote, R. 'Kant's Refutation of Problematic Material Idealism.' In *New Essays on Kant*. ed. B. Den Ouden, 111–138. New York: Peter Lang, 1987.
– Space and Time and Objects in Space and Time: Another of Kant's Transcendental Idealism.' In *Minds, Ideas, and Objects: Essays on the Theory of Representation in Modern Philosophy*, ed. P.D. Cummins and G. Zoeller, 275–90. Atascadero, CA: Ridgeview, 1992.
Melnick, A. *Kant's Analogies of Experience*. Chicago: University of Chicago Press, 1973.
Moore, G.E. 'Four Forms of Scepticism,' In *Philosophical Papers*. London: George Allen and Unwin, 1959.
Müller-Lauter, W. 'Kants Widerlegung des materialen Idealismus.' *Archiv für Geschichte der Philosophie* 46 (1964): 60–82.
Locke, J. *Essay concerning Human Understanding*. New York: Dover Publications, 1959.
Palmer, D. 'Kant's Refutation of Idealism.' *Dialogue* 39, nos. 2–3 (1997): 49–55.
Parsons, C. 'The Transcendental Aesthetic,' in *The Cambridge Companion to Kant*. ed. P. Guyer, 62–100. Cambridge: Cambridge University Press, 1992.
Paton, H.J. *Kant's Metaphysics of Experience*. New York: Humanities Press, 1936.
Prauss, G. *Kant und das Problem der Dinge an sich*. Bonn: Bouvier, 1974.
Pippin, R.B. *Kant's Theory of Forms*. New Haven: Yale University Press, 1982.
Prichard, H.A. *Kant's Theory of Knowledge*. Oxford: Clarendon Press, 1909.
Putnam, H. *Reason, Truth, and History*. Cambridge: Cambridge University Press, 1981.
– 'Sense, Non-sense and the Senses: An Inquiry into the Powers of the Human Mind.' *Journal of Philosophy* 91 (1994): 445–517.
Quine, W.V. *Ontological Relativity*. New York: Columbia University Press, 1969.
– *The Roots of Reference*. La Salle, IL: Open Court, 1974.
Reid, T. *An Inquiry into the Human Mind*, ed. T. Duggan. Chicago: University of Chicago Press, 1970.
– *The Roots of Reference*. La Salle, IL: Open Court, 1974.
Reinhold, C.L. *Beyträge zur Berichtigung bishiriger Missverständisse der Philosophen*. Jena, 1790.
– *Briefe über die Kantische Philosophie*. Leipzig, 1790.

- *Versuch einer neuen Theorie des menschlichen Vorstellungsvermögens*, Prague and Jena. 1789.
Robinson, H. 'Two Perspectives on Kant's Appearances and Things in Themselves.' *Journal of Philosophy* 33 (1994): 411–41.
Roser, A., and T. Mohrs, eds. *Kant-Konkordanz: zu den Werken Immanuel Kants (Bände I-IX der Ausgabe der Preussischen Akademie der Wissenschaften).* Hildesheim: Olms-Weidemann, 1992–5.
Rousset, B. *La doctrine kantienne de l'objectivité.* Paris: Librairie philosophique J. Vrin, 1967.
Russell, B. *Our Knowledge of the External World.* London: George Allen and Unwin, 1914.
Schaper, E. 'The Kantian Thing-in-Itself as a Philosophical Picton.' *Philosophical Quarterly* 16 (1966): 233–43.
Scharper, E., and W. Vossenkuhl, eds. *Bedingung der Möglichkeit. 'Transcendental Arguments' and transzendentales Denken.* Stuttgart: Klett-Cotta, 1984.
- ed. *Reading Kant.* Oxford: Basil Blackwell, 1989.
Schopenhauer, A. *The World as Will and Respresentation*, trans. E.F. Payne. New York: Dover, 1969.
Schulze, G.E. *Aenesidemus oder über die Fundamente der von Herrn Professor Reinhold in Jena geliefertnen Elementar-Philosophie. Nebst einer Vertheitigung des Skepticismus gegen die Anmaassungen der Verfunftkritik.* Könisberg: Hartung, 1968. Reprinted in *Actas Koutiana.* Brussels: Culture and Civilization, 1969.
Sellars, W. '... This I or He or It (the Thing) Which Thinks ...' *Proceedings and Addresses of the American Philosophical Association* 44 (September 1971): 5–31.
Skorpen, E. 'Kant's Refutation of Idealism.' *Journal of the History of Philosophy* 6 (1968): 23–34.
Stephens J., and L.M. Russow. 'Brains in Vats and the Internalist Perspective.' *Australasian Journal of Philosophy* 63 (1985): 205–12.
Strawson, P.F. *The Bounds of Sense.* London: Methuen, 1966.
Stroud, B. *The Significance of Philosophical Scepticism.* Oxford: Clarendon Press, 1984.
Tichy, P. 'Putnam on Brains in a Vat.' *Philosophia* 16 (1986): 137–46.
Turbayne, C.M. 'Kant Refutation of Dogmatic Idealism.' *Philosophical Quarterly* 5 (1955): 225–36.
- 'Kant's Relation to Berkeley.' In *Kant Studies Today*, ed. L.W. Beck, 88–116. Lasalle, IL: Open Count, 1969.
Tymoczko, T. 'In Defense of Putnam's Brains.' *Philosophical Studies* 57 (1989): 281–97.
Van Cleve, J. *Problems from Kant.* Oxford: Oxford University Press, 1999.

Vaihinger, H. *Kommentar zu Kants Kritik der reinen Vernunft*. Stuttgart: W. Spemann, 1881–92.
– 'Zu Kants Widerlegung des Idealismus.' In *Straßburger Abhandlungen zur Philosophie: Eduard Zeller zu seinem siebenzigsten Geburtstage*. Freiburg and Tübingen, 1884: 85–164.
Vogel, J. 'The Problem of Self-Knowledge in Kant's Refutation of Idealism.' *Philosophy and Phenomenological Research* 53, no. 4 (1993): 875–87.
Walker, R.C.C., Ed. *Kant on Pure Reason*. Oxford: Oxford University Press, 1982.
Warren, D. 'Kant and the Apriority of Space.' *Philosophical Review* 107 (1988): 179–224.
Washburn, M. 'The Problem of Self-Knowledge and the Evolution of the Critical Epistemology, 1781–1787.' PhD dissertation, University of California, San Diego, 1970.
Werkmeister, W.H. 'Kant's Refutation of Idealism.' *Southern Journal of Philosophy* 15 (1977): 551–65.
Wilson, M.D. 'Kant and 'The Dogmatic Idealism of Berkeley.' *Journal of the History of Philosophy* 9 (1971): 459–75.
Wolff, C. *Gesammelte Werke*, ed. J. École, H.W. Arndt, C.A. Chorr, J.E. Holfmann, and M. Tholmann. Hindesheim: Olms, 1962.
Zimmermann, R. '"Der Skandal der Philosophie," seine sprachanalytische Aufhebung und Kants "Widerlegung des Idealismus."' In *Akten des fünften Internationalen Kant-Kongresses*, ed. G. Funke, 462–72. Bonn, 1981.
Zoeller, G. 'Making Sense out of Inner Sense: The Kantian Doctrine as Illuminated by the Leningrad *Reflexion*.' *International Philosophical Quaterly* 29 (1989): 263–70.

Index

actuality, 54, 129–30, 171
Adickes, E., 33, 152
affection, 94, 102, 118, 120, 171
Allison, H., 37, 57–60, 67, 72–3, 99, 139, 147
alteration, 18, 24, 33, 45, 49, 131, 139–40, 143
Ameriks, K., 33
analogy of experience, first, 131, 138–44
analytic of principles, 131
antinomy of pure reason, 45–8, 122, 124
appearance(s)/phenomenon(/a): 4, 7; and conflation of things in themselves, 102–3; in *Dissertation*, 24–6; and illusion, 43; in Letter to Herz (1772), 29–30; in Metaphysics Herder, 16–17; and object of inner sense, 123; in Metaphysics L_1, 31–3; in Reflexion 5400, 33–4; as representations in us, 49–51 and secondary qualities, 39–40; as (mere) representations, 44–6; and things in themselves, 10–11, 35, 42–4, 72–4
apperception: as based on a perception, 86–7; as different from empirical self-knowledge, 132–3; I of, 85, 116, 121, 137–8; as immediate transcendental consciousness of ourselves, 161; inference from a priori certainty of, 167; and refutation of idealism, 137–8, 145. *See also* self-consciousness
Aristotle, 77
attention: and inner sense, 133; as reconceptualization of representations of outer sense, 145

backdrop thesis, 139
Baumgarten, A.G., 17, 32
Beck, J.S., 155
Berkeley, G., 5, 7, 16–17, 20, 37, 39, 41, 44, 48–9, 52–4, 93, 115–19, 153–5

Carnap, R., 81, 105–7, 109, 175
Cassirer, E., 14, 19
category: as involved in perception, 89; modal 82–3, 130–1; pre-formation system of, 71, 78; transcendental deduction of, 167
causal argument: abandonment of, 14–16, 27–30, 35; of *Dissertation*, 24; in Metaphysics Mrongovius 118–

19; of *Nova Dilucidatio*, 11–14; in *Prolegomena* 110–21
change: and alteration, 139–40; as condition of experience of time, 143; conditions of experience of, 139–42; reality of, 28–9; of representations in inner sense, 145; in substance, 11–12. *See also* alteration
coexistence: of contradictory predicates in a substance, 12; as mode of time, 138–9. *See also* simultaneity
cogito, 85, 88, 96, 134–8
condition of representing outer objects, 57–64
consciousness: contents of, 41, 168; as immediate perception of external objects, 35, 84
Copernican revolution, 4

Descartes, R., 3–8, 26, 37, 39, 41, 48–9, 76, 80, 82, 85–8, 96–7, 99–102, 104, 110, 116, 122, 125–7, 129, 132, 134–8, 145, 148, 155, 167, 172–4
dogmatism: in the *Nova Dilucidatio*, 15; in interpreting transcendental distinction, 27, 42. *See also* idealism (empirical)
dualism, 98
dualist, 103
Dummett, M., 107–10
duration, as mode of time, 139

Eberhard, 153–5
egoista, 17
empiricism: paradox of, 20; in pre-critical period, 19
existence, category of, 82–3, 130
evil genius, 3, 5, 21, 36, 40, 78, 81, 100, 102–4, 110, 123, 135, 160, 169, 172, 174

Falkenstein, L., 73–4
Feder, J.J.H., 7, 38–9, 115, 117, 119
form(s): of appearances, 72–4; as filters in mind, 74–9; of sensibility, 28–9, 69–72, 94
freedom, 11

Garve, C., 7, 38–9, 115, 117, 119
God, 56; as cause of all our ideas, 119; concept of, 68; God's-eye point of view, 101–2, 112–13; as possible deceiver, 16–17, 40; proof of existence of, 14, 18
Guyer, P., 9, 24–5, 37–8, 55, 74–9, 94, 153, 167–9, 175

Hanna, R., 37, 142
Heidemann, D.H., 153, 155, 170–2
Hoyos Jaramillo, L.E., 24–5
Hume, D., 19–20, 22, 47, 93, 134

I think: of apperception, 85, 116, 121, 137–8. *See also* apperception
idea: innate idea of space, 70–1, 94–5; as mental representative state, 19–21, 24, 26, 37, 39–41, 45, 48, 72, 82, 100, 118; of sensation, 93
idealism (empirical), 90, 99, 115, 122–3; dogmatic 32, 39, 107, 109, 155; material, 39, 45, 161; problematic, 30–3, 48; sceptical, 39, 107
idealism (transcendental): formal (critical) nature of, 41–8; foundation of, 55–72; as only refuge, 105–13
illusion: and appearance, 43; reduction of knowledge to, 78; transcendental, 7, 82–8
imagination, 13, 15, 26, 32, 34; delusion by, 97–100, 147–9, 156–66;

super-power of (unknown faculty of), 101–3, 118, 172
immediacy, of outer perception (immediacy thesis), 89–97
in us/outside us (things), in empirical and transcendental sense, 50–1

Jacobi, F.H., 48–9
judgment, as mediate relation to object, 89–90

Kemp Smith, N., 48, 54

Lambert, J.H., 28–9, 132
Langton, R., 37
Leibniz, G.W., 11, 13–14, 32, 52, 64, 70–1, 74
Locke, J., 16, 19–20, 26, 40, 48, 77, 93

manifold: apprehension of the, 157, 168–9; of inner sense, 133
matter: of cognition 45; as dependent on senses, 51–3; indistinguishable from soul if taken in itself, 101–3; laws of, 18; as permanent substratum 143–4; proved in same manner of soul, 96
McDowell, J., 9
Melnick, A., 37
metaphysical exposition, 57–72
metaphysics: as knowledge of first principles of intelligible world, 23; method of, 14–16; as science of limits of reason, 21

Newton, I., 70–1
noumena. *See* things in themselves

object: empirical, 26, 37, 49–52 (*see also* appearances); in general, 120; intelligible, 162; transcendental, 102, 105, 120, 161–3

paralogism, fourth: alternative strategy, 100–5; antisceptical argument of, 80–113; official strategy, 97–100; phenomenalistic reading of, 48–55; and refutation of idealism, 150–2; and transcendental illusion, 82–8
paralogisms, and transcendental illusion, 83
passivity, original, 160–4
perception: and existence of outer objects, 129; identical with things perceived, 53–4; immediacy of outer, 89–97; as necessary for self-consciousness, 84–8; transcendental realist's model of, 104, 106
permanence, as mode of time, 138–9
permanent object, 131–2, 138–47; and fatal objection, 147–51, 156, 159–60
phenomena. *See* appearance(s)
phenomena/noumena distinction. *See* appearance(s): and things in themselves
phenomenalism: and Fourth Paralogism, 48–55; and Kant's idealism, 4, 38–48
Pippin, R.B., 37
postulates of empirical thought, 127–30
psychology, rational, 31, 80, 83–5, 121
Putnam, H., 3, 6, 8, 108, 110–13, 175

quality, primary/secondary, 39–41

realism (empirical), 11, 27, 54, 173; immune from scepticism, 103, 108, 123
realism (transcendental), 25, 38; defi-

nition of, 44–5; as inevitably linked to empirical idealism, 90–3; *reductio* in Antinomy, 46–8
reason, euthanasia of 46; and transcendental illusion, 82–3
receptivity, 69. *See also* passivity
Reid, T., 8, 82, 92–7, 175
Reinhold, K., 153
representation: and appearance, 49–51; two senses of, 146
Rousset, B., 53, 121–2

Schulze, G.E., 153–5
self-affection, 15, 26, 171
self-awareness. *See* self-consciousness
self-consciousness: empirical, 87–8, 132–4; pure, *see* apperception; and Refutation of Idealism, 134–8
self-knowledge. *See* self-consciousness: empirical
sense (inner): and empirical self-knowledge, 87–8; form of, 28–9; manifold of 133; more reliable than outer sense, 28–9, 31–2; object of, 128
sense (outer): form of, 28–9, 69–79. *See also* sense (inner)
simultaneity, as mode of time, 139, 157, 165–8
soul, as object of inner sense, 128
space, a priori nature of representation of, 57–64; as condition of the possibility of the representation of outer objects, 57, 59–62; as form of intuition (form of outer sense), 69–72; as formal intuition, 91–2; as infinite, 66–8; intuitive nature of the representation of, 64–8; transcendental ideality of, 47, 69
Strawson, P., 127, 167
Stroud, B., 3
substance: and causal argument, 12–3; as intellectual form, 63; material, 52; matter as basis for application of concept of, 143–4; and object of inner sense, 128, 131; spiritual, 20, 26, 32; and time determination, 139–40
succession, as mode of time, 138–9, 165–8
Swedenborg, E., 20–2

things in themselves (noumena), as cause of phenomena, 25, 110–21, 118–19. *See also* appearances: and things in themselves
time: as a priori intuition, 56–7; determination of appearances in time, 138; as form of inner sense, 28, 38; modes of, 138–9; as not perceivable, 138; order of inner representations, 132; transcendental distinction, 35; transcendental ideality of, 28–9, 55–6; as two perspectives on same set of objects, 42–3
Turbayne, C.M., 49

Van Cleve, J., 37
verificationism, 107

Wolff, C., 13
world, intelligible, 23; idea of, 46; perspective from outside empirical, 101–2

www.ingramcontent.com/pod-product-compliance
Lightning Source LLC
Chambersburg PA
CBHW030317080526
44584CB00012B/600